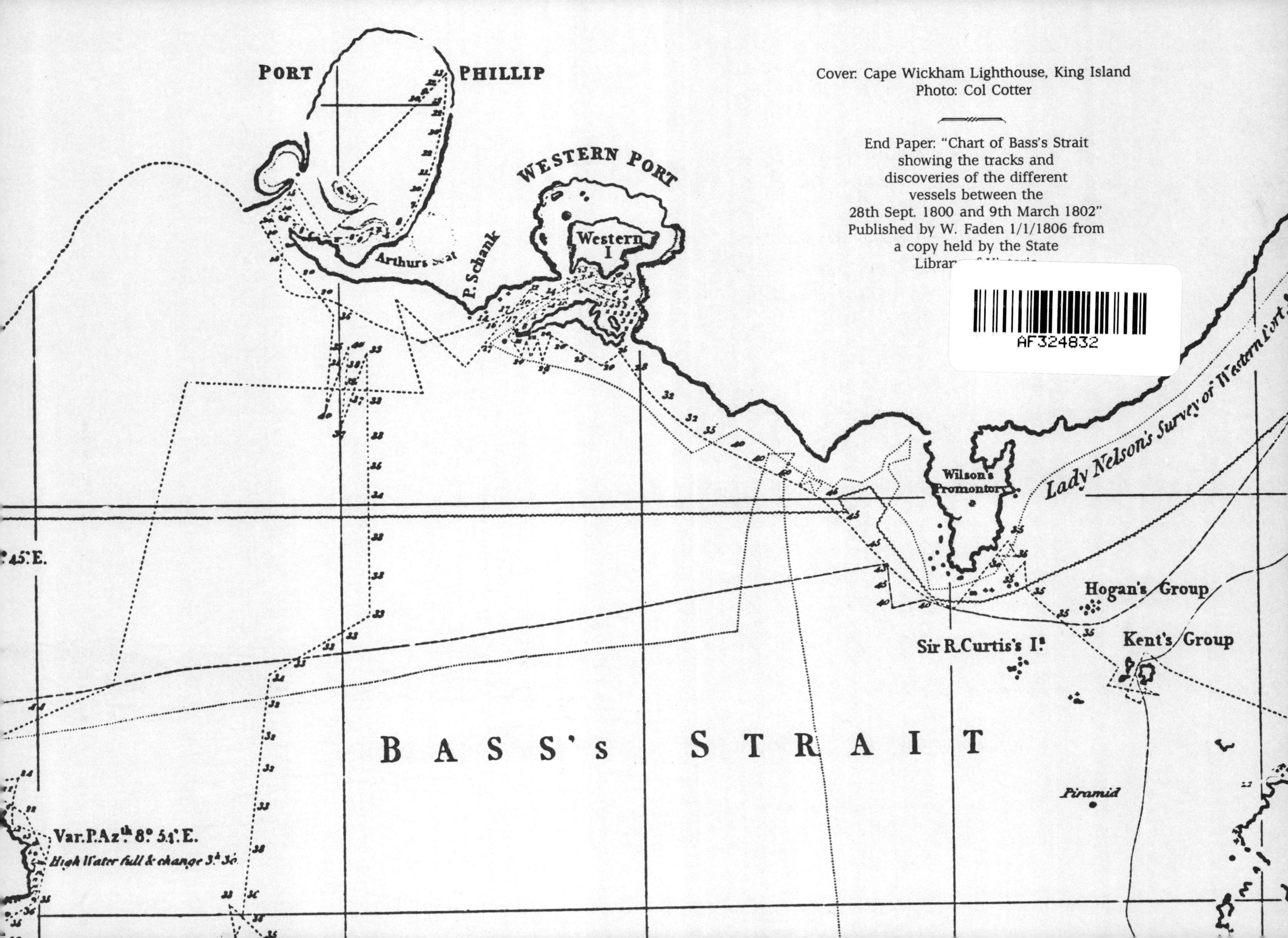

PORT PHILLIP
WESTERN PORT
Western I
Arthurs Seat
P. Schank
Wilson's Promontory
Lady Nelson's Survey of Western Port &
Hogan's Group
Kent's Group
Sir R. Curtis's I.
Piramid
BASS's STRAIT
45° E.
Var. P. Az.th 8° 54' E.
High Water full & change 3.h 30.
Cover: Cape Wickham Lighthouse, King Island
Photo: Col Cotter
End Paper: "Chart of Bass's Strait
showing the tracks and
discoveries of the different
vessels between the
28th Sept. 1800 and 9th March 1802"
Published by W. Faden 1/1/1806 from
a copy held by the State
Library of Victoria

Cape Otway Lighthouse
November 29th 1871

Sir

As the road from here to Birregurra
Post Office is now not used being blocked
with fallen timber would you be so good
as to address the letters for here to the care
of Mr Stevenson Camperdown as I shall
be enabled to get them by there people
coming to the Cape

Would you be pleased to grant me the usual
annual leave of absence in the beginning of
January next as I anticipate I shall have
to travel round by the western district in
consequence of the other road not being passable would you be so kind as to let me
know by telegraph when my leave is granted
as by so doing should any one be travelling
that way I would get the opportunity of a
guide as I have not been that way before

Enclosed is the returned letter

I have the honor to be
Sir
Your humble Servant
[signature]
Lighthouse Keeper

BEACONS OF HOPE

AN EARLY HISTORY OF CAPE OTWAY AND KING ISLAND LIGHTHOUSES

Extracts from "The Lighthouse" by Nancy McDonald is printed by permission of Angus & Robertson Publishers.

BEACONS OF HOPE
DONALD WALKER

AN EARLY HISTORY OF CAPE OTWAY AND KING ISLAND LIGHTHOUSES

ATHELSTONE TRUST

© Donald Walker 1981,1991,1998.
All rights reserved
No part of this publication may be
reproduced without permission.

First published 1981
Neptune Press Pty. Ltd.
Reprinted 1991
Deakin University Press

Reprinted by Atheletone Trust 1998
IBSN 0-646-35985-1

Book Design: Donald Walker and John Pescott.
Front and Back Cover design by Michael Roberts,
Computer Art Trends.

Set in: 10 point Itek Book
Printed by Australian Print Group
Maryborough Vic.
1998

ACKNOWLEDGEMENTS

This book would never have been written without the support and advice of many of my friends who share with me an interest in the history of Bass Strait and its lighthouses. This interest developed with my University studies and before completing them in 1971, I realized that a book deserved to be written on why the early landfall lighthouses of Bass Strait are where they are and at what cost in lives and energy our forbears built them.

I would not have been able to complete this book without the ready co-operation of officers, both past and present, of the Department of Transport, Navigational Aids Branch and Surface Operations Branch. I would especially thank Mr. M.C. Card, Mr. J. Leyden, Mr. Greg Jones, the late Mr. L. Ault, Mr. R. J. Barling, Mr C.C. Robinson, Mr. F. Wotzko, Mr. John Box, Mr. C. Tindall, Mr Bernard Meagher and Mr. M. Komesaroff.

A number of other institutions and libraries which have helped me greatly are the La Trobe Library, Melbourne (in particular Judy Wells, Shar Jones, Gill Nicholls, Mary Lewis, Graeme Johanson, Merril Lowenstein, Alannah Kelly, Mary Kehoe, Jenny Carew, Ross Gibbs and Tony Marshall), the Mitchell Library Sydney, the State Library of South Australia (in particular Caroline Spooner), the Libraries Board of South Australia, the Archives Office of Tasmania, the Archives Office of N.S.W., the John Oxley Library, Queensland, the Royal Historical Society of Victoria and the Geology Faculty at Melbourne University.

Much of my early research work was completed in the old basement quarters of the Public Records Office of Victoria, La Trobe Street, before they shifted to a new home. I would like to record my thanks to Mr. K.A. Patterson (now retired) and Mr. H.W. Nunn, for making my task so much easier.

The Historical Division of Telecom, the Department of Science, Antarctic Division and the Forests Commission of Victoria have also been most helpful in supplying illustrations to me.

Overseas, the National Maritime Museum London and the Public Records Office of N. Ireland have been of assistance to me, as has the Archives Nationale, Directeur General, Mr. Jean Favier with regard to material on the Baudin expedition.. I am also grateful to the Royal Navy Hydrographic Department of the Ministry of Defense, in particular Lt. Cdr. Andrew David for information and drawings pertaining to their surveys in Bass Strait.

Many people share with me an interest in the history of Bass Strait. In this regard I would like to thank Mr. J. Loney, Mr. P. Stone, Capt. D. Wharington, Mr. P. Williams and Capt. C. Jackman. On King Island my friends Peter and Margaret Blackney have also been especially kind in assisting me, also Michael and Dorothy Crow, Len and Cecily Sullivan. To Mr. Col. Cotter and his wife Pearl my sincere

thanks for their hospitality and the photographs of the Wickham quarters as well as that of the tower used on the cover of this book.

My thanks to Mrs. K. Stanley, Mostyn and Gay Veith for locating information in Hobart., Mr. John Tulley for his photograph of Blanket Bay, my old friend Mr. George Cox for his counsel, Mr. R. Spreadbrough at the Crown Lands Department of Victoria for locating the Smythe material, Iain Stuart for information on the Aborigines of the Otway Coast, Mr. T. Wicking of Warrnambool and M. P. Brown of Geelong for their preparedness to assist me in tracing La Trobe's journeys, Mrs. P. Kinnear of Allansford, John and Diane Bonney, Dick Mandziak and Stan Valaitis.

Whenever I have visited Cape Otway Lightouse the keepers and their families have always made me feel welcome. In particular my thanks to Mr. Ern Jones, Mr & Mrs R. (Bob) McNeill, Mr. & Mrs. Harry Dodemaide, Peter and Irene Scott, Fred and Janet Armstrong.

Many people who share my interest in the Otway Coastline have helped me, in particular I would mention Mr. Cyril Speight and the late Mrs. Bell Speight, Mr. Perc Hampshire and Paul Hampshire, Mr. Cyril Marriner, Mrs S. Anderson, Ron and Jenny Cunnington of Yuulong, Mr. Bob Davis, Mr Alec Neave, Mr. W Evans (grandson of keeper William Evans), Mr. Stewart Webster. To Ross Ferrier and Allan Simms, my sincere thanks for the photographs of Cape Otway and Cape Wickham taken from their fishing boats. Mr Fisher of Ocean Grove; Mr. W.F. Renshaw and Mrs. K.D. den Hollander for the use of family diaries. Also of my good friend Mrs. Rosamund Duruz who has helped me understand a little better the history of the Heytesbury country she knows so well, I record my appreciation.

Many past residents of Cape Otway have provided information on the lifestyle there before the turn of the century, they include Mrs. Laura McColl (nee Skilton) and the late Mrs. Edith Gosney (nee Franklin) with their descriptions of the Blanket Bay Disaster, the late Mr. Louis Keys shared memories of Theodore Prolius, Miss Mason provided photographs of Lemuel Ford's return to Cape Otway and the changing of the mechanism in 1891. Of further assistance to me were Mrs. I. Russell and Mrs. E. McColl who gave information on their father Jack Dunk and Mrs. R.H. Livingstone who provided information on her late father-in-law, Captain Livingstone, Mrs. Lawson and Mrs. Till of Princetown; my thanks to all these people.

The late Mrs. Rosemary Gibbs, granddaughter of R.A. Murray and Jane Lousia Otway Ford, supplied invaluable information on the family of Henry Bayles Ford. Mrs V.F. Letcher, a granddaughter of H.B. Ford has kindly supplied me with photographs of the long serving keeper and his wife. Mrs. M. Morgan has helped me with material on the Cataraqui wreck - for this and information on emigration, my thanks. I am indebted to Mr. C.F. Gibbens of Tackley U.K., for locating the photograph of this village. The photograph is

owned by Mr. John Tyrell of Tackley and he has kindly given me permission to publish it.

For help and advice regarding production of this book my thanks are owed to Mr. H.E Booth and Lois Holt. My many friends know how much I have needed their encouragement and I acknowledge my dependency on it over the years.

Professor Stephen Murray-Smith of Melbourne University has supported me in this attempt to record the history of Bass Strait's lighthouses and I wish to record my sincere thanks to so fine an ally. My good friend Mr. Don Charlwood has given unstintingly of his time and expertise on the subject matter of this book while advising me of pitfalls a novice writer such as myself is prone to fall into. Aware of this books shortcomings, I record my thanks for being so faithful an escort through it. To Nell and the Charlwood household, my thanks for their support.

My parents' encouragement has meant much to me, especially my mother. Assisting me with the preparation of the manuscript she invested countless hours into its predecessors. On those labours of earlier days, this book rests.

It was my wife Anne, who first introduced me to the Otways, its coast and her parents' farm. The hospitality I found there from Mr. & Mrs. C.D (Mick) Edwards induced me to tarry and learn more of the Otways. But without Anne's gentle urging and the tolerance of our daughters, Meredith and Alexandra, I know that this book would never have appeared. Aware, I trust, of my gratitude, they may now breathe a sigh of relief!

DMW   February 1981

Sadly, many of the aforementioned are no longer with us. Some were close family members – others were friends who shared an abiding interest in the Otway Coast, its lighthouses and the countless ships who depended on those towers for safe landfall. Happily, new generations of interested researchers and Otway devotees are beginning to fill out the depleted ranks. One such is Michael Roberts whose splendid photograph of the Otway is on the back cover.

Thank you to the many individuals and organisations, including FOCOS (Friends of Cape Otway Station), who have encouraged me to produce a revised edition of this book for the 150th Anniversary of Cape Otway Lighthouse commencing operation as it did in August 1848. The Bowker , Robinson and Evans families now administer the Lighthouse complex under lease from Parks Victoria, they and in particular Bill Bowker have been of encouragement to me.

Finally, once again this work would not have appeared without the support of my wife of 27 years Anne and our (now three) daughters, Meredith, Alexandra and Laurine.

DMW   August 1998

PREFACE TO THE THIRD IMPRESSION

The Cape Otway Lighthouse is now 150 years old.

Since 1848 this structure has marked the boundary between the seemingly limitless Southern Ocean—in particular to those who crossed it in sail crowded ships bound for Australia—and treacherous Bass Strait. For all those many nights, a revolving light has shone out to sea from the Cape Otway tower, turning its back, as is the custom of lighthouses, on the land whose presence it announces.

However this mechanical contraption is a relative new comer to an ancient landscape so well appreciated and understood by the region's original inhabitants. A lighthouse is by definition an intruder. It makes no attempt to blend with the landform—instead it is compelled to dominate it in order to do its job. The clash of approach is obvious. Certainly such notions as "touch the ground lightly" were not entertained at the time of its building and only now are we starting to acknowledge the pain its construction might symbolize to some.

One hundred and fifty years on, this unassuming building has outlasted nearly all its metropolitan contemporaries, many far grander and pretentious. Night and day, Cape Otway Lighthouse has routinely conducted aspiring citizens and their nation building cargoes past its high cliffs. That was its job! Scores of keepers and mechanics with the support of their families have ensured that it did that job well.

Keepers are gone from the Otway now. The original tower's light was extinguished on the morning of January 7 1994 to be replaced that night by a solar powered beacon at its base. We know that lighthouses were built for very practical commercial purposes in their day, namely the saving of lives and cargoes and not always in that order. They were, in one sense, the airport landing lights of the 1840's! Still, in losing the old light many of us felt we had lost a good friend, something that by its constancy, regardless of weather conditions had become synonymous with Cape Otway and could not go out permanently.

As with lighthouses, so with books, this 3rd edition attempts to incorporate in places updating information that has emerged since 1981 regarding Cape Otway.

Cape Otway is entering a new phase of its history. A National Park stretches either side of it. Visitors are now encouraged to see this place just off the internationally famous Great Ocean Road and connect with one aspect of their heritage. You may even stay overnight in the keeper's quarters. A sealed road ensures you have a smooth ride to the front gate – something inconceivable to families faced with a three-day ride on horseback to fetch a doctor on the other side of the Otways for a sick child.

Not surprisingly many Australians have in recent years conferred a status approaching that of "sacred site" on Cape Otway because of its vital role in making safe landfall for an emigrant people who came further than any other.

Were elevation to such a status being decided on the basis of the number of tears of joy and relief shed by our forebears at seeing its light after two or more months of ship bound nights — then it is supremely well qualified.

August 1998

AUTHOR'S NOTE

One clear night, high in the Otways, I saw the flash of a light I presumed to be a plane. With all sense of direction numbed by my drive from the city, I asked my host, what it was. "King Island Lighthouse," he said. He said it in a way that left me with no doubt that I was the only person south of Colac who did not realize that from these ranges, when the Otway's weather relents, the Cape Wickham light is plainly visible. I replied that the place he mentioned must be over sixty miles away. "We are 1200 feet above sea level here" he said, "you can see a long way."

That was in 1969. Far away though that light was, I understood for the first time just how narrow the western entrance into Bass Strait is. Cape Otway on the Victorian side and to the south Cape Wickham, King Island are the two "door posts" of Bass Strait. These two capes, only fifty miles apart, are flanked by long coastlines that present themselves to the Southern Ocean. Vessels bound from Europe making for Bass Strait knew to avoid them but were not always able to do so. Whether driven off course by storms, pushed south by the fickle currents or just poorly navigated, many vessels found the "lee, low, rocky" western shore of King Island. Mariners needed a light to guide them into Bass Strait but till 1848 there was only the darkness. Spurred on by mounting loss of life along their landfall coasts, the authorities agreed to erect lighthouses. The central theme of this book is the struggle involved in the building and manning of the beacons at the inhospitable locations of Cape Otway and later Cape Wickham.

In order to place these achievements in context, I have sketched in the background history of this section of Bass Strait – a more detailed study must wait till another time. In the first two chapters I have attempted to convey how, following their discovery, these waters were quickly seized upon by opportunists. Whether they were sealers plundering the seal colonies; Eng-lishmen and Frenchmen seeking new spheres of influence for their European masters; or mariners anxious to avoid the run south around Van Diemen's Land when bound for ports on Australia's eastern seaboard: they all converged on Bass Strait.

The courage of the men who sought out Bass Strait without the benefit of a lighthouse for the first half of the last century was matched by the devotion with which the lighthouse keepers at Cape Otway tended the light in the second half. Joined by their companion keepers at Cape Wickham in 1861, the concluding chapters are an inadequate attempt to document their little known story. With supplies only arriving twice annually, the tending of the light every night, the upkeep of the station during the day, this was the lot of a lighthouse keeper before the turn of the century and for a good many years of the present one. But there were compensations – many families embraced the solitude willingly, the continual wind, the forest backdrop, the sound of the sea always there and the satisfaction of knowing that one was responsible for a light which could bring safety or, by its extinction, tragedy to the landfall of those at sea seeking out Bass Strait.

Keepers came and went – H.B. Ford remained thirty years at Cape Otway as Superintendent until his retirement in 1878. E.C. Spong served for some twenty years as Ford's equivalent at Cape Wickham. But by 1896, the year at which I have chosen to conclude this account, the isolation of these lighthouses was beginning to deminish. A century that had commenced with James Grant and John Black discovering Bass Strait's principal western entrance, was almost concluded. Importantly though, this was the year of the Blanket Bay Disaster near Cape Otway involving the lighthouse supply ship. Shortly after, the supplies ceased to be brought ashore there and a safer overland route was adopted. Keepers no longer listened for the *Lady Loch's* siren.

Today few people remember life at a lighthouse station before 1900. One who can, firmed my resolve to write this book as she shared with me her memories of Cape Otway and the other lighthouses she had known as a keeper's daughter. Her name is Mrs. Laura McColl (nee Skilton). I dedicate this book to her, trusting that through it, many others will be able to share her recollections and appreciate why such important light-houses were built by concerned men as *Beacons of Hope*.

February 1981

Note to the second impression, 1991

On a winter evening ten years ago, at Duke & Orr's dock, the late Stephen Murray-Smith launched the first edition of this book. Our surroundings and the weather, I remember, were appropriate to the occasion. Outside, a biting wind swept the Polly Woodside jetty and at sunset a rain shower turned her poop deck to gold; near at hand were past mooring places of long-vanished sailing ships whose names had once been household words.

It has been gratifying to receive the thanks of people who read that first edition, as well as a few corrections they made. Descendants of the Fords of Cape Otway and of poor suffering George Morwick (not Morwich as stated in Chapter 13) were among the many who made them-selves known to me.

Happily, the grave of Henry Bayles Ford and his wife, Mary Ann Ford, in the Melbourne General Cemetery - unmarked for over eighty years - now has a plaque affixed to a piece of Cape Otway sandstone salvaged from their first lighthouse quarters. It was placed on the grave by some of their direct descendants and by Ford's old colonial employer, the Victorian Government. Thus the couple's long vigilance at 'the Otway' has received some recognition by a later generation. These pages themselves are a small memorial to all those who kept Bass Strait's lights burning.

August 1991

THE LIGHTHOUSE

A lighthouse on the Australian coast in the 1860s

Thundering surf on the blind and driven coast,
Out of the south the long cry of the gale,
Seas bursting here like guns on Black Man's Head
The answering boom as they swing against Cape Fell.
But that rage comes muffled here by double walls
Of thick-hewn stone; the air hangs still in the tower
Grey in the light of lowering afternoon
That dims or whitens as the squalls fly over.
Only at times a shudder, a jar runs upwards
From the rocky base, and a sly smell of damp
Creeps through the stone. But all is in order here
And safe enough.

                              Nan McDonald

CONTENTS

"*The land that we coasted .. is almost completely wooded right down to the shore, except, however, for some large white patches in various places which could serve as landmarks.*" *Nicholas Baudin. March 1802.*

A French view of the coast in the region of Cape Otway. The names Baudin gave to prominent features were later changed by his contemporaries in order to reflect a less "Republican" attitude.

...THROUGH THESE STRAITS...

1

All the early ships bound for Port Jackson rounded Van Diemen's Land. Only the French explorer D'Entrecasteaux, in 1792, noted the likely existence of a strait between the mainland and Van Diemen's Land from his observations of the current and wave patterns in the adjoining waters. However, this experienced navigator had orders to reach the Pacific Ocean speedily in order to conduct a careful search for his colleague La Perouse and his vanished ships and had no time to verify his assumptions.

It was left to Bass and Flinders with their voyage along the northern coast of Van Diemen's Land in 1798 to prove the existence of Bass Strait. The strategic and trade implications were obvious to all as this shorter route became known, for use of it promised to cut five or six days off the voyage from England. Two more years passed without a ship passing from west to east through Bass Strait on its way to Sydney. The first vessel to attempt such a passage was the *Lady Nelson* under Lieut. James Grant.

Grant was a friend of Captain John Schanck, Commissioner of the Navy Transport Board, the man who had supported construction of the *Lady Nelson* with its unusual sliding or retractable keels. A brainchild of the sometime naval architect the Duke of Northumberland, the ship's novel design permitted the raising and lowering of three keel boards in response to weather and sea or depth of water. It was in short, an ideal surveying vessel.

Earlier while wintering at Capetown, Grant had received Admiralty Orders to attempt a passage west to east through the newly discovered Bass Strait. An uneventful voyage across the Indian Ocean was climaxed by the sighting of land on the 3rd December in the region of present day Mount Gambier. Grant then proceeded eastwards along the coast noting its principal features. Having named the southernmost point of the coast Cape Albany Otway, Grant described the shore-line:

"I never saw a finer country, the valleys appeared to have plenty of fresh water meandering through them. At eleven a.m. I ordered the boats out manned and armed and went in search of a place to land on or anchor in. The land here is truly picturesque and beautiful resembling very much that about Mount Edgecumbe near Plymouth, which faces the Sound. It is moderately high but not mountainous. We did not see any fires on it, probably from the shore being inaccessible, and much surf breaking on it."[1]

1. *His Majesty's Armed Surveying Vessel, Lady Nelson.*
"*... I now reflect with much pleasure that I had conducted my little vessel safely out ... fulfilling ... orders to search for a passage through these straits.*" – *Grant.*

Although Grant himself approached the coast in one of the ship's boats, he could see no safe landing place. With unconcealed frustation, he records that he had to content himself with naming of the coastline between Cape Patton and Cape Danger. He called it Wight's Land. This is the region of present day Apollo Bay. The name joined the growing list of appellations recorded in the *Lady Nelson's* journal for the first week of summer: Cape Northumberland and Cape Bridgewater, Lady Julia Percy Island — each a fresh discovery by this vessel that many had assumed would never stand the rigours of so long a voyage. These names do survive today on charts of the Victorian coastline, but Wight's Land was very soon forgotten.

James Grant brought the *Lady Nelson* to anchor in Sydney on December 13, 1800, "with the satisfaction of being the first vessel that ever pursued the same track across that vast ocean."

Captain John Black of the brig *Harbinger* followed the *Lady Nelson* through Bass Strait less than four weeks later. The resourceful Black had fallen in with Grant in mid-Atlantic. at that stage of his voyage Black was in command of a Spanish prize ship. Grant offered to escort Black to Capetown. While there, undoubtedly

Black learnt of Grant's instructions and saw the commercial advantages offered by a new route that eliminated need to round the southern reaches of Van Diemen's Land in trading with Sydney. While working his way into the strait Black sighted and named Governor King's Island – that island that was before many years to become known as the "Graveyard of Ships."

Governor King himself was keenly aware of the strategic value of the straits and instructed Grant to return there in the *Lady Nelson* and survey more thoroughly the coast he had sighted. He was also to examine King Island. In the event bad weather prevented Grant from sailing further than Western Port Bay.

Lt. John Murray succeeded Grant in command of the *Lady Nelson* and took her south once more into Bass Strait. King thought it likely that Murray would encounter Matthew Flinders in the *Investigator* who was completing his survey of the entire Australian coastline. A French expedition under Post Captain Nicholas Baudin was similarly believed to be working in Bass Strait but Murray encountered neither party in his exploration of Bass Strait's extremities. After discovering Port Phillip Bay, Murray followed instructions and examined all but the western shore of King Island. This he was unable to reach because of contrary winds. Before departure from Sea Elephant Bay on the Island's east coast, he wrote:

"Thus we took leave of this large and fine island where the benevolent hand of Providence has fixed the chief necessities of life and the means to procure some of its luxuries."[2]

Not until January 1802 did the French expedition that King had been warned of, sight Van Diemen's Land's southern shores preparatory to examining Bass Strait. This splendidly equipped scientific expedition comprising the corvette *Geographe* and the store ship *Naturaliste*, had left Le Havre under Baudin in October 1800. Himself an educated man, Baudin had instructions to examine thoroughly the southern shores of New South Wales. In particular he was to complete a thorough survey between Bass Strait's western extremities and that point on the coastline of the Great Australian Bight where the exploration of his countryman, D'Entrecasteaux had terminated in 1792. French

2. *Post Captain Nicholas Baudin. Commander - in - Chief of the Corvettes Geographe and Naturaliste.*
"*Be severe if circumstances require it, but be fair.*"
– *Instructions to Baudin.*

charts referred to these lands as *Terre Napoleon* – much to the consternation of certain English administrators.

The two French ships were separated by storms off the Van Diemen's Land coast. Thus they completed independent assessments of Bass Strait. Hammelin, commanding *Le Naturaliste*, only inspected Western Port and sailed to Sydney after searching unsuccessfully for *Le Geographe*. But Baudin was able to carry out orders and by 30 March 1802 was abreast Cape Otway. Unaware that this entire coastline had been named by James Grant fifteen months earlier, this Republican naval officer wrote in his journal:

"During the afternoon we continued along the coast. The

3. Lt. Matthew Flinders. "The very one who discovered the strait which should bear his name, but has most inappropriately been called Banks Strait." – Baudin.

nature and aspect of it changed here, although the land along the seafront is steep and cliffy and appears arid as far back as some well wooded mountains in the interior. In the morning we noticed some smoke to the West, which indicated that this part of the continent was inhabited. It was on top of a rise on the shore, but was not very big."[3]

The coastal elevations rendered by the expedition artists depict this smoke. Soon afterwards the high cliffs near Moonlight Head and Cape Volney came into view:

"All the coast that we saw looked to me to be unapproachable and not even to offer shelter for a vessel, although it is divided into several more or less large bays which would seem to indicate an easy landing. The sea breaks along the entire stretch of shore. We made absolutely sure of this, for we were very close in."[4]

After exchanging observations with Matthew Flinders a week later at Encounter Bay, Baudin discontinued his survey westward. By now scurvy had devastated his crew. Undermanned as he was, he avoided unknown waters and rounded Van Diemen's Land on his way to Sydney. When he entered Port Jackson on June 18 he had to seek assistance to bring *Le Geographe* to her berth. Hammelin, having returned to Bass Strait in search of his commander, joined Baudin in Sydney by the end of the month.

Baudin only became aware of the existence of King Island and Port Phillip during his stay in Sydney which lasted until the start of summer. By this time Flinders had completed a detailed survey of Port Phillip Bay and had examined most of King Island's shore. At the southern extremity of the island he had located wreckage from an unknown ship. No conclusive identification has ever been made as to what ship it was, but King Island's reputation as a marine graveyard had commenced.

After grateful farewells in Sydney both French ships sailed on 17 November 1802 direct to Sea Elephant Bay on King Island's eastern coastline. They anchored preparatory to commencing the first scientific investigation of the island, particularly of its plants and animals. However, shortly after arriving, the French observed the schooner *Cumberland* approaching. She also dropped anchor in Sea Elephant Bay and next day Baudin was visited by her Commander, Lieut. Robbins. Robbins handed him a letter from Governor King. Part of this read:

"You will no doubt be surprised to see a ship so close on your heels. You are acquainted with my intention to establish a settlement in the South, however it has been hastened by information communicated to me immediately after your departure. This information is to the effect that the French wish to set up an establishment in D'Entrecasteaux Channel. [Near present day Hobart] It is also said that these are orders from the French Republic."[5]

Baudin's response to the deliverer of this unexpected communication was civilized indeed. He told the English

4. Governor Phillip Gidley King – "Myself and family join in the kindest good wishes for your health and shall long remember the pleasure we enjoyed in your society." – King writing to Baudin on the occasion of the Cumberland's dispatch to King Island.

of what time his party dined and added that the Englishmen were welcome as guests of the French Republic. A reply to King's letter he saved for later.

Soon the English intentions were made even plainer. Robbins had the Union Jack hoisted – albeit upside down and wet – to a tree overhanging the French scientists' tents on the beach. As instructed by Governor King, he then proclaimed the entire region for King George. The gunpowder with which the Royal Marines fired the salute, like much in the following days, was borrowed from the amazed French.

Robbins' actions had magnified King's distrust of the

5. *Sea Elephant Bay, King Island. "... I hope that we may meet again in London or in Paris. Despite the prevailing westerly winds Le Naturaliste left to order the dinner for which you will have to pay." – Baudin writing to King from Sea Elephant Bay.*

French party's intentions. King understood that whoever controlled King Island, controlled Bass Strait. Any idea of establishment of a settlement by England's traditional rival had to be squashed quickly. Understandably, Baudin felt insulted and wrote to King, informing him of what he thought of his actions and his island namesake. Portion of the letter reads:

"I am very sorry that King Island bears your name, because it appears to me to be of no use whatever, offering merely a temporary source of supply for the fishery of the fur seal and the seal, which the sealers call the sea elephant. Sea Elephant Bay is good only for ruining ship owners by the loss of anchors and cables. I have no knowledge of the claims which the French Government may have upon Van Diemen's Land, nor of its designs for the future; but I think that its title will not be any better founded than yours. However, if it were sufficient, according to the principle you have adopted, to have thoroughly explored a country in order to vest it in those who made it known first, you would have no claims" [6]

The letter concluded with a greeting and a wry comment, the significance of which we will never know – though no doubt King understood Baudin's meaning:

"Please present my respects to Madame King, and recall me to her rememberance as also to Miss Elizabeth, and all the other people whom I had the pleasure of meeting at your home. I expect to receive a letter from you at the Isle de France and I hope that we may meet again in London or in Paris. Despite the prevailing westerly winds *Le Naturaliste* left to order the dinner for which you will have to pay." [6]

Baudin was to die at Mauritius; the dinner appointment was never kept.

While the French and English had been playing out their games of statesmanship, private enterprise sought the seal and sea elephant. Sealing had grown in only four years to be a major component of the New South Wales export trade, the pelts fetching high prices in Canton. [7] The seals were hunted by methods so ruthlessly thorough that a gang from the snow *Harrington* was able to take 4,300 and hundreds of sea elephants in one month. Most of this haul were killed on the New Year Islands at King Island's northern end.

By May 1803, King was concerned by the sealers depredations. He wrote to the Colonial Department in London:

"I shall find it expedient to restrain individuals from resorting there (Hunters Islands and King Island) in too great numbers, and to fix certain times for them visiting these places, to prevent the destruction of that commercial advantage." [8]

King had good reason for his concern. The French party had recorded the habits of the sea elephants and the brutal methods used to kill them. Francois Peron, the chief naturalist and historian of Baudin's expedition wrote:

"This large species will be wiped out like so many others, pursued into its most hidden retreats, reached in its most distant places of asylum, defeated by the irresistible force of human intelligence the species will disappear from the surface of the globe; one will see only remnants of this huge species; its remains will become dust that the winds will disperse ..... It will live on only in the memory of men and in the pictures of the species." [9]

The pace of the slaughter did not lessen. As the animals became fewer the nomadic sealers with their aboriginal harems settled on various islands. Superb boatmen, they left little written record of their island communities, but in years to come their descendants would be called upon to bury the victims of the strait that now sustained them.

The sealing industry was responsible for the elimination of many animal species and the abandonment by others of their traditional habitat. The sea elephants of

King Island are a good example of this abandonment; today only infrequent visits are made by them to the island. Possibly they sense the tragedy of a shoreline that two hundred years ago they ruled unchallenged.

To Bass Strait the sealers brought ruthless change but they also pushed back many of the boundaries of uncertainty concerning its safe navigation. Navigators and mariners in general began to think of it as the main route to Sydney so that by 1810 numerous ships were passing Cape Otway into Bass Strait in preference to the southern Van Diemen's Land route. The final decision was the captains and was very often dictated by prevailing winds and his vessels ability to work its way into the strait.

A soldier of the 73rd Regiment accompanying Governor Macquarie to New South Wales in 1809 – 10 wrote on board the *Hindostan:*

"The Captain seemed determined to go through Basses Straights. He offered to go through with the *Hindostan* and let the *Dromedary* go by Van Diemen's Land ... today we are 2020 miles from Governor Kings Island." [10]

In fact both ships proved to be following a course which offered no such option. King Island and the strait it guards was not sighted and instead it was De Witt's Island at the southern extremity of Van Diemen's Land, that provided their landfall. This demonstrates just how uncertain landfall could be for these early mariners.

Belief in the strategic importance of Bass Strait was further demonstrated by the establishment of the short lived settlement at Sullivans Cove, Port Phillip. [11] Sent direct from England, this party under a Lieut. Gov. David Collins, had instructions to establish a presence at either King Island or Port Phillip, or at both places. This was in order to secure uncontestable claim to the strait and the adjoining coastline, but Collins withdrew from Port Phillip and moved the settlement to Hobart in January of 1804.

In the years that followed, French naval expeditions continued to explore the waters of Bass Strait but more usually they employed it as a shorter route to the Pacific and New Zealand.

Both Louis de Freycinet commanding the *Uranie,* and Hyacinthe Bougainville commanding the *Thetis* and

6. *Doubtless this ceremony might appear frivolous in the eyes of those who know little of English politics ... Thanks to these public and repeated declarations, England seems daily to strengthen her claims ..." – Peron.*
The beach at Sea Elephant Bay with the French tents and English flag above, as sketched by N.M. Petit.

7. *Young Sea Elephants at Macquarie Island. "I myself have seen one of these young females shedding abundant tears, whilst one of our sailors, a mean cruel man amused himself by breaking its teeth with the broad end of one of the oars ..." – Peron.*

8. Sea Elephants. Macquarie Island.
"This great species will be wiped out like so many others; discovered in its most hidden retreats ... it will disappear from the surface of the globe: one will only see some remnants of this huge species; its remains will become dust that the winds will disperse ... It will live on only in the memory of men and in the pictures of the species." – Peron's journal.

Esperance worried the English authorities. [12] But the greatest concern was reserved for a French expedition commanded by Dumont D'Urville in 1826-27. Aboard his ship *L'Astrolabe*, D'Urville attempted to examine the landfall coast seen by his fellow countryman Baudin, 24 years before. West of present day Warrnambool and moving eastward he recorded: [13]

"At 2 p.m. the wind having strengthened, and finding ourselves not more than eight or ten miles from land, I went about and took the seaward tack. As we turned a sounding gave thirty fathoms, the seabed gravel and shells. This portion of the coast is flat, sandy and of a sad and monotonous aspect. The S.E. and S.W. both combined and in opposition put immense strain on the ship. I really regretted that these awkward east winds did not permit me to hug the coast as far as Cape Otway in order to compare the work of Baudin and Flinders, which differ so much in these latitudes. In the evening the wind finally changed to S.S.E. and S.S.W., freshening considerably. We took advantage of it to make headway during the night. At midnight a sounding gave fifty-five fathoms, the seabed coarse sand and coral; at 4 a.m. we caught sight of Cape Otway from N. to E.N.E. at a distance of ten to twelve miles; high land, well wooded and of a very pleasant aspect. As soon as we rounded the cape I came back slowly to starboard to steer for Westernport."

D'Urville's careful examination of Western Port Bay aroused Governor Darlings' suspicions.

Accordingly, H.M.S. *Fly*, with a party of convicts, soldiers and settlers was despatched to Western Port in a move reminiscent of King's reaction to Baudin. [14] The French did not return. The settlement was abandoned thirteen months later and the region left to itinerant sealers D'Urville had met there. The French were drawn back to the Pacific and their expanding possessions there. They would also ascertain the fate of La Perouse's expedition – by then missing for nearly forty years. With D'Urville's departure French interest in the region waned and the Australian Colonies sea route through Bass Strait could be considered strategically secure. By 1830 the shipping hazards at the western entrance to Bass Strait had been better publicized. The Hydrographical Directory placed great emphasis upon locating of Cape Otway correctly: [15]

"in order that the commander in steering for it from the

9. *The coastline just east of Cape Otway. "I ordered the boats out manned and armed and went in search of a place to land in."*
– Grant.

westward, may not be deceived in the real situation of his ship."

There followed a warning to ships of the reef at Cape Otway's base:

"While passing this cape in H.M. Ship *Volage,* on the 11th of October, 1826, the sea was observed to break high upon a rocky reef, which extends from it nearly 2 miles in a south direction. This reef was also observed by Captain Lamb, in the *Baring,* August 28, 1815, who considered its extent to be 1½ mile from the pitch of the cape; the sea broke high upon it, but none of the rocks appeared above water."

Most mariners were able to heed these warnings. Others unsure of their position or running before strong south-westerly gales, desperately needed a beacon to show them the way into Bass Strait.

The ensuing pages tell the story of the three light-houses at the western entrance to Bass Strait, of the establishment and manning of them in the years of sail.

QUOTATIONS AND REFERENCES

1. Lt. James Grant. R.N., *The Narrative of a Voyage of Discovery*, (Facsimile Edition), Heritage Publications. Melbourne. 1976, p.73.

2. Ida Lee. *The Logbooks of the "Lady Nelson"*, Grafton & Co., London. 1915.

3. Nicholas Baudin (translated by Christine Cornell) *The Journal of Post Captain Nicholas Baudin.* Libraries Board of South Australia, Adelaide, 1974 p. 373.

4. ibid. p. 373

5. ibid. p. 441

6. Francois Peron, Chapters XII and XIII of *Voyage of Discovery to the Southern Lands,* translated by Helen Mary Micco in *King Island and Sealing Trade 1802,* Roebuck Society Publication No. 3, Canberra, 1971. p. 43 and 44.

7. J. S. Cumpston. *First Visitors to Bass Strait,* Part II. Oiling at King Island. 1800 - 1810. Roebuck Society, Canberra, 1973 p. 46.

8. *H.R.A. 1. Vol. IV.* p. 249. King to Nepean.

9. Peron/ Micco. p. 34

10. Ensign Alexander Hue. (D.834/2) *Diary held by P.R.O. Northern Ireland.* p. 17.

11. H.G. Turner, *History of Colony of Victoria. Vol. 1.* Longmans, Chap. 2.

12. John Dunmore. *French Explorers in the Pacific. Vol 2.* Clarendon Press, Oxford.

13. Dumont D'Urville. *Voyage de L'Astrolabe Vol. 1. (1826 - 1827)* Chapter VII. 10 and 11 November 1826. English translation, unpublished manuscript by Helen Rosenman; held by S. Murray - Smith.

14. Turner. p. 63 - 67.

15. Hydrographical Office, *The Australia Directory Vol. 1,* Admiralty, London 1830. p. 89 and 90.

ILLUSTRATION SOURCES

Facing Page – Archives Nationale. 5JJ51 ARGI reel 16, view No 30 – held by the State Library of South Australia on microfilm.

1. Narrative of a voyage in the *Lady Nelson.* Grant

2,3,&4, Picturesque Atlas of Australia. Garran. Vol 1.

5 & 9 D.M.W.

6. Archives Nationale. Copy held by the State Library of S.A. Ref No AR61 Reel 33 Frame 70.

7 & 8 Dept. of Science. Antarctic Division

10. Mitchell Library, Sydney. ML. A1. 214. p. 327.

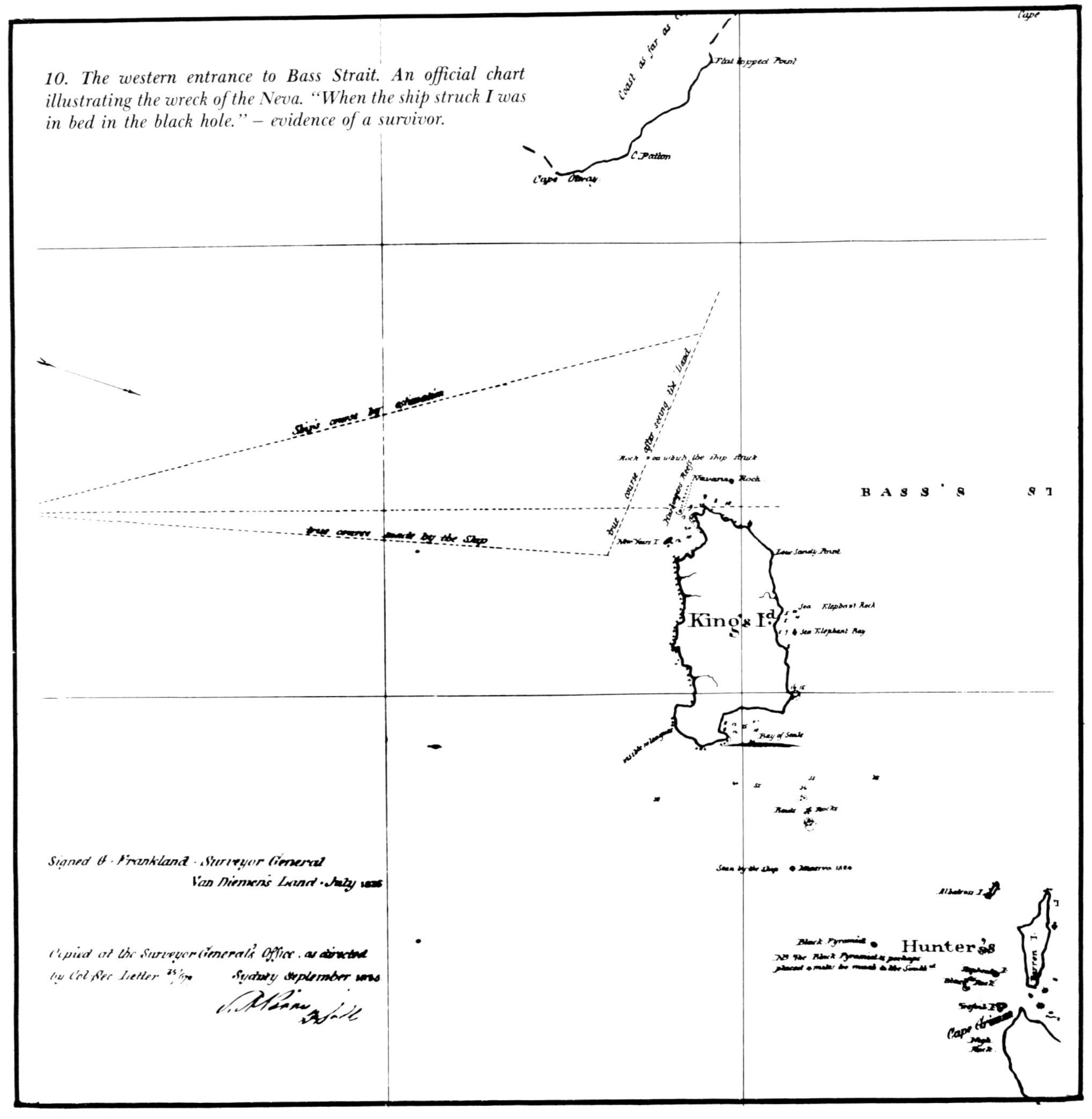

10. The western entrance to Bass Strait. An official chart illustrating the wreck of the Neva. "When the ship struck I was in bed in the black hole." – evidence of a survivor.

...AN ANXIOUS PASSAGE...

On the night of the 12th May 1835, the convict ship *Neva* was entering Bass Strait from the west. This ship had left Cork in Ireland four months earlier with 135 female convicts and their 55 children. The master, a mariner of long experience, was Benjamin Peck.

At 2 a.m. on the morning of the 13th with good visibility afforded by moonlight, the ship, a Hull built vessel of 331 tons, struck the Navarine Reef off the northern coast of King Island. By morning 218 persons had drowned of whom 138 were convicts. Another seven survivors died from exposure during the first night. Peck suggested at the inquiry that the deaths of these seven had been contributed to by their drinking too much of the rum that had been washed ashore. [1]

To see the Navarine Reef today is to marvel that any one at all reached shore. Two miles off shore, the reef is flanked by the East and West Harbingers, first seen by John Black. Peck in his evidence said that he was endeavouring to give the Harbingers a wide berth when he struck the Navarine Reef. Reference to a chart of these waters will show that if Peck's evidence and his reported course were correct, he could not have struck the Navarine Reef. Peck blamed his charts, alleging that the Harbingers were laid down too far to the east and that this, taken in combination with set of the current to the southward, had brought about the loss of his ship.

The evidence of the female convicts is revealing as to conditions on board at the time of the tragedy: [2]

"Rose Anne Hyland, a prisoner per *Neva*, states, I am a native of the County of Down in Ireland. I embarked at Cork with other prisoner women on board the late ship *Neva*. For the first three weeks after sailing the provisions were short in quantity, but the captain upon a complaint being made to him took the duty of opening the provisions upon himself, and after that everything was quite right. I have no complaint to make against the Master or Superintendent or any of the crew, they always did their duty correctly as far as related to the prisoners. When the ship struck I was in bed in the black hole that night. I got up and observing the water rushing in, I and another woman broke open the black hole prison door and went into the main prison. The Captain ordered the ladder to be hauled up and that we who had been in the black hole were to be kept down — but myself and other two succeeded in getting on deck. Most of the other women who had been in the main prison had got on deck and into the cuddy where they were drinking and some of them were so drunk as to be unable to help themselves. I was on the poop when the ship opened,

1. *Sir John Franklin – Governor of Van Diemen's Land, the originator of moves to see lighthouses erected in Bass Strait. ". . . the master of any merchant ship . . . looks upon this portion of his voyage with the greatest apprehension."*

and it fell in when there was several women drinking in the cuddy. I stuck to this part of the wreck, and went some part of the way on shore upon it. When we came close to another part of the wreck upon which were some of the sailors, I endeavoured to get upon it when one of the sailors caught hold of me and pulled me upon it. I fell off and was a second time caught hold of by the same man and placed again upon the wreck – when we got near the shore this man (Sharp) jumped off the wreck and carried a boy on shore, he returned for me, and then for another woman. I have no complaint to make of any person since the wreck. As far as relates to my own conduct on the morning of leaving the island, I only left the boat to go back for some shirts, having had a little rum which had got into my head."

Port Officer at Launceston, Lieutenant Friend R.N., who presided at the *Neva* Enquiry strongly recommended the construction of a lighthouse at Cape Wickham. The suggestion was lost somewhere between the Admiralty and the Colonial Office, although Lord Glenelg did inform Governor Bourke that, in consequence of the *Neva's* loss: [3]

".... it is the intention of His Majesty's Government to avoid sending out the Convict Ships at that period of the year when they are exposed to a greater danger of shipwreck.

Six years were to elapse and Van Diemen's Land was to have a new Governor before the matter of Cape Wickham lighthouse was again raised. These six years had seen the establishment of Melbourne and the settlement of the Port Phillip District. The *David Clarke* arrived on 27 October 1839 with the first immigrants for Port Phillip. In 1841 the ship *Duchess of Cumberland* arrived with the first direct mail from England. All of these changes meant increased passages through Bass Strait.

It was Van Diemen's Land and not the fledgeling District of Port Phillip that took the iniative in easing the difficulties of mariners negotiating Bass Strait. The Governor of the island colony was Sir John Franklin. He came to the position with a naval career as a background – he had in fact been a midshipman aboard Flinders' *Investigator* during his circumnavigation of Australia.

The following letter from him appears in the appendix to the Report on "Lighthouses proposed to be erected in Bass Strait" made by a committee of the New South Wales Legislative Council. With this letter the tortuous history of Bass Strait lighthouses can be said to commence: [4]

> Government House,
> Van Diemen's Land,
> Feb 3, 1841

"My Dear Sir George, [Gipps, Governor of N.S.W.]
 . . . I intended to have written to your Excellency on the subject of rendering the navigation of Bass' Straits more secure than at present, by the erection of Lighthouses.
 . . . This matter has occupied much of my attention from the time of my arrival in the Colony, and recent occurences in

2. *Sir George Gipps – Governor of N.S.W. – in 1845 forced to explain to the Home Government why lighthouses had not been built in Bass Strait.*

Bass' Straits have given increased importance to the subject; within the four years of my residence here, two large barques have been entirely wrecked there, a third stranded, a brig lost with all her crew, besides two or three Colonial Schooners, whose passengers and crew shared the same fate, not to mention the recent loss of the *Clonmell* steamer. ... I consider that the passage through Bass' Straits would be rendered secure, as far as the knowledge of a vessels exact position would make it, by placing Lighthouses on Cape Otway, the south west part of Sir Roger Curtis Island, and on Cape Howe, if the "Harbinger" Reefs had not been six or seven miles distant from the north west part of King's Island, I should have recommended the western Light being placed on that Island rather than on Cape Otway, but I fear if it were so placed, ships might be running on those reefs."

Franklin concluded with an expression of his concern for mariners forced to use the unlighted straits:

"... the prevalence of strong winds, the uncertainty of either the set or force of the currents, the number of small rocks, islets, and shoals, which, though they appear on the chart, have been but imperfectly surveyed, combine to render Bass' Strait under any circumstances an anxious passage for a seaman to enter; and I will venture to say that the master of any merchant ship trading from the northern hemisphere to Sydney, or in the opposite direction, looks upon this portion of his voyage with the greatest apprehension.

> Believe me my dear Sir George,
> Yours very faithfully,
> John Franklin."

The alarm engendered by an unlighted King Island may be seen in the diary of Anne Drysdale, writing in 1839 aboard the *Indus* as she records the circumstances of their entry into Bass Strait: [5]

"Thursday evening a hurricane got up. At daylight there were high cliffs two miles off, to which we were drifting towards King George Island [King Island] as we could not carry sail, and must trust in Providence ... "

Franklin's opinion that lighthouses strategically placed in the Straits would assist the safe passage of vessels was shared by William Moriarty, Port Officer at Hobart. This officer was dispatched to investigate the best position for lighthouses on the Tasmanian side of the Straits, however his report concludes with the remark: [6]

" . . . I should not desire to overlook the lighting of Bass' Strait, and were the points situated within this Government, would not hesitate to recommend Lights to be fixed on Cape Otway, Kents Group, and Cape Howe; as it is I fear to be considered intrusive and presumptuous, yet, when I state that sixty thousand tons of shipping pass annually to and from Launceston, and the different Ports of New Holland, we are not without an interest in the question at least. ..."

Of course ships masters were "not without an interest" but the New South Wales Legislative Council Report that sprang from Franklin's letter notes a difficulty in obtaining witnesses with sufficient expertise in the subject. One they did question was Captain J.W.C. Wickham, R.N. of *H.M.S. Beagle*. He had been a companion of Charles Darwin on the *Beagle's* most memorable voyage and was now back in Australian waters on survey work.

Wickham touched on what was to become a contentious point: the wisdom of lighting the north end of King Island when the off-shore Harbinger and Navarine Reefs were so close to the shore: [7]

" ... but as the position of these rocks has been carefully ascertained by the Officers of the *Beagle* and their distance off shore found not to exceed four and a half miles ... I am induced to consider the hill near the north point of King's

3. "All the coast that we saw looked to me to be unapproachable ... the sea breaks along the entire stretch of shore." – Baudin. 1802.
Wave cut platform and flanking cliffs at Ryans Den, twenty miles west of Cape Otway.

4. Skull Rock near Wilson's Promontory – "the number of small rocks, islets, and shoals ... combine to render Bass Strait under any circumstance an anxious passage for a seaman to enter."

Island, the most desirable situation for this light. The Harbinger rocks, although dangerous, are by no means so formidable as they are generally supposed to be, as instead of being a continuous reef some miles in extent, they are two single detached rocks, with a clear passage between them, through which the *Beagle* sailed and did not find less than sixteen fathoms water ..."

It seems fitting that the name of the man who expressed this opinion is perpetuated at King Island's northern tip: Cape Wickham.

Wickham was supported by a number of other ships masters who expressed concern over the dangers of King Island and also the possibility that any alternative lighthouse at Cape Otway be obscured by fog. In consequence the Committee recommended the erection of two lighthouses, Cape Wickham King Island at the Western entrance to the strait and Kents Group at the Eastern entrance. Unfortunately no realistic assessment was made of the cost of such structures, let alone an assessment of maintenance problems.

For a short time it appeared that the wreck of *Neva* might bring some benefit to later ships. The Governments of Van Diemen's Land and New South Wales were supposedly united in their vision for Bass Strait. It appeared that approval, when it was forthcoming from England, would mean that lighthouses would be established at critical points and the Straits dangers reduced. But events soon to unfold would run a different course. Bitter fruits of inaction would be harvested on the exposed western shore of Governor King's Island.

QUOTATIONS AND REFERENCES

1. Charles Bateson. *Australian Shipwrecks. Vol 1.* Reed, Sydney, 1972. p. 110
2. Mitchell Library. MS An 7 – Account of the wreck of the Neva. Minutes of Launceston Enquiry.
3. HRA 1. Vol. 18. p. 274.
4. N.S.W. Legislative Council: Lighthouses in Bass' Straits, Sept. 1841. Appendix p.1.
5. Anne Drysdale. Voyage aboard the Indus, 1839, manuscript MS. No. 9249. La Trobe Library, Melbourne.
6. N.S.W. Enquiry 1941. Appendix.
7. ibid.

ILLUSTRATION SOURCES

1 & 2 Picturesque Atlas of Australia. Vol. 2.
3. D.M.W.
4. Capt. D. Wharington.
5. Don Charlwood.
6. John Oxley Library, Brisbane.

5. Wilson's Promontory, presides over eastern Bass Strait. The lighthouse was erected in 1857.

6. Capt. J.W.C. Wickham of H.M.S. Beagle. King Island's northernmost cape is named after this friend of Charles Darwin.

...A LEE LOW ROCKY COAST ...

Admiralty concern for the perils to Bass Strait shipping was ably demonstrated when Commander J. L. Stokes was instructed to conduct a thorough survey of these waters by the Admiralty:[1]

"The number of vessels which are now in the habit of passing through Bass Strait, and the doubts which have been recently expressed, not only of the just position of the dangers it is known to contain, but of the existence of others, show the necessity of this survey being executed with that care and fidelity which will give confidence to all future navigators."

1841 gave way to 1842. In the September of that year the N.S.W. Committee reconvened and requested Stokes' opinion as to where lighthouses would be best placed in Bass Strait. Stokes had conducted extensive surveys of the various islands and reefs preparing the second generation of naval charts – for these waters Flinders' had been the first. He provides a telling description of the dangers of Bass Strait:[2]

"I would prefer Cape Otway, to the north end of King's Island. Ships entering the Strait generally make the land in the neighbourhood of Cape Otway, but from the want of some object on the shore to determine their position, are obliged to sight Kings' Island, and are in consequence brought in the neighbourhood of the dangers off the north end of that Island, called the Harbinger Reefs, and which I think is one great objection to the Light being on King's Island; ..... supposing a ship running in a westerly gale for a Light placed on the former [Otway] should happen to be on the southward of her true place, she would enter the strait safely; but had this vessel been running for the Light on King's Island, she would have been brought on the western side of that Island. A lee, low, rocky coast, with outlying rocks, and in all probability the ship would be wrecked."

Not surprisingly the committee changed their preference from Wickham to Otway. But this is only of academic interest, as over the next three years nothing further was done.

When Stokes published an account of his voyages he recorded the name used for Bass Strait by the early settlers[3] – "The Funnel" – "from the constant winds that sweep through it." In his journal are his impressions of the approach to Cape Otway from the direction of present Barwon Heads:[4]

"Passing this [the mouth of the Barwon River] the nature of the country begins to change, and high grassy downs with rare patches of woodland present themselves, which in their turn give place as we approach Cape Otway, to a steep rock coast

with densely wooded land rising abruptly over it."
"The above mentioned Cape is the northern point of the western extremity of Bass Strait, and is swept by all the winds that blow into that end of the Funnel. the pernicious effect of these is evident in the stunted appearance of the trees in its neighbourhood."

Stokes also noted the off shore Otway Reef. Both this and the wind assailed vegetation may be still seen by today's visitor to Cape Otway.

At King Island Stokes recorded his encounters with some of the early settlers of these lonely places while noting the isolated islands suitability for a penal settlement. He wrote of a New Year Islands man: [5]

"A sealer had established himself on the north island with two wives, natives of Tasmania. They were clothed in very comfortable great coats made of kangaroo skins, and seemed quite contented with their condition. Their offspring appeared sharp and intelligent."

Stokes also described a Captain Smith living on the adjacent west coast of King Island and records: [6]

"The house in which this modern Robinson Crusoe dwelt was what is called a slab hut formed of rough boards and thatched with grass. He had a garden in which grew some cabbages and a few other vegetables, but he complained sorely of blight from the west winds ...... I could not help pitying the condition of this gentleman and his interesting family, a wife and a daughter and three or four fine boys. They had retained a few of the tastes and habits of civilised life, and I observed a good library with a flute and music in the slab hut."

Stokes' commission had arisen because of the increasing trade through Bass Strait. Many of the vessels negotiating these waters were intercolonial vessels. Working their way along the coast as they did, their need

1. Commander John Lort Stokes — carefully surveyed Bass Strait and testified to the necessity for lighthouses there.

for lighthouses was acute and would be made clear at future inquiries.

Between 1842 and 1845 intermittent pressure was applied by the Melbourne and Sydney Chambers of Commerce for the erection of lighthouses but sadly the lessons implicit in the loss of a few hundred convicts and their children in the *Neva* were forgotten by the general public; so was the lighthouse inquiry itself. It must be admitted that the economy of the colonies was in a depressed condition during those years – drought and consequent reductions in wool exports produced a curtailing of funds for government work. The British Government, so far removed from the area of concern, had much more pressing matters on its doorstep.

2. Northern New Year Island – considered by many mariners giving evidence at later enquiries to be the ideal location for a lighthouse marking the entrance to Bass Strait.

Ireland and much of Scotland were in the grip of famine. Rioting by the impoverished, against the export of corn overseas by landholders, threatened to spread over the entire country. Australia was, in every sense of the word, a backwater with no one to argue her case.

The British Admiralty, concerned with safe passages for its convict transports and warships maintained the call for lighthouses. Later they were to criticize harshly those who abandoned Franklin and Moriarty's vision for the Straits.

A namesake of Moriarty, Merion Moriarty, Port Officer of New South Wales, was one of the few to press the issue. As late as July 1845 he wrote: [7]

"the advantage which will accrue to the Colony from the establishment of Lighthouses at Cape Howe and Cape Otway, and from the constant intercourse I have with the masters of all ships from Europe, I am enabled to state with confidence, that the expense attending them would be cheerfully met and amply repaid by the increased security in the navigation, which would result from their erection."

Even as the 1842 lighthouse inquiry gathered dust, ship wrecks about Bass Strait continued. The barque *Rebecca* was totally lost on King Island in 1843 while attempting to claw her way into 'The Funnel'. In September of the same year the schooner *Joanna*, so typical of the intercolonial trading vessels, was totally wrecked on the long beach that now bears her name, only 8 miles north west of unlighted Cape Otway. Bound from Launceston to Portland and Port Fairy, Victoria, she had sought the high Otway coastline to afford some shelter from strong northerly winds. However during the night of the 20th the wind swung around to the south west – a change typical of the Otway coast. Heavy seas pounded the *Joanna* that night and all next day with the result that three feet of water had entered the hold by evening. Her master Captain Irvine attempted to seek the little shelter afforded by Moonlight Head and Point Reginald. During the night however, she was driven further east and eventually dawn on the 22nd saw her broached by the waves in the surf. She was fortunate not to have chosen the uncompromising cliffs under Cape Volney as her graveyard, for it is certain that the Captain and crew would not have waded ashore there as they

3. *Warrnambool Harbour (circa) 1865 – not only masters of vessels from overseas needed lighthouses in Bass Strait – small coastal craft transported cargoes regularly through the strait and their owners pressed the need for lighthouses at the 1841 and 1845 enquiries.*

were able to do next day. Victualling themselves as best they could from the wreck they set off to walk for help. Their story was recorded two years later in notes made by C.J. La Trobe while he was visiting the vicinity of the wreck: [8]

"The master, Irvine, made his way in 8 days time to the neighbourhood of Geelong, having been in great distress and torn to pieces by the scrub; living upon dead whale and pig's face and in great dread of the blacks. The *Joanna* was a new vessel from Launceston to Portland, rigged in a manner which disabled her from sailing, went on shore off the mouth of the river. "Pime" and "North Wester" names of the two blacks who fell in with the crew. Captain goes to Launceston, and then comes back to Port Fairy, having arranged that a boat should be brought over from Launceston by one of the coasters, taken to the part of the coast where the vessel lay, and there dropped with its crew. He hoped to get the vessel off. Meanwhile the blacks had found the vessel, and had been helping themselves to the flour and sugar, which with cherry brandy etc. etc. composed the loading. The Captain engages Mr. Henry Allen to accompany him coast wise to the wreck, with his carpenter.

They manage to reach it and find it in entire, though in such a position as to preclude all hope of removal. Carpenter, Knowledge by name, blows off his fingers in igniting something at his powder flask, as they went; at the creek called by me after him. They after seeing the wreck return to Allan's. Boat comes afterwards, is swamped coming ashore, and two hands drown. The two other crawl their way without shoes to Allan's and one goes on to Port Fairy, and gathers together by his description of the wreck and its contents, all the loose fellows in the neighbourhood, who determine to go down to the wreck in a body for Xmas jollification. They manage to get there by aid of the blacks, cut the vessel in half, she breaks up and one half drifts ashore and breaks up. They have here a six weeks "spell", drinking quarrelling and fighting; half mad with the exposure, heat and debauchery, every man but one becoming blind by the explosure and the fly bites. They return to Allan's led by the seeing man with a stick, only part of the forecastle now left."

While plainly a light at Cape Otway would never have saved the *Joanna* from foundering, all wrecks added weight to arguments calling for the building of Bass Strait lighthouses.

As there were no railways or all weather roads to serve new settlements east and west of Melbourne, there was heavy reliance on coastal shipping. These coastal settlements served the growing number of squatters taking up vast land holdings. This was particularly so in the County of Grant, west of Geelong. With large flocks of sheep and no fences to contain them there was a desperate shortage of shepherds and general farm labourers. It is ironic that many of the Scottish rural poor were forced to leave the land at this time because of the enlargement of sheep holdings at home. The new country in the region of present day Colac was enthusiastically described by a James Malcom to the New South Wales Legislative Council Enquiry into Immigration in 1845. [9]

"Who shut up the sea behind doors
When it burst forth from the womb,
When I fixed limits for it and set its doors and bars in place,
When I said 'Thus far you may come and no farther;
here is where your proud waves halt'?"

Job 38.

4. Johanna beach at sunset. (See opposite page).

"There are thousands of acres adjoining Lake Colach [sic] clear of timber, and the richest land I ever walked or rode over, ... the district from Lake Colach, for about two hundred miles is very rich; I do not think there is richer land in any part of the world, it is as good a land as plough was put into."

In 1841, 32,625 assisted immigrants had come to the Australian Colonies (including New Zealand) however by 1844 the number had dropped to 2,229 and would at the end of 1845 stand at only 830. [10]

With such vast distances of travel involved across the most inhospitable oceans in the world, it is not surprising that the great percentage of emigrants chose not to come to the Australian Colonies but instead the far closer, well established Canada and United States. New homes made in these countries did not involve the almost certain surrender of hope to ever see loved ones and birthplace again. The disparity is shown in the figures for 1838; in that year for every passage to Australia and New Zealand, twelve others were for Canada and ten for the United States. [11] Not even with the discovery of gold some fifteen years later would this trend be substantially reversed. Not gold but the stigma of a remote prison was the image most potential emigrants from Great Britain had of Australia during the 1840's.

The emigration program as it evolved had employed two basic methods. [12] The first was where the Land and Emigration Commission chartered a ship and whole boatloads of aspiring settlers sailed together – this was particularly true in the 1830's whereby a shortage of young women in Sydney was partly alleviated.

However the Land and Emigration Commission also employed the Bounty System whereby shipping companies applied to the Commission for a contract to carry a given number of people to a prescribed destination. The contract would have to be completed by a certain date and advertisements were placed in newspapers giving locations that applicants would be received – a very large percentage of the people being illiterate.

In other cases various parish churches, on which the burden of social relief largely fell, were formed into unions and put forward the names of those within their individual parishes most in need of the new opportunities afforded by emigration.

5. Johanna Beach. "... the loose fellows in the neighbourhood ... determine to go down to the wreck ... for Xmas jollification." La Trobe 1846.

The owners or charterers of emigrant ships were paid by the head for those they delivered at the journey's end. The passage included food and medical care. The gratuity to the ship's master, first and second officer and surgeon superintendent was usually 5/-, 2/-, 1/- and 10/6 per "statute adult" respectively, and proportionately less for children depending on age. The money to make these payments came from the sale of Crown Lands in the Australian colonies – hence the dual name Land and Emigration Commission.

In 1843 the Liverpool firm of W.M. Smith and Sons had entered into a contract with the Commission to convey emigrants to Melbourne. The last of the quota of families drawn mainly from the English counties of Bedfordshire, Oxfordshire, Cambridgeshire and from Ireland were aboard the Quebec built *Cataraqui* on the night of August 3, 1845. One hundred days out from Liverpool, 369 emigrants plus the crew aboard, the *Cataraqui* was wrapped in darkness and blinding rain. Running before a winters gale, she was seeking the entrance to Bass Strait. Even by this date there was no light showing to guide or warn shipping.

QUOTATIONS AND REFERENCES

1. Capt. J.L. Stokes. Discoveries in Australia, HMS. Beagle. 1837 - 1843 p. 11.
2. N.S.W. Legislative Council. *Lighthouses proposed to be erected in Bass' Strait.* 1842.
3. Stokes. p. 257
4. ibid. p.262
5. ibid. p. 263 and 264.
6. ibid. p. 266
7. 30/7/1845. N.S.W. Port Officer to Colonial Secretary, printed in 1845 N.S.W. *Legislative Council. Report on Lighthouses.*
8. C.J. La Trobe, *Memoranda of Journeys and Excursions,* Journey No. 41. unpublished manuscript, 1856, M.S. No. H. 93166, La Trobe Library.
9. N.S.W. Legislative Council Immigration Enquiry 1845 Parliamentary Papers.
10. Edited by C.M.H. Clark. *Select Documents in Australian History.* 1788 - 1850. Angus and Robertson, 1950. p. 214.
11. ibid. p. 214.
12. P.B. Madgwick. Immigration into Eastern Australia, 1788 - 1851. Sydney University Press, Chapters 7, 8 and 9.

ILLUSTRATION SOURCES

1. La Trobe Library – lithograph by S. Pearce. H. 5227 PS 56.
2. Mr C. Cotter. King Island.
3. Mr. T. Wicking. Warrnambool.
4,5 & 6 D.M.W.

6. Johanna River joins the sea – through only one outlet for the past seventy years. The old western outlet may still be distinguished when walking along the sand hills – in the distance coastal spurs and gullies that were at first to defeat men who sought Cape Otway.

...BY A BRIGHTER STAR...

4

On the morning of 15 September 1845 the *Port Phillip Patriot and Melbourne Advertizer* carried a heading: "APPALING WASTE OF LIFE." The article commenced "We are painfully compelled to chronicle the most disastrous waste of human life that has hitherto occurred by any vessel in these seas." There then followed a detailed account of the loss of the *Cataraqui* at King Island, in the early hours of Monday the 4th of August. The article named the married emigrants and the number of their children who had perished with them. Typical entries read: [1]

"..... children, James and Hannah Rollins and six
children, Anthony and Edith Mery and nine
children, W. and Deborah Simmons and seven
children, Ephraim and Sarah Stafford and four
children, John and Sarah Savings and three
children..."

Names of the single followed. Over 350 persons were listed. From these five lines the readers eyes might have moved down to the forgotten Legislative Council proceedings in which this day, as if to mock the sad account that preceeded it, the following untimely notice appeared: [2]

"Mr Robinson to move. That a Select Committee be appointed to enquire and report as to the best positions for Light Houses or Beacons, in Bass' Straits, or on the coasts adjacent."

Two days later the *Port Phillip Gazette* gave further details of what J. Phelps Robinson, Member for Port Phillip had argued so prophetically in the Council. [3]

"This matter (lighthouses) . . . was so plain and the necessity for some proceeding of this description so self evident, that he would not detain the House by any argument in support of his present proposition . . . however . . . nothing had yet been done; but he should deem it a disgrace upon that House if another session was suffered to pass over without some further steps being taken in the matter."

Robinson, a consistent advocate of the lighthouse cause was fittingly elected as chairman of the Select Committee. He stood in ignorance of news of the *Cataraqui's* fate — a calamity that today remains Australia's worst peace time marine disaster in terms of loss of life.

At 4 a.m. the *Cataraqui* had struck the west coast of Governor King's Island, there the east bound waves are halted after an uninterrupted journey across the Southern Ocean. Within two days they broke up this well-built ship on rocks angled like shark's teeth. None of the women or children lived. Solomon Brown the one male emigrant survivor, lost his wife and family.

The following account of the wreck was given Supt. La Trobe by Thomas Guthery, the only surviving officer: [4]

"Sir,   Melbourne, 17th September
               1845

The painful duty devolves on me of informing your Honour of the total wreck of the Emigrant Ship "*Cataraqui*", C.W. Finlay Master, which sailed from Liverpool on the 20th April last, bound for Port Phillip having on board 369 Emigrants of all ages – exclusive of Mr. C. Carpenter Surgeon Superintendent and his brother Doctor Edward Carpenter and a crew of 44 men and boys."

For Master and Surgeon Superintendent alike it was the second trip to New South Wales. The *Cataraqui* had been inspected by the Lloyds examiners before leaving and with everything in order had set out for Port Phillip 13000 miles away. Guthery continued:

"Nothing particular occurred during the voyage, until about a fortnight prior to the 4th August when we experienced boisterous weather and a strong gale of wind from the N.W. to S.W. accompanied with heavy rain which continued without intermission until Sunday the 3rd. August – the ships course being during this period from E. by S. to E. by N. At 7 o'clock on Sunday Evening the 3rd. The ship was hove to under close reefed main topsail, and fore topmast staysail. The wind about this time was N.W. At midnight the gale wearing from the S.W. wore ship with her head to the southward and continued laying to until 3 a.m. On Monday the 4th I went on deck at 4 a.m. to relieve the watch, when I found the ship running free under three close reefed topsails and reefed foresail. The Captain was

2. "*... the ship struck, going at the rate ... of about 7 knots, through the water.*"
Cataraqui Beach, King Island – the reef on which the Cataraqui foundered.

3. The village of Nethercott in Oxfordshire where two families aboard the Cataraqui had originated. This photograph was taken around 1900 and shows the main group of labourers cottages there together with some of the residents. It was in this group of buildings that Anthony Merry, his wife Edith and their nine children, John and Hannah Ryman and their three children lived, before leaving to emigrate to Port Phillip. They never arrived.

on deck at the time and gave the orders to continue the course E. by N. to keep a good look out and let him know at day light. About half past 4 o'clock a.m. the tempest still continuing, rain falling in torrents, and the darkness of the night such as not to allow any object to be seen within a few hundred yards of the vessel, the ship struck, going at the rate, I suppose of about 7 knots, through the water."

Later it was alleged that the surgeon and his assistant wished to reach Melbourne as soon as possible so as to avoid outbreak of sickness among passengers kept below for days by the rough weather. Loss of passengers would have meant loss of bounty money. At Carpenter's urging Captain Finlay had decided to proceed before daybreak. After the initial grounding the vessel continued on, according to Guthery, for another 15 minutes before:[5]

"she struck the 2nd time after which she ran ahead for a few minutes and on striking the third time she struck and fell over on her larboard side. At this time the sea commenced breaking

on board, the passengers at this time rushing on deck and crying for assistance. The whole of the crew were instantly on deck and assisting to get the passengers from below, and I should say, to the best of my knowledge about 300 were got on deck. Seeing there was no possibility of saving the ship, the Captain ordered the masts to be cut away which was promptly done, with a view to righting the ship, as well as to form rafts for the people to get on shore. The sea by this time was breaking on deck, and carrying everything away, with part of the crew and passengers nothing could be done from this until daybreak. At daybreak observed the land ahead of the vessel, I should say about 130 yards, and could likewise see that the vessel was breaking up aft. The sea was breaking at this time over the vessel and washing away at every sea some of the passengers and crew. No possibility of reaching the shore was afforded. At 10 a.m. the only remaining boat was launched, and instantly capsized no one reached the shore until about 4 a.m. on the 5th, when one of the passengers got on shore by means of clinging to a small part of the wreck. About 5 p.m. the ship parted by the forerigging and left about 50 on the forecastle head. At daybreak she commenced breaking up altogether, when I was washed away from the spitsail yard, and do not remember scarcely anything until I found myself on the rock where I had been washed by the violence of the sea. I found two on shore at this time, and shortly afterwards we found six more that had been washed from the bows when she finally broke up. On my looking round I could not see any part of the vessel above water. Out of all on board 9 only were saved.

I remain,
(signed)   Thos, Guthery,
late Chief Mate of the Ship,
Cataraqui

The *Port Phillip Gazette* reported of Captain Finlay:[6]

"The last words he was heard to utter were, "God grant some one may be saved to tell the tale." ... he has left a wife and two children to regret his loss."

The *Gazette* article described the escape of one of the eight crew members, a young boy named Blackstock:[7]

" ... on the night of the Monday he was sitting on the anchor holding on along with another boy named Robertson, at this time there were about twenty five on the wreck, who had given up all hopes of being saved, and sat calmly awaiting their fate. Blackstock and his companion were at one time during the night washed off the anchor, but... [he] ... regained his position

4. David Howie — this man was responsible for collecting the remains of the Cataraqui victims and burying them in four large graves. He was dubbed Special Constable of the Bass Strait Islands in 1847.

and stooping down drew his companion upon the anchor. He had not been up more than five minutes when he died, and Blackstock pushed him down into the water again. Soon afterwards the sea washed the bowsprit away and as it could no longer afford them any protection all of them laying hold of whatever spars came in their way, trusted themselves to the water."

Guthery and probably the eight other survivors, believed themselves to be on the Australian mainland coast. At first they feared attack by Aborigines. They had no means of lighting a fire and two days passed before men belonging to David Howie's party found them. This farmer, trader and sealer had settled on Robbins Island south of King Island and alert for signs of shipwrecks, voluntarily visited the neighbouring islands every quarter. Howie had guessed there to be a wreck on King Island when a rosewood couch had drifted ashore on Robbins Island. When the *Cataraqui* survivors were found, he lacked means of alerting Melbourne to the disaster.[8] The delay might have been longer had not a Capt. Kirsopp of the cutter *Midge*, when passing King Island, noticed signal fires on the shore and put in to investigate. They learnt from Howie of what had happened and then brought he and the survivors back to Melbourne.

The newspapers reflected a shock felt by the entire population of Port Phillip. Within days the mood changed from shock to indignation and the papers mounted a vitriolic attack on the New South Wales Government and its servants. Condemnation followed condemnation. The wreck bore out their long-held contention that Port Phillip's real interests were matters of little moment to the government of New South Wales. Before long the papers raised the possible effect on future immigration to the Australian Colonies: [6]

"It is to be regarded as almost a national calamity; in as much, as the District was starving for labour, and we find this supply of healthy emigration snatched from us when almost within our reach, could anything be more tantalizing to the country ... It is to be regretted from the influence it will exert on the minds of labouring classes in Britain, who are naturally afraid to brave the dangers of the ocean, and henceforth will be tenfold more adverse to emigrate to Australia."

and then:

"That great blame must be attributed to some quarter is evident. Upon a spot more dangerous than any in the wide seas which surround us, and this vortex of destruction and death too, at the entrance of Bass's Straits — the high road to Sydney, Port Phillip, New Zealand, Van Diemen's Land, etc. for the vessels of all nations to traverse — there is no beacon to warn the mariner of his danger..... The Government of New South Wales and also of Van Diemen's Land and New Zealand are culpable, if this waste of property and human life is allowed, without measures being instantly adopted to prevent its recurrence."

The article demanded erection of lighthouses at the eastern end of Bass Straits. As for the western end: [10]

"We do conscientiously assert that the Government will be culpable if it should not proceed at once to have a beacon erected at King's Island."

A public meeting was called in order to raise money for the survivors and there again the New South Wales authorities were loudly criticized for their failure to act.

Superintendent La Trobe, seen as representing New South Wales interests at heart, was similarly castigated. Years later Garryowen's "Chronicles of Early Melbourne", recalled the wording of a resolution from this meeting which declared that the best monument to the *Cataraqui* victims, that the Government could erect on King Island, was a lighthouse. It went on to suggest that should a plaque be affixed to such a tower then something in the following vein would be appropriate: [11]

"Erected by the Government of New South Wales to commemorate its neglect which caused the wreck of the ship *Cataraqui* upon this coast, occasioning thereby measures to be taken to meet such a calamity when too late, by George Gipps and C. J. La Trobe."

La Trobe's relationship with the press were to reach their nadir not long after this when the *Melbourne Argus* advertized for a new Superintendent.

While meetings were being held and relatives mourning their loss, the problem remained of how to dispose of scores of bodies littering the coast near the wreck.

La Trobe's dispatch to Governor Gipps conveying news of the *Cataraqui*, reached Sydney on the morning

5. *Cataraqui Beach. "... bury the bodies sufficiently inland and of a good depth to save them from being washed out of their graves by the surf which runs very heavy on that Island ..." Howie. 1845*

of the 26th September. That same afternoon, the Colonial Secretary replied: [12]

"Sir George Gipps desires me to express to your Honour the extreme pain with which he has received your account of this dreadful catastrophe, at the same time to convey to you His Authority for incurring such expense as may be necessary in order decently to inter the dead at the Island, and to provide for the reasonable wants of the few Persons who have escaped."

La Trobe had not waited for this authorization and accepted a written offer from David Howie to inter the remains. His letter makes clear the difficulties of his undertaking: [13]

Most Honoured Sir,   Melbourne. Sept 19, 1845.
Having been informed that the humane inhabitants have convened a meeting this day at the Royal Hotel Melbourne for the purpose of employing some person to bury the unfortunate remains of the Sufferers lost in the *Cataraqui* Emigrant Ship which was wrecked on the Kings Island.
I most respectfully advise you and trust should there be any preference given having exerted myself in every respect both to the saving of the few now existing and also by interring many bodies which myself and men found on the Island prior to my proceeding up to Melbourne by the *Midge* Cutter — it may be offered to me — not that I wish it for any other purpose than well knowing the case such an undertaking required to bury the bodies sufficiently in land and of a good depth to save them from being washed out of their graves by the surf which runs very heavy on that Island, with due respect I beg leave to be

> Most Honoured Sir,
> Your most Obedient Humble Servant,
> David Howie
> of King's Island
> now in Melbourne."

An agreement for payment by the Government of £50 plus tools was signed with Howie on the 24th and he departed for King Island to collect remains that the sea had not taken. He later reported burying these in four graves the largest measuring 18 feet by 16 feet and 12 feet deep containing 206 bodies, the others 50, 20 and 18 bodies respectively. It was to be over two years before any memorial was placed there. This was reported in the *Port Phillip Gazette:* [14]

"Monument to the Emigrants who perished in the wreck of the "Cataraqui" ... The Government is about having metal plates manufactured in the foundary of Messrs. Langlands, Fulton and Co., to be erected as a monument to those who perished in the unfortunate "Cataraqui". These plates are made so that they may be easily conveyed to the spot where the bodies washed on shore. We do not admire the petty economy which prevents the Government from erecting a proper monument to these unfortunate persons who suffered more through its negligence than from the perils of the ocean."

For many years the location of the largest mass graves in Australia has passed from local memory. The dunes have covered them.

In the meantime money raised for the survivors was distributed by a committee consisting of leading Melbourne citizens. [15] "and the unfortunate survivors have every reason to be satisfied with the liberality of the inhabitants of Port Phillip."

A benefit concert on the evening of the 25th was held and a young midshipman survivor drew a sketch of the sinking ship. This was copied by an artist and used as a backdrop in the theatre. It was advertized widely by George Coppin, later the founder of J.C. Williamson's, as a special attraction. Amazingly the sketch has survived and is held by the La Trobe Library. [16]

At La Trobe's request immigration authorities were instructed to assist Thomas Guthery, the surviving officer. Their recommendation read as follows: [17]

"The number of Immigrants reported to have been on board the *Cataraqui* at the time of her loss comprised about 275 Statute Adults on who the Mate's gratuity (i.e. the mate serving out the provisions) at 1/- would amount to £13/15/-. Perhaps £20 might not be an unreasonable sum to allow to Mr. Guthery."

There was a lull in the Port Phillip newspapers fury for some weeks at the start of October. Once again attention was given to long accounts of Charles Sturt's latest expedition northwards.

Sir George Gipps knew what reaction at home could be expected to the news of *Cataraqui's* loss. There would be questions in the House, accusations and counter accusations. Not surprisingly, when informing

6. *C.J. La Trobe, Supt. Port Phillip District – the man who was charged with the task of having a lighthouse built at remote Cape Otway.*

Lord Stanley of recent events in Bass Strait, Gipps said very little, waiting as he was for the findings of the Select Committee to be presented. [18]

It is to that belated Committee that our attention will now be turned. From it would come urgent recommendations for the lighthouses that may still be seen nightly in Bass Strait.

QUEEN'S THEATRE

QUEEN-STREET, MELBOURNE.

Under the immediate Patronage of His Honor
the Judge, and His Worship the Mayor.

Upon which occasion the proceeds of the Evenings Entertainments will be given in

AID OF THE SURVIVORS

From the late

Melancholy Wreck

Of the Emigrant Ship 'CATARAQUI,

AND

To REWARD Mr. HOWIE'S PARTY for their meritorious assistance.

The Manager does not think it necessary to solicit the support of the Public for this evening, feeling assured (from the well-known liberality of the Melbourne Inhabitants) the above announcement will, in itself—without taking into consideration the attractive entertainments — fill the Theatre for the relief of the unfortunate.

THURSDAY EVENING,

18th September, 1845,

The Entertainments will commence with SHERIDAN KNOWLES' celebrated play received last Thursday evening by a numerous audience with universal approbation, entitled the

HUNCHBACK;

OR, WOMAN'S LOVE.

Sir Thomas Clifford....Mr. NESBITT.   Master Walter..Mr. HAMBLETON.
Fathom................Mr. COPPIN.
Lord Tinsel ...Mr. YOUNG.   Modus....Mr. THOMSON
Master Wilford........Mr. WATSON.   Thomas............Mr. OFIE
Master Heartwell..Mr. ROGERS.   Stephen......Mr. WILKS.
Julia...........Mrs. COPPIN.   Helen......Mrs. MERETON

7. "On Thursday last each man was supplied with a quantity of wearing apparel and £2 in cash ..." – a handbill for the benefit concert held to raise funds for the survivors of the Cataraqui.

QUOTATIONS AND REFERENCES

1. P.P.G. 15/9/1845.
2. ibid.
3. P.P.G. 17/9/1845.
4. Port Phillip District, Superintendent's Inward Correspondence. Letter No. 45/1616 *P.R.O. Vic.*
5. ibid. p.2.
6. P.P.G. 17/9/1845.
7. ibid.
8. ibid.
9. P.P.G. 15/9/1845.
10. ibid.
11. Garryowen. The Chronicles of Early Melbourne. p. 586
12. P.P.D. Supt. In. Correspondence. No. 45/1095.
13. ibid. 45/1622.
14. P.P.G. 24/9/1845.
15. P.P.G. 27/9/1845.
16. La Trobe Library. Coppin Collection. Ms. No. 8827.
17. P.P.D. Supt. In. Correspondence. No. 45/1874. (enclosures)
18. H.R.A. Ser. I. Vol. 24. Gipps to Stanley p. 575

ILLUSTRATION SOURCES

1. Chronicles of Early Melbourne, Garryowen.
2. D.M.W.
3. Mr. J. Tyrell of Tackley, U.K.
4. Winters Photographic Studio. Burnie.
5. D.M.W.
6. La Trobe Library. H. 30625 CB5/28/12.
7. ibid Coppin Collection MS 8827.

...NAVIGATOR, BE CERTAIN..

5

"Bass' Strait may be passed without more than common danger at any time of the year, provided that the navigator be certain of his latitude ... he should not however, enter the Strait in the night, unless he has previously seen the land, or be certain both of latitude and longitude." – Admiralty.

The Select Committee on Lighthouses began hearing evidence in Sydney on Monday 22 September 1845. Word of the *Cataraqui's* loss reached there at the end of that week. The Committee Chairman, J.P. Robinson, Member for Port Phillip, had consistently warned of just such a disaster in his frequent calls for lighthouses in Bass Strait. It was largely Robinson's agitation that had brought about the formation of the Committee.

This sequence of events explained how the Port Phillip papers had been able to publish word of the loss of the *Cataraqui* alongside a report of the new enquiry's commencement. It would be seven months before word reached the Admiralty of the loss of the *Cataraqui* and Governor Gipps recognized the wisdom of having lighthouses well under way before word of the likely Home Government's censure was dispatched. The first witness called was Merion Moriarty, Esq. R.N. Port Master of New South Wales. Moriarty stated: [1]

"... a light should be erected at Cape Otway, it being the Southern extremity of the mainland at the entrance of Bass's Straits; it was the commencing point of this Government; it was a bold coast, and might therefore be run for without fear; no danger being near, it would be a direct guide for vessels bound to Port Phillip as well as the Straits."

During the three days the committee actually sat it became evident that a great diversity of opinion existed on how best to navigate Bass Strait. The deepest rift was on the question of any proposal to place a lighthouse on Cape Wickham. After speaking in favour of King Island witness Edward Kirsopp continued: [2]

"... vessels from England generally make the north end of King's Island, and rapid currents appear to set towards the southward; when I was on the island I found a man who had lived there for thirteen or fourteen years; he kept a journal, and told me that during that time, one or two vessels hove in sight almost every week ... standing to the north east, apparently for the Straits."

In the middle of his evidence Kirsopp changed his preference to Cape Otway after having been asked to take Port Phillip into account. He then enumerated points in Otway's favour:

" ... the Cape is a bold projection but it is not altogether a precipitous cliff, there is a slope towards the extremity; and it is also to be remembered that it would be accessible by land."

1. Cape Albany Otway. "... is a high bluff projection of reddish coloured cliffs, having hills well clothed with verdure rising gradually above them." Hydrographic Office, Sailing directions. A wave breaks on the Otway Reef.

However others voiced concern over the possible obscuring of Cape Otway by fogs, particularly in the wintertime while the necessary measures to counter currents in the area could not be agreed upon.

Most witnesses expressed preference for revolving, that is flashing, lights. In the case of Otway this would avoid confusion with native fires. There were no aboriginal inhabitants on King Island.

Such a light, said Alexander Sproule, Master of the brig *Corsair* out of London; [3]

"would enable masters of vessels, who might find themselves there at night, to steer with confidence for the light, as the extremity of the danger."

The critics of King Island repeatedly stressed the danger of the Harbinger reefs. Supporters of the motion for lighting King Island conceded the danger but urged that the northernmost of the New Year Islands or the Harbinger reef itself should be the site of the tower. The latter proposal would have been beyond the colony at the time; the building of wave swept towers on the United Kingdom's worst reefs, required all the sophistication the motherland could muster.

Additional opinions received from Port Phillip tended to favour King Island: [4]

" ... had a Light House, in that position, been then erected, [after the *Neva* was lost] I am of opinion that the *Cataraqui* would be in our harbout this day ... A light in that position, when once seen, would leave the Commander ample room to choose his own course for the safety and protection of his ship and the lives under his charge."

C. J. La Trobe while leaving the choice of sites to experts, pressed for rapid means of construction. Remembering prefabricated lighthouses he had seen during his European travels, he said: [5]

" ... the whole materials, both wood and iron, may be fully prepared at the localities where the labour and materials are most readily at command, and transhipped piecemeal to the spot of erection." In this La Trobe was correct and at that time prefabrication was making significant advances into the area of light house building.

The Committee settled on the safest option by recommending four lighthouses, one each on King Island and Cape Otway at the western end, and Kent Group and Gabo Island at the eastern end. They furthermore recommended that convict labour be employed — presumably from Van Diemen's Land. The Government were optimistic enough to state: [6]

" ... that fifty men employed at each of the situations ... would complete the respective buildings in a very few months."

They thought that £12,000 should cover the cost of erecting the four towers.

Even as the Committee was hearing evidence Governor Gipps was writing to Lord Stanley in London, introducing his report with masterly understatement,

"The Committee was already sitting when intelligence reached Sydney of the wreck of the Emigrant Vessel *Cataraqui* and it will readily be believed that this calamitous event added fresh interest to the *enquiry.*" [7]

Word of the wreck had in fact reached London in early February 1846 well before Gipp's official notice, and immediately questions were raised in the House of Commons. Relevant authorities were informed. The *Cataraqui's* condition, history and the records of her captain and officers were examined. *Cataraqui's* owners officially informed the Secretary of State for Colonies: [8]

"It is our painful duty to communicate to you, for the Information of Her Majestys Land and Emigration Commissioners, the total loss of the Ship *Cataraqui* ... Capt. Finlay was a well educated steady and experienced person who was strongly recommended to us by former employers ... Deeply lamenting the melancoly nature of this communication ..."
                    W. M. Smith & Sons.
                    Liverpool.

Within a week of hearing news of the wreck, the Admiralty made its position abundantly clear. The letter remains one of the most important in the history of Bass Strait:

2. Secretary of State for Colonies, William E. Gladstone who bore the censure of Admiralty and Parliament for the failure to erect lighthouses in Bass Strait.

3. Swan Island Lighthouse. This tower, with its companion at Goose Island was erected at the instigation of Sir John Franklin, Governor of Van Diemen's Land to guide shipping through Bank's Strait. The drawing is by Capt. Owen Stanley of H.M.S. Rattlesnake.

Admiralty,
14th February 1846

"Sir,

I am commanded by my Lords Commissioners of the Admiralty to request you will bring the following facts to the notice of Mr. Secretary Gladstone.

"1. The number of disastrous wrecks that had occurred in Bass's Straits, determined my Lords to have it thoroughly surveyed, which has been done, and the chart published, and nothing is wanted to its free navigation but judicious lights.

In the years 1841 and 1842 a Committee of the Legislature of New South Wales examined our surveying officers, and other evidence, on the best positions for these lights. Similarly steps were taken in Van Diemen's Land; sites were fixed, and the Lieutenant Governor laid the first stone of one or two of them at the eastern end of the Straits.

Since that nothing has been done, though each year has been marked by more or less loss of life, and the last mail from Sydney adds to the catalogue an account of the wreck, on King's Island, of the *Cataraqui*, in which four hundred and fourteen emigrants perished.

A single light on that island, or on Cape Otway, would have prevented this frightful misfortune.

2. Under these circumstances, my Lords trust that Her Majesty's Government will take such measures as they deem proper, to insure proper Light Houses being erected to prevent such disasters in future; and in the meantime my Lords will consider it their duty to prevent transports, with troops or with convicts, to attempt navigating the said Straits till Lighthouses have been built; and they would recommend that emigrant ships should be also prohibited from navigating them for the same period.

I have, etc.,
W.A.B. Hamilton."

The Admiralty was, of course, correct. It was fully three years since Stokes had given his evidence. This was the first time anyone had spoken of closing Bass' Strait; the proposal was a measure of the concern felt by the Admiralty. With still no official details from Gipps in Sydney, Colonial Under Secretary Stephen was forced to acknowledge in his reply, "no information has been received at this department, relative to the proposed erection of Lighthouses by the Government of New South Wales."

The Admiralty having taken such strong action, Gladstone made the decision to caution emigrant shipping masters from using Bass' Strait. The seriousness of this step was appreciated by the Land & Emigration Commissioners in London. In replying to the directions they pointed out certain difficulties: [10]

"We have to acknowledge your letter of the 17th instant informing us that the erection of Lighthouses is contemplated in Bass Straits and that in the meanwhile the Lords of the Admiralty have prevented Transports with troops and Convicts from navigating those Straits.

In compliance with Mr. Secretary Gladstone's Instructions we will take care that a similar stipulation be made in respect to any vessels which may be engaged under this Board for carrying Emigrants to Places beyond the Straits in question. But Launceston and Port Phillip (to which latter Port the *Cataraqui* was destined) being situated within the Straits, it will be perceived that the same precaution will not admit of being applied to Vessels bound to those places.

We have etc.,

T. F. Elliot,

C. Alexander Wood.

It is difficult to determine now whether these instructions were ever put into operation. In June Gipps' dispatch covering the lighthouse enquiry arrived at Downing street. Coincidentally an unrelated drop off in passages by emigrant ships occurred.

The Admiralty was informed of Gipps' despatch and expressed their "satisfaction at learning that the Legislative Council of New South Wales has so humanely and promptly taken measures to render secure the navigation of Straits hitherto so dangerous." [11]

In reply to Gipps, Earl Grey was able to say that the lighthouse machinery would be ordered promptly. He went on to give Admiralty recommendations regarding elevations and characteristics of the four lighthouses now planned.

While the news of the *Cataraqui* was being pushed off the front pages of the London newspapers by word of further corn riots and famine in Ireland, Charles Joseph La Trobe was fighting his way through the Otway Ranges, endeavouring to reach one of the sites the Admiralty had agreed to: Cape Albany Otway.

QUOTATIONS AND REFERENCES

1. N.S.W. Parliamentary Papers. Legislative Council Select Committee on Lighthouses. 1845.
2. – 6. These quotations are all drawn from the 1845 enquiry.
7. H.R.A. VOL. 24 SER. 1. P. 618. 21/11/1845.
8. ibid. P. 763.
9. ibid. P. 820.
10. P.R.O. London. Entry Book No. 386. letter 63. P. 209.
11. H.R.A. VOL. 25 SER. 1. P. 138.

ILLUSTRATION SOURCES

1. Ross Ferrier, Apollo Bay.
2. D.M.W.
3. Mitchell Library, Sydney, ML PXC 281
4. D.M.W.

4. The Otway coast awaited La Trobe – the high cliffs near Point Reginald.

..ON FOR THE CAPE...

In fact La Trobe had moved very quickly. On 7 October, not waiting for instructions from Sydney, he had attempted to reach Cape Otway overland. The *Port Phillip Patriot* later ridiculed their Superintendent's readiness to "play explorer":[1]

"... we cannot think it exactly fitting, that the representative of Her Majesty should be employed in seeking a path through scrubs and ranges, for the purpose of executing a duty which could be quite as well perhaps better, performed by either of the pilots, any one of whom would have had no difficulty whatever in reaching the point in a boat. It would, we think be about as consistant for the Governor to have joined Leichardt's expedition as a volunteer."

However La Trobe, in a record of his various Port Phillip excursions wrote:[2]

"The first of a number of attempts personally made to get at Cape Otway and secure the erection of a Lighthouse."

Accompanied by two native troopers named Bluebeard and Noggy as well as a mounted trooper, La Trobe failed to find available those settlers whose assistance he sought. But he did reach the Allan brothers' station near present day Allansford and Warrnambool. Before La Trobe returned to Geelong he skirted the Otway foothills and saw first hand how this country was going to test any man who wished to attain Cape Otway. La Trobe writes:[3]

"Try for Hamilton's and get entangled in forest and bends of Creek. Heavy rain. return to Tarang [Terang] and finally make and reach Kilambeit [Thomsons]. Chilled and unwell ... back to Tarang and to Hamilton's ..."

Gipps informed La Trobe of the £9000 budgeted for the lighthouses and instructed that he should organise the necessary exploratory parties to widely separated Cape Howe and Cape Otway. La Trobe dispatched to Cape Howe and nearby Gabo Island, Charles Tyers, Crown Lands Commissioner for Gippsland, while the Government of Van Diemen's Land undertook to erect the recommended tower on Deal Island. King Island was another matter as a rigorous campaign against the building of a lighthouse at Cape Wickham was being mounted.

La Trobe's second attempt was made before the close of 1845 and would take him much deeper into the Otway or Barrier Ranges. Accounts written shortly after La Trobe's expeditions, but before the Otways had been changed forever by the hunt for land and timber, give a vision of forest clad ravines and ridges. With pressure in

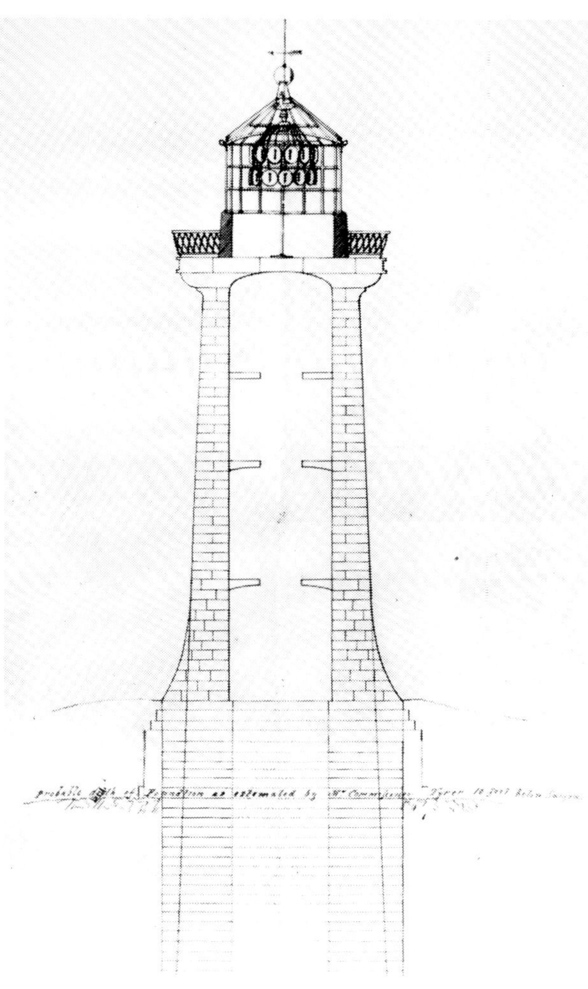

1.
Gabo Island Lighthouse was commenced concurrently with Cape Otway but the choice of the highest point on the island, as the site for the tower, proved unfortunate as no solid foundation could be found within 60 feet of the surface. The contractor was dismissed and the work abandoned.

2. The splendid isolation of Deal Island. Governor Franklin undertook to erect this lighthouse as the Van Diemen's Land contribution to the quartet of beacons recommended by the 1845 Enquiry. (See opposite page.)

Sydney mounting, La Trobe knew that another attempt to reach Cape Otway would have to be made before the end of the year. The following diary by Edward Snell, engineer for the Melbourne-Geelong railway, written in 1856, gives a description of people and country encountered in a journey to Apollo Bay: [4]

Christmas day. Dec. 25th 1856.
Started about 7.30 for Apollo Bay, crossed the Barwon river twice near its source, rode about 5 miles through an undulating country well watered and plentifull, sprinkled with wild cattle, after this, the country became gradually more hilly

and thickly timbered until we at last found ourselves in a track cut through a dense forest only wide enough for one horse to pass at a time. The road was execrable – fallen trees lying across the track every few yards over which our horses had to leap, the bottom was soft mud and roots of trees and the forest was so dense that the sun never shone down on the track which was about 25 miles long and carried up and down the ranges the whole way most of the hills being about as steep as the roof of a house. The trees were magnificent hundreds of them being at least 400 feet high and 20 feet diameter at the base running up as straight as if turned in a lathe and without a branch until near the top. The undergrowth was principally

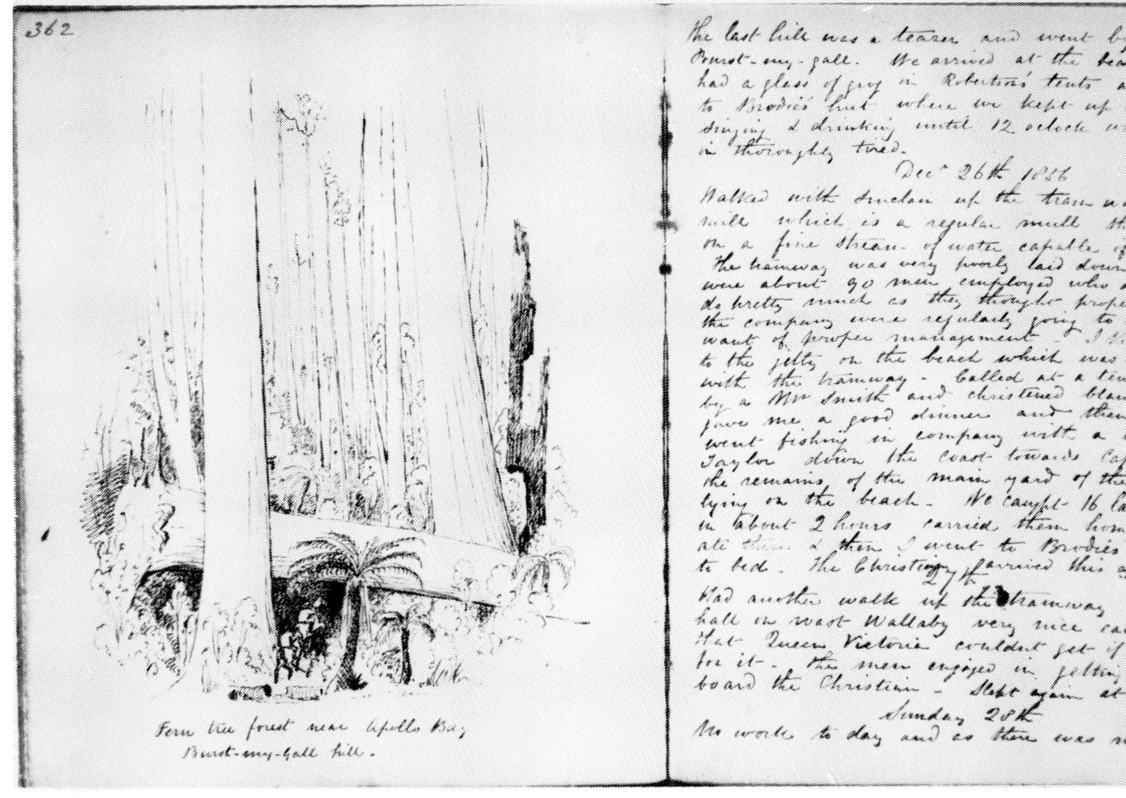

3. When Edward·Snell entered this drawing into his journal in 1856, ten years had elapsed since La Trobe and companions had made their first attempts to reach Cape Otway overland. The country was no less uncompromising but unlike his predecessors,

Snell had the benefit of a bridle track to reach Apollo Bay. From there the track continued on to Cape Otway whereas La Trobe's western route around the coast had by then been obscured by the encroaching scrub. (By courtesy of the La Trobe Library).

fern trees and bottom plants like the sketch on the next page, the last hill was a teaser and went by the name of Burst-my-gall. We arrived at the beach about sunset had a glass of grog in Robertson's tents and then went to Brodie's hut where we kept up Christmas by singing and drinking until 12 o'clock when we turned in thoroughly tired."

No such bridle track existed for La Trobe. Often his thoughts on his arduous journeys must have turned to the explorers Gellibrand and Hesse who had disappeared somewhere in the Otways in 1837. On his second journey Henry Dana accompanied him. La Trobe had appointed Dana as Superintendent of the Port Phillip Native Police in 1842. Acting upon the advice of his native troopers, it was undoubtedly he who persuaded La Trobe to attempt to reach Cape Otway from the west. The party rendezvoused at Geelong and set out that evening for Beale's Inn at Winchelsea: [5]

"not a noisy, filthy bug-infested hostelry, as might have been expected ... but as clean and quiet and well-ordered a little place as you might wish to meet with on a Derbyshire trout stream or in a Welsh valley."

5. *Henry E.P. Dana, Superintendent of Native Police, Port Phillip and a frequent companion of La Trobe on expeditions away from Melbourne.*

4. *The Allan brothers Station on the Hopkins River. "Henry Allan not at home, but William and John give every assistance."*

Two days later they reached the Allan brothers station at Allansford. Unfortunately the eldest Allan brother, the most qualified to act as guide, was not at home, however La Trobe stated: "but William and John give every assistance. Tommy of the Coast tribe engaged to go with us." [6]

The party set out at dawn on the morning of December 5, 1845 for the coast, travelling as light as possible in anticipation of the difficult country about to confront them: [7]

"Cavernous and elevated Coast with one deep indenture. Then bold projection. Country falls inland ... The peculiar character of the Coast. Perpendicular Sand Cliff. The Bay of Martyrs, Cudgee Cudgee Creek, 26m. from Allans. A wide estuary — salt. Fresh water 2m. beyond. breakfast 10 a.m."

6. Native Police. La Trobe used their knowledge of the forest to good advantage and finally reached Cape Otway on his third attempt.

The estuary spoken of marks the present day township of Peterborough. La Trobe rested there after a five hour ride at one of the rivulets that the highway of today sweeps down into. Continuing, he gives us in stacato notes his impressions: [8]

"Iron-bound coast. Ravines and Open heathy lands. Port Campbell – Sherbrooke Creek. Valley above Port Campbell spacious and deep, with divers branches. Scrubby wood near Keenans. Deserted Station since murder of shepherd by the blacks."

Coastal features that are shown on calendars of today, were not dwelt on, for La Trobe's over riding concern was to reach Cape Otway. He pushed on past tall rock stacks referred to laconically as the Sow and Pigs. To later generations these would be the famed Twelve Apostles.

The next obstacle was the mouth of the Gellibrand which the party crossed after waiting for the tide to fall. Today the Gellibrand's outlet can be seen from the isolated Post Office of Princetown, as the river finds its way around the bluff known as Point Ronald.

Camp was made that night in sandhills that start their run up to the shoulders of Moonlight Head. Half a

century later *Rivernook* guest house would be located nearby and host many a holidaying Western District squatter. Premiers of Victoria would later fish where La Trobe wrestled with his rheumatism and the despondency of the aboriginal guide: [9]

"A gusty, bad night; no feed for horses and Tommy frightened and restless, I in pain and without appetite, bad sign!"

From this point the expedition was a defeated one. Next day's events, matched an emotional impasse with a physical one: [10]

"Up and off early over the heathy and scrubby back of Moonlight Head into the forest, where, in perfect miscalculation of distance from the Cape, and difficulties in the way, we fasten our horses and start without provisions. Fight our way by following native track and Tommy many miles through the scrub, ascending a range, till we come to a dead halt at the edge of an impenetrable scrub of mimosa, where all indications of passage fail, and Tommy sulks. After many trials to get forward, we come to the decision, however unwillingly, that we were beaten, and must return. From "Tommy's furthest", glimpse from one point, of a long spit many miles in advance on the other side of range."

La Trobe's route is shown on his chart. After skirting behind Moonlight Head, they had been defeated in the region of present day Yuulong. It was from there that they saw the coast tending toward what they suspected was Cape Otway. On starving horses a quick return was made to the Gellibrand. The belief that these coastal regions were frequented by Aborigines in the more agreeable months of the year was supported by the last entry for that day: "The wild blacks reported on our track ahead –Leeches."

1845 gave way to 1846 and it was not till the end of March that La Trobe was able to organize a third expedition. By this time the Colonial Secretary was writing of the necessity to obtain detailed information on the site's characteristics, particularly its elevation. In Sydney, Mortimer Lewis the Colonial Architect wished to commence the drawings. Meanwhile the Government of Van Diemen's Land had undertaken to erect the Deal Island tower but an offer by William Moriarty to similarly erect the Cape Otway and Gabo Island light-

7. Point Ronald – near present day Princetown, east of here the Otway foothills commence. "To lose one's reckoning in the Otway ranges is no enviable thing." A Wandering Maniac 1879.

houses from that colony was declined by Gipps. News of these developments when transmitted from Sydney, placed further pressure on La Trobe to reach Cape Otway. Memoranda of Journey No. 41 commences with: [11]

"To Geelong, overland, sending horses before and borrowing "Hottentot" of Bell. By the same route as before, the two next days to Colac, Lloyds and Hamiltons, calling on the Nicholson's and Cobhams as before."

La Trobe's party on this occasion consisted of Corporal William Poynton and Trooper Bird of the Native Police with a Sergeant McGregor of the Border Police. At the Allan brothers Station, Henry Allan joined them. The journal moves to the party's arrival on the banks of the Gellibrand which was found to be "one wide lake from the formation of a bar across the

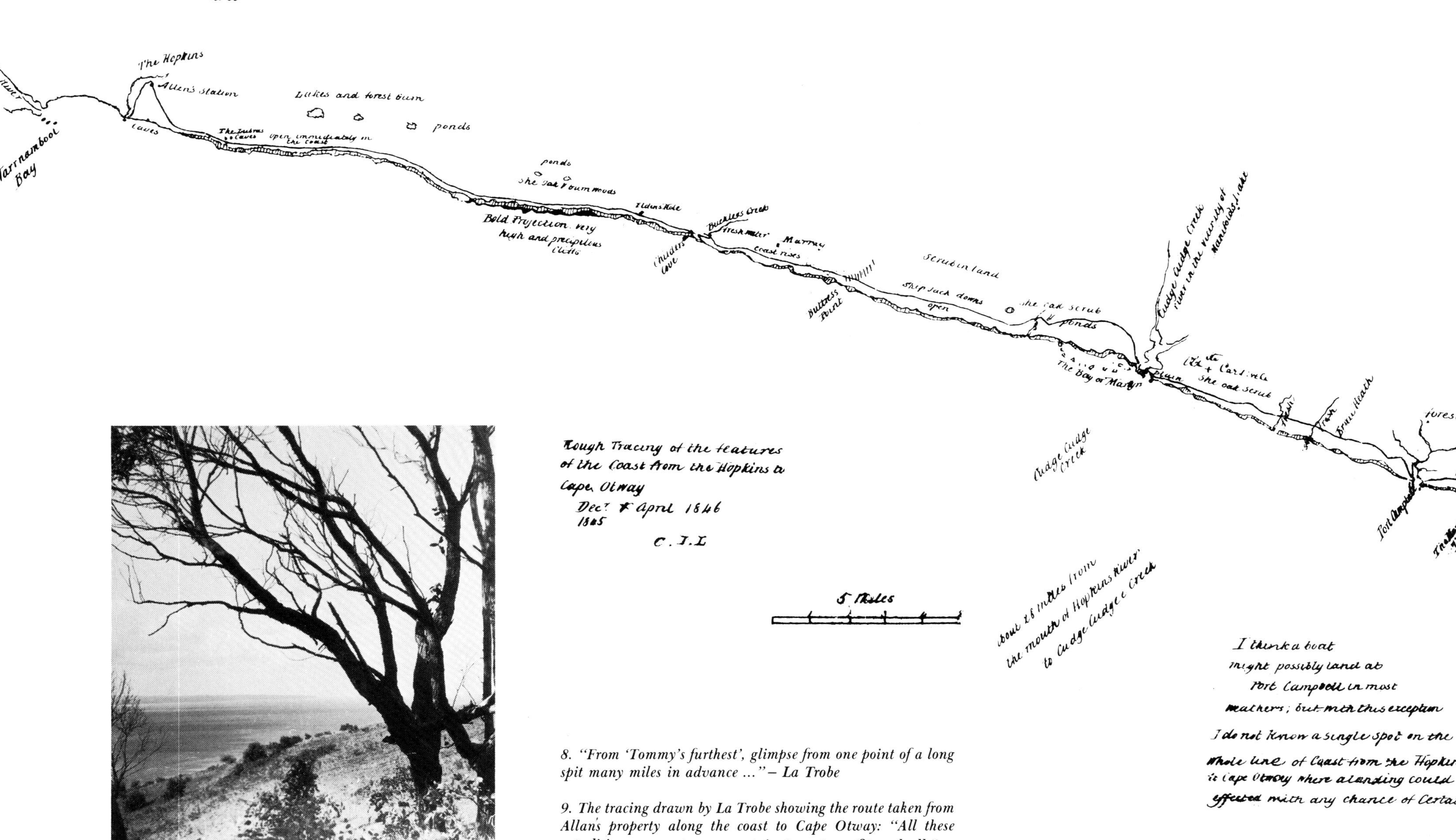

8. "From 'Tommy's furthest', glimpse from one point of a long spit many miles in advance ..." – La Trobe

9. The tracing drawn by La Trobe showing the route taken from Allan's property along the coast to Cape Otway: "All these expeditions were at my own private cost, outfit and all." – La Trobe.

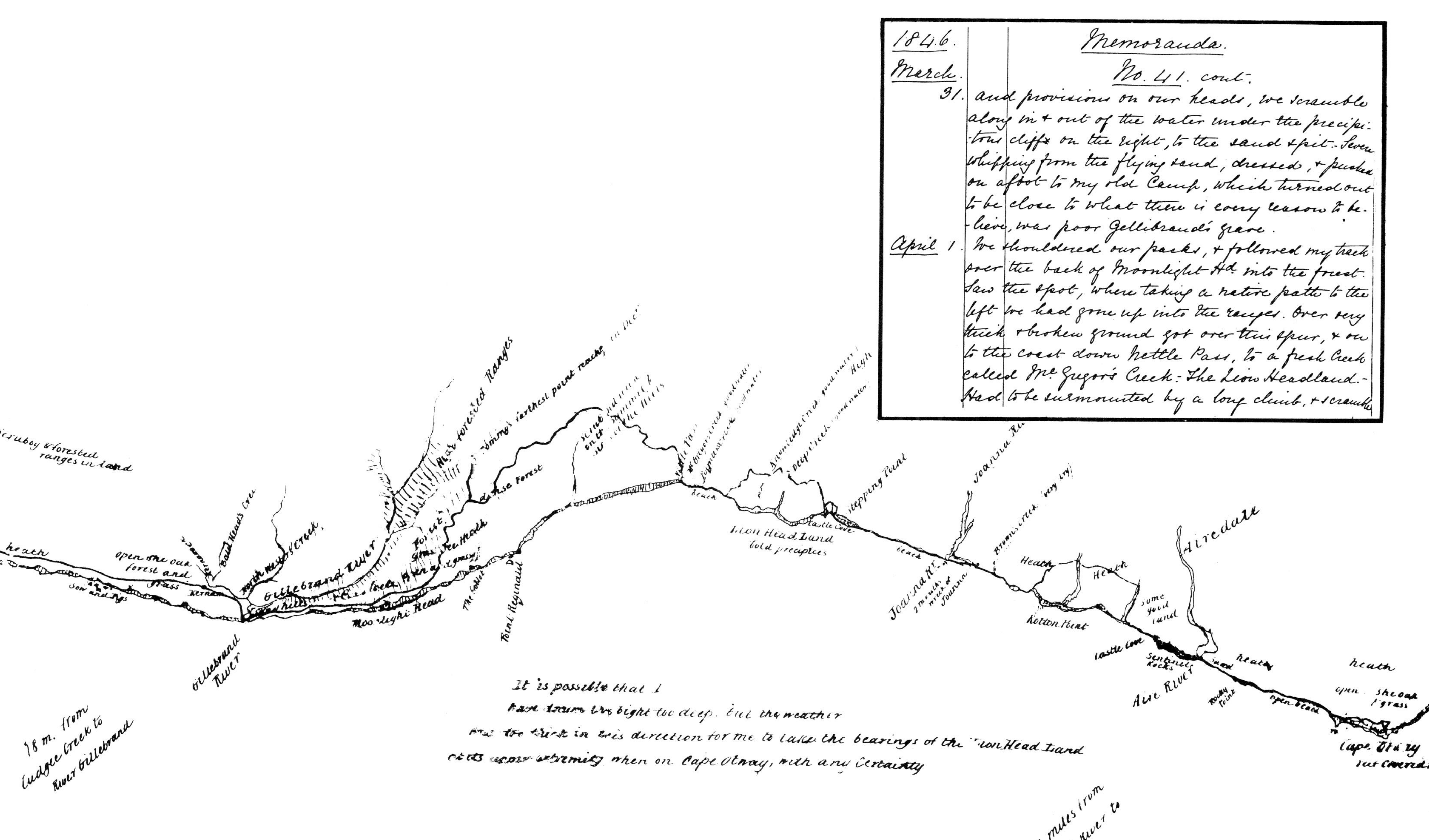

1846.   Memoranda.
March.   No. 41. cont.
31. and provisions on our heads, we scramble
along in & out of the water under the precipitous cliffs on the right, to the sand spit. Seven
whipping from the flying sand, dressed, + pushed
on afoot to my old Camp, which turned out
to be close to what there is every reason to believe, was poor Gellibrand's grave.
April 1. We shouldered our packs, + followed my track
over the back of Moonlight Hd. into the forest.
Saw the spot, where taking a native path to the
left we had gone up into the ranges. Over very
thick + broken ground got over this spur, + on
to the coast down Nettle Pass, to a fresh Creek
called McGregor's Creek: The Lion Headland.-
Had to be surmounted by a long climb, + scramble
Scrubby & forested ranges inland
Most forested Ranges
Stormy's farthest point reach, in the
dense Forest
beach
Lion Head Land bold precipices
Castle Cove
Stepping Point
Airedale
open one our forest and grass
Gellibrand River
North West Creek
Bald Heads Cree
Moonlight Head
Point Reginald
Nettle Pass
Joanna R.
mouth of Joanna
Joanna R.
Heath
Rotten Point
some good land
Castle Cove
Sentinel Rocks
Aire River
Rocky Point
open beach
Heath
open she oak & grass
Cape Otway not covered
Gellibrand River
18 m. from Cudgee Creek to River Gillebrand
It is possible that I
have drawn this bight too deep, but the weather
was too thick in this direction for me to take the bearings of the Lion Head Land
at its western extremity when on Cape Otway, with any certainty
about 32 miles from Gillebrand River to Otway

entrance." They were forced to leave their horses there with Trooper Bird and half waded, half scrambled around to the bar under Point Ronald to effect a crossing. They reached the camp site at which La Trobe had had the uncomfortable night on the previous expedition.

The track that had led to a dead end on that expedition was ignored and instead, they chose to come down off the ridge and fight their way down to what is today known as Milanesia Beach. The route they took they called Nettle Pass, naming the two creeks that flow into this still isolated beach, McGregors and Poyntons Creek. Unfortunately the names did not come into common usage. Remains of midden grounds are still to be seen at this beach and by their extent testify, to a long occupation by the coast tribe whose country this was.

The party scrambled around the back of Lion Headland and after crossing a number of deep gullies, two of which they named Deep Creek and Knowledge Creek, they found themselves walking along the beautiful Joanna Beach. (Corrupted to Johanna c. 1901 through an uncorrected error by a signwriter on the Post Office there, which was left unaltered.) It was possibly around their campfire that night that Henry Allan recounted the story of the *Joanna* and the circumstances attending the fate of its sought after cargo — La Trobe mentions that a dead whale and part of the ships forecastle were all they shared the beach with that night.

Until about 1912 the Joanna had two mouths; gradually the western one silted up. It was from the eastern mouth that La Trobe's party set off at dawn next day for the Cape.

Brown's Creek was crossed and progress was rapid along the beach to Rotten Point. There by scrambling over the back of these "remarkable rocks", La Trobe gained his "First view of the valley of the Aire."

Implied in the narrative is the fact that this was the first time any white man had seen this peaceful world. Certainly life would soon be very different for "the wild Blacks, 7 men and women" whose trail La Trobe noted.

Midden grounds high above the Aire River flats, a mile from the sea, speak of the way of life of this tribe so soon to be exterminated. These vantage points offered shelter from the southerly winds, while schools of fish could be seen in the river over a hundred feet below. Stone and bone tools show how well these people had utilized the resources of this sanctuary. La Trobe's concession to the original inhabitants was to "make our breakfast on shell fish."

The journal now gathers pace; [12]

".... then push on for the Cape, which we held Limestone Point to be. Remarkable point, lime, water, and fossil trees. Land rises, more open and better grassed. Push forward and reach the highest sand hill amongst the cups and saucers, and know that we have really found Cape Otway. Receding line of coast on both sides, E. to Cape Patten [sic] and W. to to Moonlight Head. An hours halt, and then return, on our steps, to our camp on the Joanna River. The *soft* deal board! A gusty night."

La Trobe might well have been pleased. His one hour inspection had shown that it would not be difficult to clear suitable ground and he had driven in a staff to mark the site. Next day they retraced their steps to the Gellibrand and shared their story with an "exultant" Trooper Bird. "An evening of rest, story telling and feasting."

La Trobe, though certainly gratified to have reached the elusive Cape, well knew that the route he had just followed was impractical for use in the construction of the lighthouse. Except for possibilities at remote Port Campbell, nowhere had he seen a place at which goods could be brought ashore safely and regularly. La Trobe had already addressed himself to the problem. At the Joanna River the night before, he decided that an

10. *"Over very thick and broken ground got over this spur, and on to the coast down Nettle Pass, to a fresh creek called McGregor's Creek." — La Trobe.*
Looking west along Milanesia Beach towards Nettle Pass with Poynton's Creek in the foreground.

attempt had to be made to find a less circuitous route to this area of coast and recognised that this would involve crossing the highest part of the Otway Range. La Trobe knew of no one better to attempt it than the man at his side by the camp fire –Henry Allan. Allan agreed to try before winter.

On the 7th April La Trobe rejoined his "anxious wife and family at the Heads". His weekend cottage was at Queenscliff. One week later he wrote to Colonial Secretary E. **Deas** Thomson, in Sydney: [13]

"In order that no time may be unnecessarily lost in making preparations for the erection of a lighthouse on Cape Otway, I take advantage of the Mail after my return to town from a visit to that part of the Southern Coast to state to you for His Excellency's satisfaction that the Cape presents a bold rocky promontory of about 3 miles across and of a general elevation of from 150 to 200 feet, as I should consider, above the ocean.

The land on the back is comparatively speaking open, and covered with grass and she oak. Good building stone lime, and water, are abundant and accessible. A rise, about a musket shot from the brink of the precipitous face of the Southern point of the promontory, furnishes as it appears to me an admirable site for the projected lighthouse, as it commands an unimpeded view of the whole of the deep bight to the Westward extending between Cape Otway and Moonlight Head and of the entire line of Coast extending to the North East towards Port Phillip Heads."

11. *"... arrived tired and soaking at Joanna – our camp for dinner was not pleasant, as we were at the mouth of the river, without shelter of any kind, and the rain and wind didn't aid us in boiling our billy." – A Wandering Maniac.*

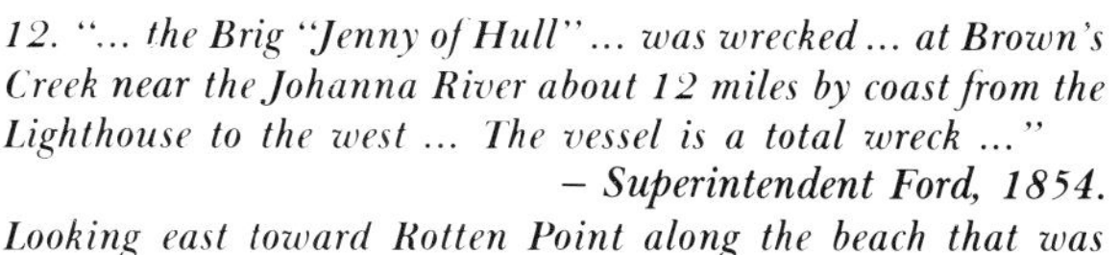

12. *"... the Brig "Jenny of Hull" ... was wrecked ... at Brown's Creek near the Johanna River about 12 miles by coast from the Lighthouse to the west ... The vessel is a total wreck ..."*
– Superintendent Ford, 1854.
Looking east toward Rotten Point along the beach that was strewn with the remains of the Jenny of Hull.

La Trobe stated that beyond Moonlight Head a suitable road was "totally impracticable for horses or oxen ..." and that

"the precipitous and rugged character of the rocky spurs of the Mountains abutting upon the straits, and the depth of the wooded ravines ... form serious impediments to approach in any manner."

After explaining the commission he had given to Allan he mentioned his desire to have the adjacent coast surveyed. He followed this up in his next letter to Sydney: [14]

47

release two lubras for the purpose. Allan's party now comprised Sergeant McGregor and Troopers Ball and Cobra of the Native Police, Corporal William Poynton, Thomas Grice and John Artler of the Border Police.

Next day, 24 April, it started to rain. From this point the journal records over three weeks of nearly continuous rain as they moved higher into the Otway Ranges. Beyond today's town of Gellibrand, Allan lamented: [15]

"25th April	"Rain all day and all night."
27th	"Still raining very heavy; engaged dividing the rations, and too late to start ... dreadful rain from 12 o'clock till daylight."
28th	"clear morning; got the horses over the ravine ... rain very heavy ... came to the River, found it had risen 10 feet and felled trees across and got over ... found in black mia-mia a large lot of implements; [some aborigines obviously did penetrate the ranges on occasions] the River still rising and covered our bridge ... Rain again till daybreak."
29th	"Heavy rains, River still rising ... weather broke up, but still heavy showers till sundown, when the River began to fall."

So the catalogue of discomfort and frustration continues. The "River" Allan mentions was most likely the Gellibrand. After this the party worked their way up to the top of the main range — possibly in the region of present day Beech Forest. From there they sought a route that would come out on the Aire River flats or the back of the Cape Otway country. In general it was a case of: [16]

"followed this [ridge] the whole of the day without finding a single spur on either side, the hill rising to an apex. Camped.,
or
"The whole of our route today [we] literally cut our way and it raining from after the first hour."

"I have not only sent in a party from the Colac District but have felt justified in availing myself of the services of the gentleman named in the margin (Mr. Douglas Smythe) formerly employed as a surveyor under contract in this District to explore and survey the unexplored portion of the coast to the Eastward of the Cape in question."

George Douglas Smythe was well known in Melbourne — he was related by marriage to Captain William Lonsdale, La Trobe's deputy. The section of coast between Cape Otway and the Lorne of today had to be thoroughly surveyed to confirm that no suitable roadstead existed from which a lighthouse might be supplied. Owing to the nature of the coast, much of the survey was done point to point by whaleboat.

Meanwhile Henry Allan in his attempt to find a route by land was dogged by losses of time. He wasted a whole day at the Colac Police Station waiting for the sergeant in charge to find his horses. The expedition still had not left three days later when Mr. Tuckfield in charge of the Wesleyan Mission named *Buntingdale* (near presentday Birregurra) refused to allow any of the **Aborigines** collected there from the local tribes to act as a guide. Allan records how in the end he ordered Tuckfield to

Allan alludes to the scrub being as heavy and difficult as that which he had encountered at Moonlight Head the month before when with La Trobe. He was now in the region of Cape Horn only eight miles from the Cape. Further progress though was impossible. By May 3 he admitted "that he had wasted three days on a route that had been totally impracticable since the first ravine."

May 4th   "Start for home with a thick fog; rain began in about an hour, and continued the whole day. It was fortunate we returned, as it was with extreme trouble and danger we crossed the River, two of the party not being swimmers; and getting a pot of tea the river rose six feet ... a perfect hurricane during the night, with hail, thunder etc."

At this stage Allan resolved to return to Colac to get fresh supplies but before doing so he named a series of ranges on the west bank of the Aire, the Lady La Trobe Range. Like the expedition, this name has been forgotten.

They did not reach Colac without a further trial.

May 5   "Arrived at the river, found it had overflowed its banks, and our bridge 8 feet under water, and still rising; our stock of provisions reduced to one Johnny cake each, and every prospect of 3 days at least if the weather cleared up, of which there was no hope; began to camp, when one of the men found an immense tree just fallen across the River, just a mile up, over which we all passed with ease, a great relief to me; arrived at "Donkey" creek and had a good meal, having left some flour and meat there, passed one of the most miserable nights I ever remember, besides being in constant dread of the trees, which were falling on every side of us."

They had four days rest in Colac and a reduced party of three men set out once more. Next day Allan wrote:

".. a fine clear day, the first since I started this expedition."

14. "...and W., to Moonlight Head." – La Trobe 1846. "... No one had come from the Westward since our party (April 1846)" – La Trobe. 1849.

This endeavour met with slightly more success but no less rain. By the 15th May Allan had crossed the highest part of the ranges and was again in the hills behind Cape Horn. Today, this country remains some of the most rugged in the whole Otway Ranges — " ... the gullies steep but passable; heard the sea quite loud." Still some miles from the Cape, his frustration showing in this, one of his last journal entries:

May 16   " ... I now determined to follow it down the bank, as I was sure I was close on the head of the large flats [this could only be Aire River flats] I had seen from the Cape when there with His Honour, but after laboring two hours I did not make a ¼ of a mile, the river running SW, and having to make bridges in that distance over several creeks and branches. I now tried to rise the same range I had been foiled at the day before, but still the same rock stopped my progress. I came down again, and tried further down, but no success, the stones and scrub like the Nettle Pass on the Sea Coast route. I was very loth to give up now, as I may say up to yesterday I had got a route, it was

possible to send supplies by if done in the summer, the creeks then being small and the banks high and plenty of saplings to make bridges of. Came to one of my old camps, heavy showers all day, and fine night."

Allan journeyed to Melbourne where he handed his diary and route map to La Trobe. (This map has not survived.) He commented: [17]

"Your Honour will perceive that altho' the whole object was not fully accomplished it was entirely on acount of the unfavourable state of the weather and the heavy floods in the Rivers and Creeks."

He explained that a potential supply route had been marked as far as the main ridge on the Colac side and commended Poynton, Grice and Artler:

"they having on all occasions shown great alacrity and willingness to assist in attaining the object proposed and having without complaint suffered much privation, fatigue and hardship."

When the task Allan undertook is viewed against the backdrop of the Otway Ranges in winter, none but the ungenerous would ascribe a less flattering testimonial to Allan himself.

As for the Otways this would be its last untroubled winter. Before the spring different men would find a way through the labyrinth.

QUOTATIONS AND REFERENCES

1. The Spectator. P. 219. 23/5/1846. A Sydney Newspaper.
2. and 3. La Trobe Excursions. No. 36. MS. No. H. 93166.
4. E. Snell. *The Life and Adventures of E. Snell from 1849-to 1859* La Trobe Library. MS 8970.
5. The Australasian VOL. 1. 1850-51. P. 459. *The Black Forest of Victoria*. Mitchell Library. Ref. No. 352/A.
6. – 10. La Trobe Excursions. No. 41. 27/3/1846.
11. La Trobe Excursions. No. 41. 27/3/1846.
12. ibid. 2/4/1846.
13. P.P.D. Supt. Outward Correspondence. 46/326. 14/4/1846. P.R.O. VIC.
14. ibid. 46/376. 9/5/1846.
15. P.P.D. Supt. Inward Correspondence. 46/841. Enclosure. Copy quoted is that sent on to Sydney some days later and now held at P.R.O. N.S.W.
16. ibid. and further quotations drawn direct from journal.
17. P.P.D. Supt. Inward Correspondence. 46/841.

ILLUSTRATION SOURCES

1. Gabo Island Folder. N.S.W. Gov. Archives, Sydney.
2. Ian Lyell, Photographer, Courtesy Prof. S. Murray-Smith.
3. La Trobe Library. *The Life and Adventures of E. Snell from 1849 to 1859*. MS. No. 8970.
4. 7, 8, 10, 11, 12, 14, 16 – 17 D.M.W.
5. Victorian Historical Magazine Sept. 1911, Vol. 1 No. 3.
6. La Trobe L. H. 11291/MC 52.
9. South – West Coast. Tracing by C.J. La Trobe. La Trobe L. MS 10852.
13. Brookes Photographic Union. Views of Western Victoria.
15. Brookes Photographic Union.
17. Forests Commission of Victoria.

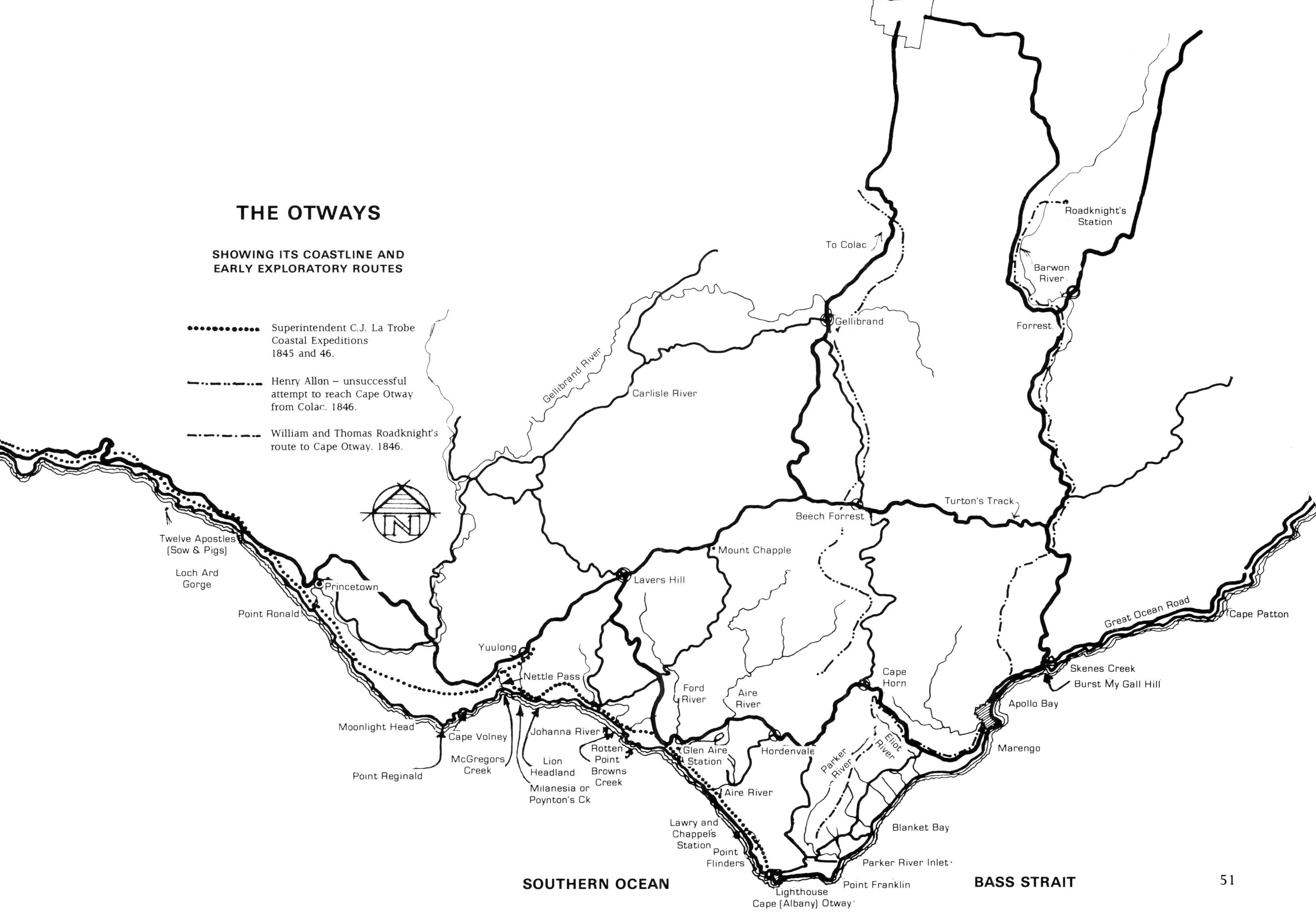

THE OTWAYS

SHOWING ITS COASTLINE AND
EARLY EXPLORATORY ROUTES

Superintendent C.J. La Trobe Coastal Expeditions 1845 and 46.
Henry Allon – unsuccessful attempt to reach Cape Otway from Colac. 1846.
William and Thomas Roadknight's route to Cape Otway. 1846.

N

Roadknight's Station
Barwon River
Forrest.
To Colac
Gellibrand
Gellibrand River
Carlisle River
Turton's Track
Beech Forrest
Mount Chapple
Lavers Hill
Twelve Apostles (Sow & Pigs)
Loch Ard Gorge
Princetown
Point Ronald
Great Ocean Road
Cape Patton
Yuulong
Skenes Creek
Burst My Gall Hill
Nettle Pass
Ford River
Aire River
Cape Horn
Apollo Bay
Moonlight Head
Cape Volney
Johanna River
Glen Aire Station
Hordenvale
Marengo
McGregors Creek
Lion Headland
Rotten Point Browns Creek
Parker River
Elliot River
Point Reginald
Milanesia or Poynton's Ck
Aire River
Blanket Bay
Lawry and Chappel's Station
Point Flinders
Parker River Inlet
Point Franklin
SOUTHERN OCEAN
BASS STRAIT
Lighthouse Cape (Albany) Otway

17. "Who shall tell during how many centuries these Patriarchs of the Forest have been attaining their enormous bulk? Are they contemporaries of the venerable "Cedar Saints" of Mount Lebanon?" – reflections of one who journeyed across the Otways in 1851. When this photograph was taken, half a century later near Beech Forest, much of the forest had been put to the match.

52

...THE STONES TO BE TRUE AND SQUARE...

7

The Otway Ranges had defeated Henry Allan but upon returning to Melbourne Surveyor Smythe reported to La Trobe that the survey of the coast in the region of Cape Otway was complete. Almost immediately he returned to the region to complete his survey of the coast west of the Aire River. The map, a copy of which La Trobe forwarded to Sydney, did not agree with his own observations. This concerned La Trobe as he recognized that if the actual Cape was twice as high as he had supposed — 400 feet not 200 feet — then the shaft of the lighthouse could be shorter and money saved. The obscuration by fogs of the lighthouse too highly elevated was a concern of the 1845 enquiry and La Trobe knew that any change would have to be notified to the Colonial Architect immediately. In addition, Smythe believed that present day Point Franklin, two miles to the east of Cape Otway, was further south and so the correct site for a lighthouse marking the western entrance of Bass Strait. After hasty consultation with Smythe, La Trobe declared: [1]

" ... not withstanding the general impression with which Mr. Smythe had returned to Melbourne ... it is found upon laying down his work that he was in error."

In fact later checks showed Smythe to be in error in both cases: Cape Otway's height was much closer to La Trobe's estimate and it extends further south than Point Franklin.

To G.D. Smythe is attributed the honour of being the first to survey if not to enter the Parker River Inlet. Sadly, though, to him is also ascribed the responsibility for the eradication of the remnants of the area's Aborigines.

Smythe had been paid 30/- per mile, he bearing all the expenses and so he was not in a position to delay with the survey. The notebook he kept on the expedition has survived and describes events leading to one of the saddest episodes in the history of this coast. His notes tell of the murder by the Aborigines, of one of his men at the Aire River. The *Geelong Advertiser* published a detailed account based almost word for word on Smythe's version of events: [2]

"Yesterday, this indefatigable explorer returned from his second expedition to Cape Otway. His return has been hastened in consequence of a melancholy and disastrous occurrence, the murder of one of his men by the blacks. After

1. *"... not withstanding the general impression with which Mr. Smythe had returned to Melbourne ... it is found upon laying down his work that he was in error." – La Trobe.*
Smythe's survey map of the Cape Otway country forwarded to La Trobe. The Parker River Inlet was surveyed in detail as Smythe recognised it to be the only point on the coast, near to the proposed lighthouse site, where supplies might be landed.

2. *The sad remnants of the Geelong Aborigines. "The next morning the blacks wanted to go further to look for more wild blackfellow declaring that there were plenty more, and 'him come by and by and kill more white fellow'..."*

the expedition left the Barwon Heads about a month ago, they encountered a succession of westerly gales; and made several ineffectual attempts to get round the Cape. The party at last landed on the eastern side, and encamped, while Mr. Smythe, accompanied by four men, penetrated to the westward to survey the Aire River. Mr. Smythe started on this excursion on Saturday, the 25th July. In proceeding along the shore they fell in with a tribe of blacks, composed of one man, four women, and three boys, all of whom had been at the tent some days before. Mr. Smythe prevailed on the man and one of the boys to act as his guide to *Gunna-waar*, or Eyredale. After travelling for about three hours they came to a part of the country with which Mr. Smythe was familiar, and as he had no further use for the blacks, he sent them back to the tents, first giving them a supply of tea, and a note to the coxswain, directing him to give them some flour. Mr. Smythe returned to the tent on the evening of the 31st — when he learned that one of the men, named Conroy, had been barbarously murdered about 200 yards from the tent, where he had gone to cut wood. This happened on Sunday morning, between nine and ten

3. One of the large aboriginal midden grounds located above the Aire River flats. Sheltered here from the prevailing westerly winds, master of this hidden valley, they could dine on shell fish carried from the beach two miles away. Today these hills and remains are a mute reminder of the Aborigines that knew this country as home before they were exterminated by fellow natives in 1846.

o'clock. The blacks had arrived at the tent early that morning, and had been supplied with damper — they then went along the beach; and just previous to the perpetration of the murder, they were seen returning making a great noise. On their again retiring the body of the deceased was found by his companions dreadfully mangled about the head, and life entirely extinct. A tomahawk was found near the spot, with which no doubt the blows had been inflicted. Mr. Brodie, one of the party who acted as surgeon, made an examination of the wounds ... The body was buried in a grave four feet deep, having being previously wrapped in a blanket. After this event, Mr. Smythe finding his stock of provisions nearly exhausted, deemed it advisable to return. The party, therefore, re-embarked, and sailed eastward to Loutit Bay (under Flat-topped Point), a well-sheltered harbour, where they beached their whale boat, and secured it above high water mark, Mr. Smythe determined to make his way to Geelong by land. It is his intention, we believe, to make a third excursion to the Cape Otway country so soon as he has given in his report to Government."

Smythe consulted Foster Fyans the Police Magistrate for the Geelong District and County of Grant on how best to deal with the Aborigines at Cape Otway. With Fyans' approval Smythe commenced assembling a squad of the local Barrabool tribe to return with him to Cape Otway and apprehend the offender.

Descriptions of the country surrounding the Aire River first seen by La Trobe then Allan and now Smythe, were circulating amongst a grazing fraternity hungry for more land. If this land had year round assured rainfall, possible access to a small roadstead such as the Parker River, then it seemed important to find a way across the Barrier Range to it.

The station of William Roadknight and his son Thomas was close to the Buntingdale Mission from which Allan had set out. No doubt the Roadknights had heard Allan's report of the Aire country. La Trobe had referred to William Roadknight in a despatch to Sydney as "an enterprising settler of the Colac District," but had gone on to express doubt that Roadknight would succeed where Allan had failed in opening a route to Cape Otway. Nevertheless Roadknight took independent action and it was a surprised La Trobe who received a letter from him. Dated in Geelong on 25 August 1846, it commenced: [3]

4. "... an enterprising settler of the Colac district ..." Thomas Roadknight who, from his station on the Barwon River near present day Birregurra, pushed his own track through to Apollo Bay and on to Cape Otway. He established his Glen Aire station on the Aire River west of Cape Otway.

"I take an early opportunity of informing your Honour that on my return from Cape Otway ... I have at length succeeded in completing a track thereto."

Roadknight went on to describe the conditions they encountered and the results of their efforts:

"From this [Mission] Station we have good sound Dray Road partly cut through a dense scrub with permanent Bridges completed to the distance of 22 miles in the direct line to the Cape, from this point we have been many times defeated in our attempts to discover a practicable track to the Coast, but have at last accomplished the task of discovering and opening [it] out for Pack Bullocks, though it is rather circuitous, being about 44 miles from the termination of the Dray Road to Cape Otway, making the distance by our track from the Mission Station to Cape Otway about 66 miles, but from the local knowledge acquired by my son during the arduous under-taking, we have no doubt (as the weather improves) of completing a good Dray Track in about 42 or 45 miles."

Unlike Allan. Roadknight worked due south when surmounting the main range. This is the region of

5. *"... First view of the valley of the Aire held a new discovery. Descend to the coast ..." – La Trobe 1846. The Aire River flats as seen from the northern side – the sea in the distance. La Trobe skirted the ocean side of this beautiful valley but today the Great Ocean Road finds its way around the northern rim of the flats.*

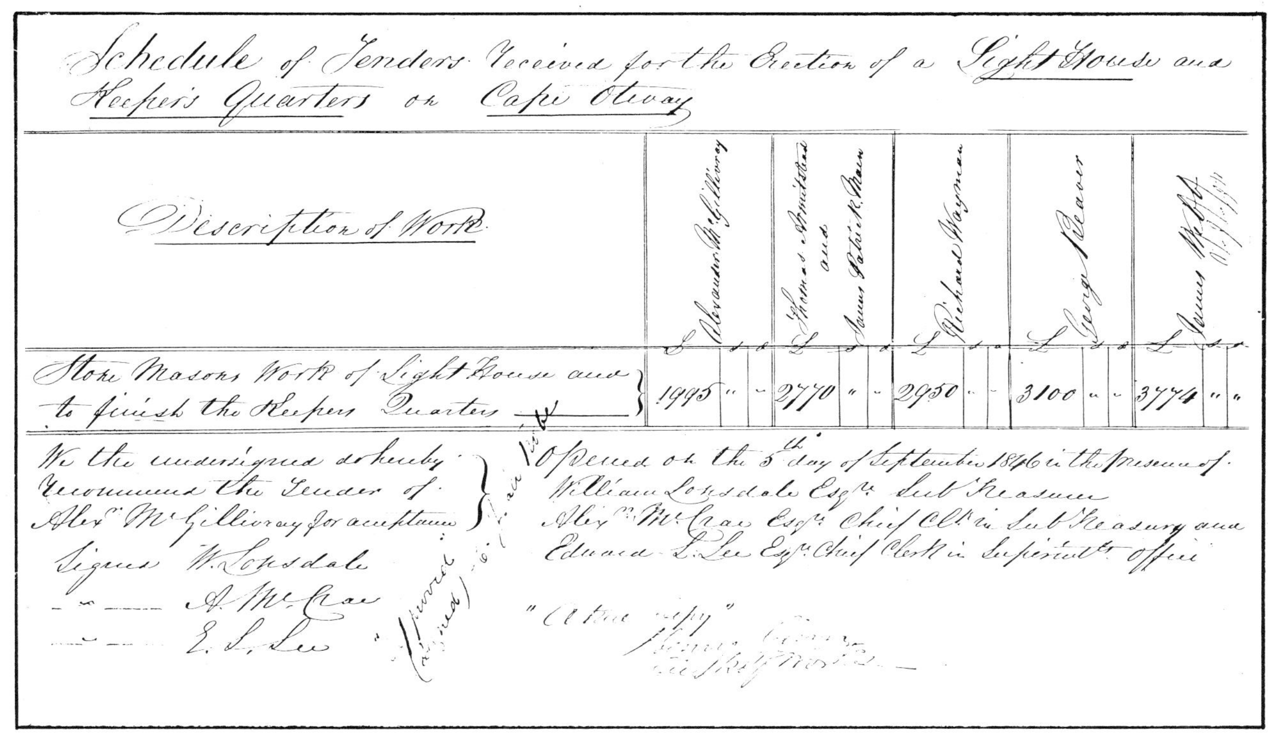

6. *A record of tenders received for the Cape Otway Lighthouse. Tenderers were confronted with uncertain access to the site and the prospect of having to obtain building stone from Van Diemen's Land if suitable material could not be found at Cape Otway. It is not surprising that tenders varied so widely.*

present day Mount Sabine and the track descended to the coast at Skene's Creek east of Apollo Bay. From there it struck in land toward the country that had defeated Allan in winter. Then employing one of the spurs Allan had searched in vain for, the track descended onto the attractive country at the back of Cape Otway.

Roadknight added that he had driven a herd of cattle to Cape Otway "where they are now depasturing." The description concludes:

"... there will be now, no serious impediment in establishing a good Dray Road, more than the great labour of cutting through and removing the immense masses of timber with which this part of the Country is encumbered. We have contrived to avoid all the deep Ravines — I observed the mark set up by Your Honour upon the hummock near the extremity of the Cape."

In the meantime Smythe had left Geelong for Cape Otway with his party of Aborigines in order to trace the murderer of Conroy. He was able to use Roadknight's track rather than the previous circuitous boat trip via Lorne. One of Roadknight's stockman returning from the Cape met Smythe's party. Over forty years later he recalled the encounter and the fate of the Cape Otway tribe in an article in the *Weekly Times*: [4]

" ... some of us travelled to the home station, taking some sheep up. On our way through the forest we met Mr. Smythe returning to the Otway, with eleven of the Geelong district blacks, armed with old muskets. Each had been served with a new blanket. They seemed delighted at the prospect of a fight with wild blackfellows. In due time Mr. Smythe and his little army arrived at the Cape and fixed their camp for the night. The next morning they went out in search of "wild blackfellow." This was the name the more civilised tribes gave to all strange blacks. During the day they sighted the enemy, and at once Mr. Smythe's band broke away from their leader, in fact they became unmanagable. They followed the strangers, and after a long chase overtook and surrounded them, all but the old man, who managed to steal away and make tracks for the river. He was followed this time by Merridong, the king of the Geelong tribe. The old man took to the water, Merridong jumped in after him, knife in hand, soon overtook him, and stabbed him in several parts of the body, killing him in the stream. In the meantime the other ten had been kept together. One of the young lubras was taken charge of by one of the Geelong blacks who subsequently brought her home with him. The others were placed singly against a tree and shot, most of the blacks firing at each victim at the same time. This was done in spite of every effort made by Mr. Smythe. In fact, the armed natives had worked themselves up into a state of frenzy and for some hours the lives of the whites were anything but safe. That was the end of the Cape Otway blacks with the exception of one. The next morning the blacks wanted to go further to look for more wild blackfellow declaring that there were plenty more, and "him come bye and bye and kill more whitefellow." They were eventually got under control, and headed toward home."

No official word of this episode was forwarded to Sydney and reactions were confined to expressions of shock by the Melbourne newspapers and the temporary suspension of Smythe.

While Smythe and Roadknight had been pursuing their different interest in the Cape Otway country the final drawings for the lighthouse had been completed. They were accordingly forwarded from Sydney and tenders were called on the 11th of August. It was only one week before tenders closed that La Trobe had received Roadknight's encouraging advice of improved access to the site.

Mortimer Lewis the Colonial architect had not provided drawings of keeper's quarters so La Trobe decided: [5]

"... to include in the advertisement for tenders the erection of a detached substantial four roomed stone building for the keeper's quarters, consisting of one sitting room, two bedrooms and one store room."

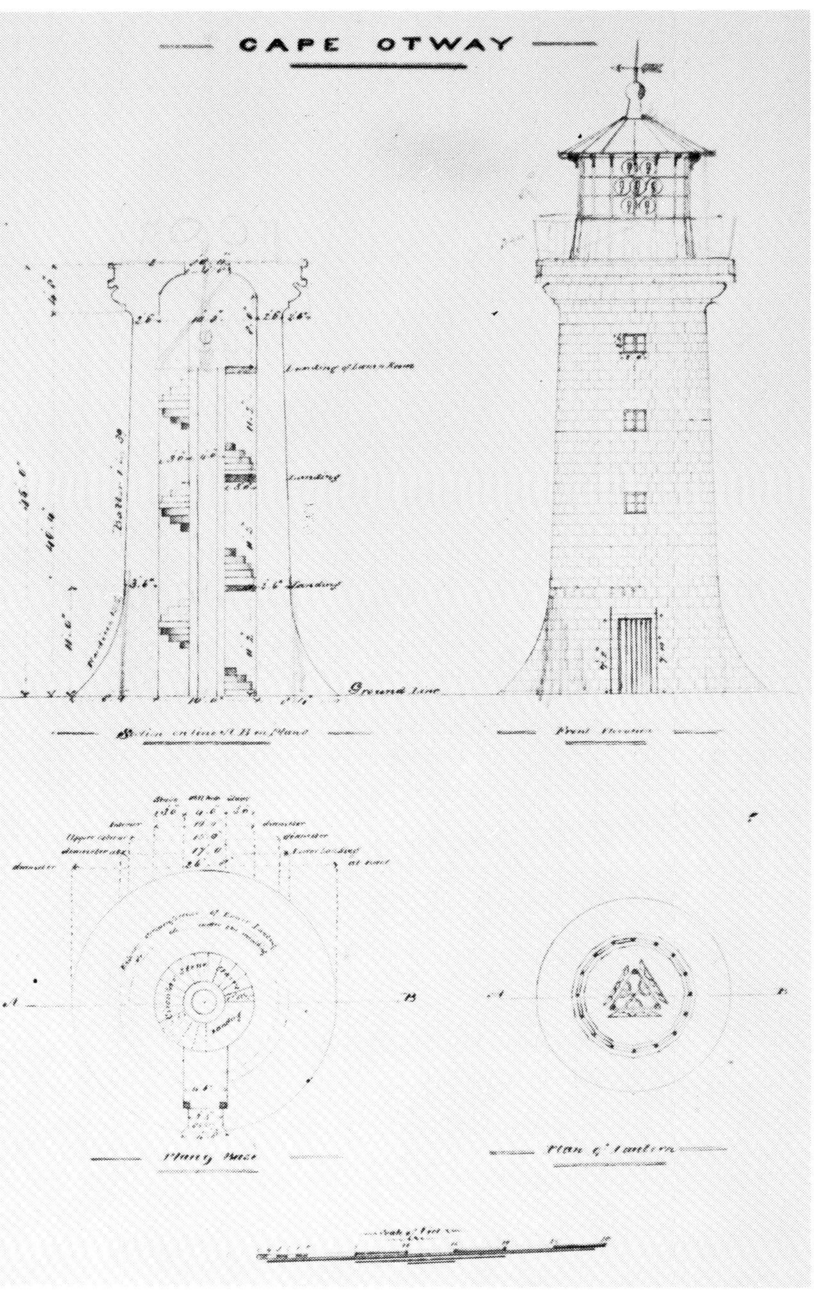

7. Henry Ginn's drawing of the lighthouse at Cape Otway. He remarked, "I have the honour to state that the materials being used in these works are of the best description of their respective kinds, they are procured within five miles of the site of the lighthouse." The shaft was never built with the fluted base but the simple squat tower that still serves today was completed by tradesmen and labourers in direct government employ.

The schedule of submitted tenders was duly forwarded to Sydney but within a fortnight the *Argus* was carrying a *Geelong Advertiser* report: [6]

" ... Mr. McGillivray of Geelong is, we understand, the successful tenderer for the erection of the Lighthouse on Cape Otway. (The announcement is rather premature; Mr. McGillivray's is the lowest tender, but it will not be known who has obtained the contract until the return of His Honour the Superintendent)"

La Trobe was in fact in Sydney discussing the serious situation that had arisen in Van Diemen's Land where the Governor Sir Eardly Wilmot had been called home by Gladstone following certain disparaging stories appearing in the English newspapers. La Trobe doubtless used the opportunity to inform the Colonial Secretary at firsthand of the moves made toward commencing the lighthouse.

Not only was McGillivray's tender lowest, it was lowest by a considerable sum. This should have alerted William Lonsdale — acting Superintendent in La Trobe's absence — to the difficulty contractors had had in preparing their tender when so much was unknown about the site. Lonsdale later stated, when writing to the Colonial secretary; [7]

" ... Should any question arise to the reasonableness of this tender, I can, I think safely say, that should the work be submitted again to competition it would not be done for a sum as low as the present. It must also be remembered that in addition to the plan forwarded by the Colonial architect, quarters consisting of four rooms were sanctioned, and are included in the present contract. The contract has also been taken on the uncertainty of a proper kind of stone being found on the site, and in the event of its not being found there the contractor has to bare the expense of procuring it from Van Diemen's Land."

Lonsdale's letter was written in the November. Already McGillivray was threatening to withdraw his tender "because," said Lonsdale: [8]

" ... of the delay which had taken place since he sent in his tender being prejudicial to him, as the rate of wages was increasing and material getting dearer."

Added to this the approaching months were the only time he could be sure of access via Roadknight's track. With pressure on to get the lighthouse established McGillivray was informed that his tender for £1995 had been accepted. The tower was to be a conventional masonry structure, fluted at the base. The technology did not exist in the colonies for erecting cast iron structures such as La Trobe had mentioned. To bring out such structures from great Britain would have meant a delay of eighteen months or more. Politically this could not be afforded.

Sir Charles Fitzroy, successor to Sir George Gipps, had informed Gladstone on the last day of August of the progress made with each of the four recommended lighthouses. [9] He was able to say of Gabo Island, that a tender had been accepted and that the same plan was being used for it as for Cape Otway. Kent Group Lighthouse had been commenced by the Government of Van Diemen's Land. The proposed King Island lighthouse was causing controversy and the Admiralty had been asked to arbitrate following strongly worded objections to its erection from Moriarty, Harbour Master at Hobart and consistent lighthouse advocate.

It is against this broader Bass Strait lighthouse program that the commencement of work at Cape Otway should be seen. Otway tower was only one of the four planned and had already been preceded by the Goose Island and Swan Island lights in Banks' Strait erected by the Van Diemen's Land Government that now objected to King Island.

The Argus of December 22 carried news of a disheartening arrival at Cape Otway by McGillivray: [10]

"The schooner *John* which was chartered to convey the contractor and workmen, with the supplies for the erection of the Lighthouse on Cape Otway, has arrived in safety at its destination, although after a stormy and protracted voyage. The *John* had arrived near its destination when the fearful gale which drove the vessels ashore at Portsea set in. The captain of the schooner judiciously stood out to sea and after beating about for a fortnight was at last enabled to approach the place of disembarkation. An attempt was made to land within a mile of the extremity of the Cape, but the shore was found to be completely fenced with a line of sunken rocks. At last a landing was effected at a small bay about six miles east of the Cape. [Blanket Bay] In this bay or roadstead the *John* lay in safety at a distance of half a mile from the shore."

McGillivray commenced excavation work at the place La Trobe had chosen nearly two years earlier. Fortunately

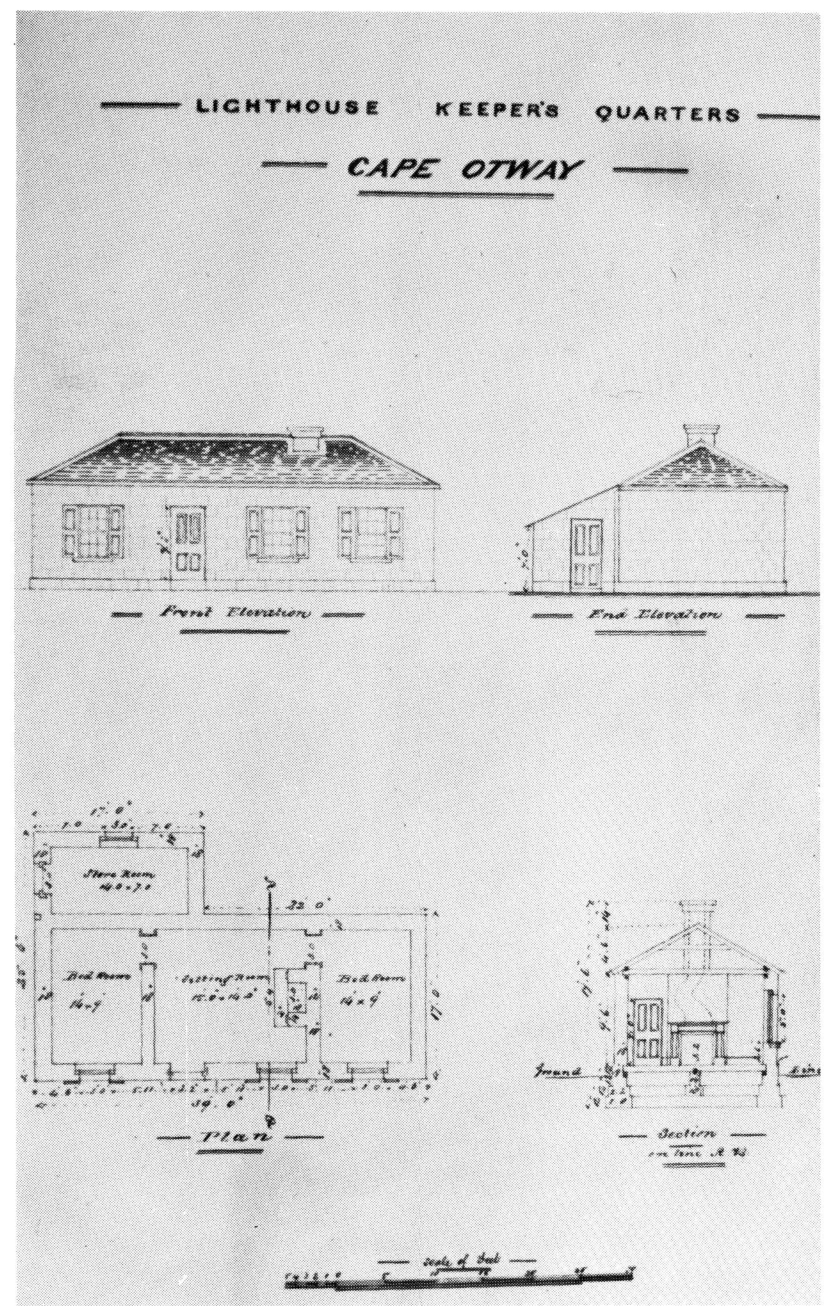

8. *". . . I find that the bedroom of my Quarters is quite uninhabitable on account of the damp coming through the end wall, as the plaster is all hanging with moisture." – Ford, 1848. This drawing of the original keeper's quarters is in Henry Ginn's Inspection Book. The building withstood only nine years of Cape Otway weather before it was replaced in 1856, by the existing quarters.*

9. Sheltered from most winds the Parker River Inlet was the principal landing place for lighthouse stores. The site of the quarry, where stone was won for the lighthouse, was also here. Operations were transferred to Blanket Bay in 1878, thirty years after the delicate lighthouse mechanism had been brought through the surf here.

10. Surf driving onto the beach near Point Franklin – the only practical landing places lay to the east at the Parker River and Blanket Bay. Early attempts to land workmen for the lighthouse here proved very dangerous.

good quality sandstone was found at the Parker River itself and a quarry was opened. The following specification of workmanship required had been drawn up for both Gabo Island and Cape Otway by the Colonial architect: [11]

"The stones to be ... true and square on the face, beds and joints are to be of the soundest description that can be procured and to be set on their natural beds (or as may be directed) alternate header and stretcher. The bonds or joints on the circumference to bond or overlap at least twelve inches and on the diameter or cross section at least nine inches. No stone to be less than two feet long and fifteen inches on the bed and the headers to be of such depth of beds as may be ordered by the Colonial architect or person superintending the work."

By January 1847 McGillivray had found that the site chosen by La Trobe was a mass of sand. It was shifted about fifty feet further back from the cliff edge. The extra expense involved in the change was borne by the Government but by the middle of May more problems had arisen. Henry Ginn, in charge of the infant Public Works Department, made a personal visit to the site and condemned the stonework prepared for the footings. The resident government overseer was dismissed. A man destined to contribute much to the building of the Cape Otway Lighthouse was sent in his place: Joseph Burns, Ginn's assistant architect.

La Trobe, in reporting these matters to the Colonial Secretary wrote: [12]

"I have directed that Mr. Burns ... in whom full confidence may be placed, should be desired to make arrangements for his immediate return to the Cape, to superintend the removal and resetting of the foundation and to continue in charge of the work until it may be completed."

La Trobe's knowledge of the Otway country shaped his concluding remarks:

"I am gratified to say that Mr. Burns has undertaken this duty though at considerable sacrifice of personal convenience and has this morning left Melbourne for his return. To facilitate this, I directed two of the Native Police to accompany him as far as the track through the Southern Forest as may be

11. G.D. Smythe is considered the discoverer of the Parker River Inlet but on so inhospitable a coast sealing gangs undoubtedly knew of this roadstead well before. Today the crack of bullock whips and the shouts of boatmen are no longer heard here – only the wind in the she-oaks and the muffled report of the surf below.

practicable at this season for horses, or to the Cape itself, if circumstances permit."

Whether Burns realized it or not, McGillivray was not to continue much longer as the contractor for the Cape Otway Lighthouse. Ginn informed La Trobe in the September that McGillivray's men were taking out writs against their employer over the quality of provisions supplied and were refusing to work.

Cape Otway in winter is never pleasant and for these men living in tents and other rude shelters, lack of proper supplies would have made their working conditions doubly difficult. As stragglers returned to Melbourne they brought news of finds on the coast of wreckage from the *Joanna*, lost to the west four years previously. There were rumours of caches of rum, but the occasional bottle of wine and numerous wax candles seem to have constituted most of the finds reported.

Foreclosure at Otway was imminent. Ginn learnt that McGillivray was on his way to Melbourne: [13]

"for the purpose of procuring additional hands; or, to foreclose the Contract in the probable event of men not engaging with him on account of the reports (whether true or not) relative to the provisions supplied."

Faced with this deteriorating situation, the Government foreclosed. Believing that the best course now was to take over the work, advertisements were placed for men on October 13, 1847. La Trobe had his men within a week. Arrangements now proceeded quickly. Sydney approved La Trobe's proposal to send, 47 men comprising — 23 stone masons, 1 carpenter, 1 blacksmith, 5 bullock drivers, 7 Quarry men and 10 labourers. When added to eight of McGillivray's men who were still at the Cape and were expected to sign on, this gave Henry Ginn the workforce needed to get the building finished. Most important of all, he had the able Joseph Burns about to return to the site.

The schooner *Teazer* under Captain Rogers was chartered and sailed for the Cape with some 43 workmen. While coming ashore at the Parker River the ship's boat overturned and the Captain and one other crew member drowned. Again the hazards of landing on the coast had been demonstrated. The *Teazer* returned to

12. Planned as Cape Otway's companion lighthouse at the eastern end of Bass Strait, the Gabo Island tower was never completed in the form intended. This drawing of Capt. Owen Stanley shows the excavation there and the contractors attempts to secure a solid foundation. He was eventually dismissed in 1849 while the present Gabo tower was not built till 1861.
Reproduced by permission of the Hydrographer of the Royal Navy.

13. Charles Yules drawing of Cape Otway. The lighthouse under construction and the earlier abandoned excavation can be seen. Although rough seas precluded Yule from landing and inspecting the work personally, he was able to determine the height of the cliff by means of sights taken at sea. Yule's estimate was half that of earlier ones and when reported, moves to reduce the height of the tower in order to save costs, lapsed.
Reproduced by permission of the Hydrographer of the Royal Navy.

Melbourne with her passengers. They were sent overland via Roadknight's track.

The Otway workmen were to be paid wages slightly above the equivalent Melbourne rates — for example the stone masons were to be paid 7/- per day, though Ginn added: [14]

"Precaution has been taken to enforce a full days work from the men; who distinctly understand that full average quantity of stone must be prepared and dressed every day by each man."

Fat bullocks were procured from Roadknight and were provided at the Cape for the men. Other rations could be purchased at Melbourne prices. On the fifth day of each month the pay abstracts had to reach Roadknights *Grannymede* station on the Barwon River for handover, so that the families of the men could be paid in Melbourne.

Work proceeded at a steady pace under Burns' supervision but one question remained to be answered. What should be the exact elevation of the lighthouse when complete? There ensued a series of memoranda between Ginn, La Trobe and the Colonial architect as to the wisdom of taking to its full design height, a tower believed to be sited 400 feet above the sea. The time and expense saved by such a measure was an obvious consideration and La Trobe stated for the Colonial Architect's benefit: [15]

"The great elevation of the Light above the sea is an acknowledged disadvantage and I do not see why it is necessary that the light should be raised the additional contemplated height above it, as there can be but little doubt that every purpose would be answered if 20 feet were taken from the proposed height of the Column [so] that the light would be equally visible on all sides by night and the Column at the summit sufficiently prominent to serve as a beacon by day."

La Trobe then requested the reaction of Captain Owen Stanley to this suggestion. Stanley had left Sydney in *H.M.S. Rattlesnake* in early February 1848, in company with the sloop *Bramble* to inspect progress on the various lighthouses in course of erection in Bass Strait. This was in answer to the Admiralty's expressed concern.

Owen Stanley visited Gabo Island and saw the sixty foot deep sand hole that was all the government had to show for progress there, then conferred in Melbourne with La Trobe before inspecting Deal Island and the newly completed Van Diemen's Land lights in Banks Straits. To Cape Otway he sent Lieutenant Charles Yule in the *Bramble*. Yule's findings were a revelation to La Trobe: [16]

14. *Capt. Owen Stanley informed La Trobe of Yule's findings regarding Cape Otway. When asked if the tower might be shortened, he replied, "... I enclose a sketch showing what an awkward appearance the column would have if curtailed of its due proportion."*

"Her Majesty's Ship
Rattlesnake
Sydney 23/3/1848.

"Sir

In answer to your memo., suggesting that the column of the Light House on Cape Otway should not be raised more than 25' from the ground.

I beg leave to state from Lieutenant Yule's report which I have just received it appears that the cliff on which the Light House is built is not more than 250 feet above the high water mark.

And that the land in shore of the lighthouse is higher than the cliff. Under these circumstances I think it highly desirable that the column should be carried up to the full height originally intended in order that it may form as conspicuous an object as possible during the day time, and I enclose a sketch showing what an awkward appearance the column would have if curtailed of its due proportion.

> Your Most Obedient,
> Humble Servant,
> Captain and Surveyor
> Owen Stanley."

This was within 50 feet of La Trobe's original estimate.

By the April Burns was able to report that he was completing the stone cornice. He was probably glad to receive Ginn's note: [17]

"The contract drawings of this part and the height of the cornice are not binding on you; act in such matters as your material will permit."

As the lighthouse moved toward completion Ginn found himself increasingly defending Burns from accusations made by the disaffected Alexander McGillivray. In March he wrote to McGillivray: [18]

"I regret exceedingly that you should be compelled to reitorate your serious charges against the Overseer of Works at Cape Otway."

He reminded McGillivray that an enquiry was to be held into his charges. To further charges, Ginn replied sharply: [19]

"I am ordered by His Honour the Superintendent to inform you that the Government decline further correspondence with you."

It was to be May 19th 1848 before Ginn was finally able to report that the estimated cost of erecting the lighthouse was now expected to be about £4,300. "the workmanship and material are of the best description."

With the waves of Bass Strait at their feet, Burns' masons dressed and placed the last cornice stones. The dead of Bass Strait could have a memorial; the living no better welcome.

---

15. "The twentieth course above the foundations of the Column is set and it is presumed that the entire of the works will be completed by the 26th day of June so that the lamps can be lighted on the first day of July next." – Ginn.

16. "... a light should be erected at Cape Otway. It being the southern extremity of the mainland at the entrance of Bass's Straits ... it was a bold coast ... it would be a direct guide for vessels bound to Port Phillip as well as the Straits – Moriarty, 1845.

By May the shaft of the lighthouse was near complete and awaited the lantern that has arrived from England. The delicate machinery had to be brought through the surf at the Parker River in an open boat. (See opposite page).

QUOTATIONS AND REFERENCES

1. P.P.D. Supt. Out. Correspondence. 9/6/1846. No. 46/528. P.R.O. VIC.
2. *Geelong Advertiser.* 8/8/1846.
3. P.P.D. Supt. Inward Correspondence. 1499/46. 25/8/1846. P.R.O. VIC.
4. *The Weekly Times.* 23/7/1892. P. 32. Reminiscences of Pioneer Days in Victoria by "Bushwhacker."
5. P.P.D. Supt. Out. Correspondence 46/761. La Trobe to N.S.W. Col. Sec. P.R.O. VIC.
6. *Argus.* 15/9/1846.
7. P.P.D. Supt. Out. Correspondence 46/993. 3/11/1846. Lonsdale to N.S.W. Col. Sec. P.R.O. VIC.
8. ibid.
9. H.R.A. Series 1. Vol. 25. P. 183.
10. *Argus.* 22/12/1846.
11. N.S.W. Legislative Council Enquiry into Bass Strait Lighthouses. 1849.
12. P.P.D. Supt. Out. Correspondence 47/587. to N.S.W. Col. Sec. P.R.O. VIC.
13. P.P.D. Supt. In. Correspondence. Letter dated 20/9/1847 from Ginn P.R.O. VIC.
14. ibid. 23/10/1847.
15. P.P.D. Supt. Out. Correspondence 47/652. to N.S.W. Col. Sec. P.R.O. VIC.
16. P.P.D. Supt. In. Correspondence 48/730. P.R.O. VIC.
17. Col. Archit. Letter Book. (Nov. 1847 – Mar. 1850) Page 62. No. 111. P.R.O. VIC.
18. ibid. No. 74. P. 76.
19. ibid. No. 148. P. 71.
20. P.P.D. Supt. In. Correspondence. 48/870. P.R.O. VIC.

ILLUSTRATION SOURCES

1. N.S.W. P.R.O. Col. Sec. inwards corresp. 46/4361.
2. La Trobe L. H19572 H Ca 6/3/8.
3. Iain Stuart.
4. La Trobe L. Picture Collection.
5. Mr. Cyril Marriner, Hordenvale.
6. P.R.O. Vic. Supt. Outward Corresp. 46/927.
7. P.R.O. Vic. Col. Architects Inspection Book.
8. ibid.
9., 10, 11, 15, 16 and 17. D.M.W.
12. Hydrographic Office, Royal Navy, Somerset. File OD. 67. No. 13.
13. ibid. OD 67. No. 2.
14. P.R.O. Vic. 48/730 Supt. Inward Correspondence.

17. *"I have the satisfaction of believing that as the work is now completely under the control of the Government and the season becoming more and more favourable that the column of the lighthouse may be erected within the time originally proposed."* – Ginn, October 1847.
*The path taken by Cape Otway's keepers for over one **hundred** and thirty years.*

...PERFECT WORKING ORDER...

The lantern for the lighthouse was received in Melbourne on leap year day 1848 and was immediately dismantled to be carefully repacked into smaller casks: [1]

"for the purpose of rendering the packages as secure as to allow for the lantern being landed through the surf, and to provide against the very probable contingency of boats upsetting in attempting a landing."

The makers Wilkins Bros, at 24 and 25 Long Acre, London, who had made the lantern then in use in the Eddystone light, were a long way away in case of serious accident.

La Trobe decided that it would be best if the Lighthouse Superintendent could accompany the mechanism to Cape Otway. This would enable the man selected to familiarize himself with the machinery while the overseer was on site; after that, Burns would be a four day ride away, weather and track permitting.

It was now two years since an application for a Keeper's position had been received from James Ross Lawrence R.N. (retired) Lawrence stated his preparedness to serve at either Gabo Island or Cape Otway. On that occasion he had forwarded a petition to La Trobe signed by the masters of vessels in port but with Cape Otway lighthouse now nearing completion, he wrote again to La Trobe.

It is worth deviating a moment to read Lawrence's more detailed statement of his background as it provides a glimpse of naval history: [2]

Melbourne
March 29, 1848.

"Statement of the services of James Ross Lawrence,
Lieutenant Royal Navy

Joined the *Bittern* Sloop as Midshipman in July 1812. Was actively employed up to the close of the War. I was a Midshipman of the *Leander* in Lord Exmouth's attack on the batteries of Algiers August 27th 1816. Was promoted 1821, into the brig *Alacrity* on the South American Station and subsequently removed into the *Owen Glendower*, as third Lieutenant of that ship. Was paid off 1822 at Portsmouth. Was appointed Chief Officer in the Coast Guard Service at Looe in Cornwall, May 1825 and remained in the Coast Guard Service until 1832 October. Received most flattering testimonials (now lost) from three consecutive Inspecting Commanders for my "gallantry and activity."

James Ross Lawrence.
Lieutenant Royal Navy."

Lawrence was duly appointed and hastily made arrangements to sail with Ginn and the valuable lantern to Cape Otway. This he did, but the ship was forced back from the Parker River to Hobsons Bay. From there Lawrence wrote to La Trobe with a chronicle of what had taken place at the Parker. It was 9 p.m. when Lawrence commenced writing: [3]

" ... the whale boat had made five consecutive trips without loss or apparent damage of any kind when in the attempt to return the fifth time a sea broke onto her (the steer oar at the instant snapping) the boat fell off broadside exposed whilst a second wave filled, and a third turned her, bottom up. You may easily imagine, Sir, that the men were in imminent peril yet most providentially all were saved. Subsequently they succeeded in reaching the *Mary* but as soon as the master learnt that the steer oar was broken and lost, he informed me that he could not incur the risk of an attempt to land any of the cargo without one, and should return to Port Phillip to procure it. I most respectfully, beg leave here to remark that the spot, although possibly the best that can be selected is still one evidently frought with danger even to the vessel and all on board and indeed all our future operations will require the greatest care and caution.

Some of the rollers were terrific and would have engulfed the finest boat that ever swam and this I noticed contemporaneously with the accident.

The Clerk of the Works has requested me to remain on board until everything is landed and in carrying out what I feel to be a most important charge, I shall invariable discourage any attempt to land, and if necessary protest against it, when danger can be apprehended, however the master has used all due precaution and I do not anticipate that interference on my part will be required. Since I commenced this letter I have ascertained that the necessary Steer oar and spare ones are provided and wind and weather permitting we sail for Cape Otway tomorrow."

The Parker River Inlet remains today little changed from that place Lawerence saw for the first time — a secluded roadstead that offers no compromise to those not prepared to respect it's changing moods.

The lighthouse was nearing completion and although it was the middle of winter the track over the ranges to Roadknight's station on the Barwon was in frequent use. Ginn had appointed two Assistant Keepers both at 4/2 per day with provisions supplied. Their names were Philip Monaghan and William Weavers. The former was also a qualified stone mason and proceeded with his wife to the Cape in the first week of June over the Barrier Range. The track was a quagmire. Either side and above, the forest walled the traveller in. This was the same country that in alliance with the rain had thwarted Henry Allan two years before. Now much lesser mortals were obliged to suffer it.

Stonemasons and quarrymen were discharged at Cape Otway and prepared to return to Melbourne, some with their families. In fact it would appear that a little community was parting. "The return of the children and women by the vessel that brings the Lantern is advisable," wrote Ginn, "however, the Government are not responsible for their passage money."

Against the forest backdrop the Cape Otway Lighthouse commenced operations on August 29, 1848. Burns words were truly an understatement: [5]

"The entire of the works were completed in accordance with your instructions and the lights exhibited on the 29th August,

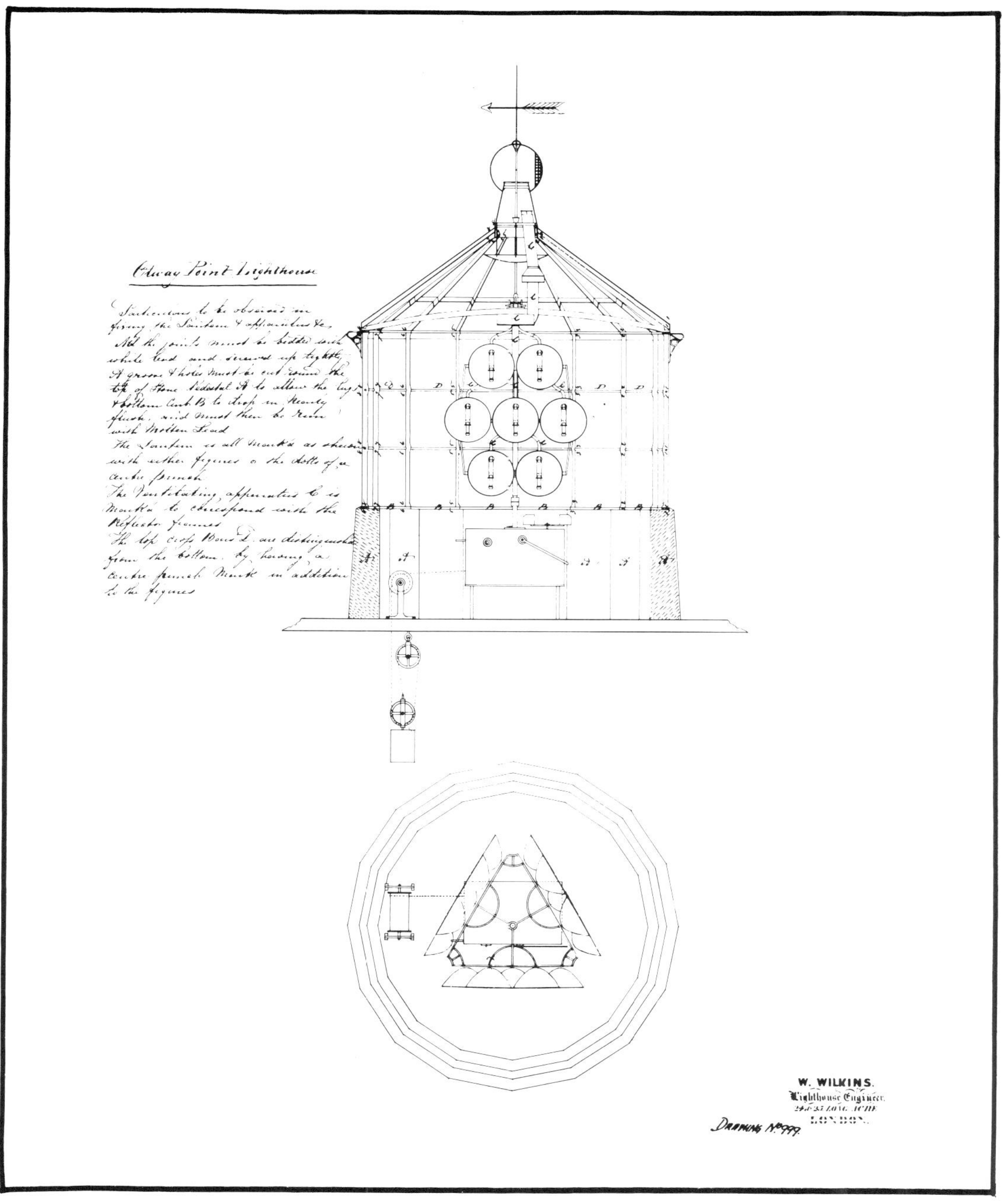

after which I remained five nights at the Cape to test the efficiency of the machinery and lamps and gave up the whole in perfect working order to the Superintendent of the Lighthouse."

The completion of the lighthouse was reported in the *Argus* newspaper and after praising the efforts of Ginn and Burns, a concluding sentence showed so well, known sentiments held toward another: [6]

"The work ... will certainly go far to give the lie to Mr. La Trobe's calumny on the province as having neither the means properly to devise nor prudently to execute such works."

Ships negotiating the entrance soon reported seeing the lighthouse. Ginn sent to La Trobe details of the towers elevation, latitude and longitude for inclusion in the New South Wales Government Gazette. With this he submitted the following extract from the log of the *Mary*, a cutter bound from Warrnambool to Melboure: [7]

"This day commences with fine weather, at 6 p.m. Moonlight Head bore W.N.W. Cape Otway light seen for the first time, distance about 30 miles."

The flash was of three seconds duration with fifty seconds of darkness. The lantern had three faces, the entire revolving every two minutes and thirty nine seconds. On each face was mounted seven Argand Lamps which burned special sperm oil. The early instruction books are filled with accounts of how the oil had to be kept up to the wicks, the wicks trimmed and monitored during the night and the individual parabolic reflectors located behind each light, kept as clean and reflective as the best French *chamois* would allow. The clockwork mechanism was worked by a large weight that slowly dropped from the top to the bottom of the

2. *"The Lighthouse on Cape Otway, Bass' Straits, latitude 38°51' south and longitude 143°29' having been completed and lighted on the 29th August, 1848: a light will continue burning from sunset until sunrise." – Ginn.*
Lanterns such as these with their individual parabolic reflectors, required the constant attentions of the keepers during the night to ensure a steady and bright light. The original Cape Otway mechanism was replaced in 1891.

shaft as the night passed. The glass chimneys would often break, and new flues had to be fitted as the light continued to revolve. In the morning the Assistant Keeper would slowly wind it up again.

But within weeks of the commissioning of the light, Lieutenant Lawrence was forced to ride over the track to Roadknight's station. He went on to Melbourne to allege that the machinery had broken down. Burns returned to the Cape with Lawrence and interviewed each of the keepers. After repairing the machinery, he returned and prepared a report for Ginn.

He had taken evidence from each of the assistant keepers. Firstly Weavers, who would say little: [8]

"I heard Mr. Lawrence say repeatedly that the whole design or construction of everything about the lighthouse was defective or some such words." Then Monaghan, "He never knew anything to be wrong with the machinery until Mr. Lawrence and Mr. Weavers had taken the cover off when he believes they were working at it for a whole day, for having gone to the Lighthouse towards evening he perceived Mr. Weavers handling and violently wrenching a great many parts."

From this report Ginn concluded for La Trobe's benefit: [9]

5. *Lt. J.R. Lawrence's application to La Trobe for the position of Superintendent, Cape Otway Lighthouse was accompanied by the above testimonial. It was signed by the masters of vessels in* **Port Phillip at the time. They may have been disappointed had they learnt of Lawrence's alleged failure to live up to their high expectations.**

6. "I heard Mr. Lawrence say repeatedly that the whole design or construction of everything about the lighthouse was defective or some such words." – Keeper Weavers. 1848. The lenses of the 1891 dioptric mechanism are still in use at Cape Otway and require far less upkeep than the original parabolic reflectors with their individual lamps.

"I am convinced that some party or parties must have tampered with it, otherwise it would have worked seven years without variation and then only have required cleaning, it being as perfect a piece of machinery, as far as materials and constructions are concerned as could be made, and I regret to add, that should the same waste of glasses (which cannot be procured of the sort in the Colony) and ill usage of the machinery continue within twelve months it would be impossible to have the lighthouse lighted."

La Trobe summarily dismissed Lawrence. Ginn sent Balmain, one of his own men, to oversee Monaghan who was in charge of the lighthouse and to give notice of dismissal to Weavers. Weavers was replaced in the December by a James Murray. It was not till then that Balmain was able to report on all that he had encountered and learnt of Lieut. Lawrence's performance:[10]

"I found the casks of beef which had been spoilt, close to the Quarters, they of course emitting a most powerful effluvia. In making a list of the stores, I found the ration of tea in an open box, a cat with a litter of kittens having taken up her quarter in it. At every hut that I passed on the road, the remark was made that the occupants had never heard anyone make use of such improper and ungentlemanly language as Mr. Lawrence."

Lawrence replied with more rhetoric than a refutation:[11]

"I have to contend against falsehood and misrepresentation but I should think that the truth would prevail at the last." Again:
"The Overseer of Works has sown the Whirlwind as just retribution he may yet reap the storm."

Lawrence's application had shown him to have been a well known man and therefore, presumably, competent. The *Argus* sprang to his defence:[12]

"Lieutenant Lawrence is an old and deserving naval officer and his offence being a very menial one a very general feeling prevails that he has been sacrificed to the malignity of a man (Monaghan) whose ill will he had incurred, by insisting upon a strict attention to the duties of his office."

The *Argus's* antipathy to La Trobe make their opinions suspect.

Joseph Burns made annual inspections of the lighthouse machinery, but with the passage of time he slipped back into the anonymity of the Public Works Department. He resigned in 1852[13] and was later instrumental in founding the Royal Victorian Institute of Architects. At the close of 1848, Ginn said of him:[14]

" ... that he was absent from his home and large family for fourteen consecutive months, that his hours of duty were nearly double what they would have been had he been stationed in Melbourne, and that he had had to undertake five journeys overland to the Cape of the nature of which your Honour is fully aware."

As a result of La Trobe's representations to Governor Fitzroy, Joseph Burns received a gratuity of £100. The Otway light remains a lasting testimony to him.

QUOTATIONS AND REFERENCES

1. Col. Architect Letter Book. Letter No. 54. P.R.O. VIC. 29/2/1848.
2. P.P.D. Supt. Inward Correspondence. 48/715. P.R.O. VIC.
3. ibid. 48/1034.
4. Col. Arch. Letter Book. Letter No. 56. Page 38. P.R.O. VIC.
5. P.P.D. Supt. In. Correspondence. 48/2109 enclosure. P.R.O. Vic.
6. *Argus* 10/10/1848.
7. P.P.D. Supt. In. Correspondence. 48/1849. P.R.O. VIC.
8. Col. Arch. Letter Book. Letter No. 264. October 1848.
9. ibid. No. 253. P. 104.
10. P.P.D. Supt. In. Correspondence. 48/2542. P.R.O. VIC.
11. ibid. 48/2519.
12. *Argus* 5/12/1848.
13. Col. Sec. Vic. In. Correspondence. BOX 172. 1/1/1852. P.R.O. VIC.

Burns deserved better from the young "gold crazy" colony. Even in this letter of resignation he comes across as an honest man:
"Having completed the term of my agreement, I beg leave to resign my appointment under the Colonial Government and in so doing I must say, that I have not been actuated by any sinister motive but am solely necessitated from the inadequacy of my salary to meet the present extravagant prices of the necessaries of life ... however should my immediate leaving cause any inconvenience to the Public service, I am willing to remain until the end of the present month."

14. Col. Arch. Letter Book. Letter No. 374. P. 138. P.R.O. VIC.

ILLUSTRATION SOURCES

1. D.M.W.
2. Dept. of Transport.
3. D.M.W.
4. Dept. of Science Artarctic Division.
5. P.R.O. Vic.
6. D.M.W.

...ARRIVED HERE LAST SATURDAY NIGHT...

The 1845 enquiry had recommended the construct-ion of four towers in Bass Strait. Lighthouses at both Deal Island in the Kent Group and Cape Otway were now in operation. At Gabo Island a large hole, speedily filling with sand, was all the N.S.W. government had to show for three years work and £1850. The Gabo Island debacle precipitated a general enquiry into the progress of Bass Strait Lighthouses in 1849 by the New South Wales Legislative Council. Of King Island nothing was said at this enquiry, as by this date the British Admiralty had bowed to pressure from William Moriarty and the Van Diemen's Land Government regarding the undesirability of placing a lighthouse there.

Shortly after the 1845 vote of £9000 for the four Bass Strait towers, the Van Diemen's Land Colonial Secretary had written to his New South Wales counter-part with extraordinary directness: [1]

"The Objections raised by Captain Moriarty to the placing of a light on the the northern extremity of King Island appear to the Lieutenant Governor to be so well founded, that he must decline entering on the consideration of the question until he shall have been informed that these objections have been over-ruled by the Lords Commissioners of the Admiralty."

Eighteen months later the Secretary of State for Colonies in writing to the N.S.W. Governor enclosed advice from the Admiralty [2]

"that the opinion of My Lords as to the propriety of having a light on the North point of King's Island was unchanged; but as the Light House on Cape Otway is in progress, and as it will be much more essential guide to the entrance of Bass' Straits than the disputed Light on King's Island and as there appears to be a decided reluctance to proceed with the latter, My Lords will abstain from pressing their objections any further, and have only to express their hope that the experiment may succeed."

This decision on King Island was a quite drastic departure from the view in March 1847. [3] Their capitulation meant that a further thirteen years would elapse and many more lives be lost, before a tower was built at Cape Wickham.

With no lighthouse on King Island and Capt. Lawrence dismissed, one man was destined more than any other to

bear the burden of watch over the western entrance to Bass Strait. As it happened that one man was well fitted for so arduous a task. He was Henry Bayles Ford. This determined independent man had gone to sea at eighteen years of age aboard the government Brig *Governor Phillip*. He came under the notice of La Trobe when in 1841 he married Mary Anne Fitzgerald, an immigrant from Ireland's County Wexford and governess to the La Trobe children. For some six years he was part owner and captain of the intercolonial trader *China*. In 1845 he entered the Customs Service from where he was approached by La Trobe to accept a position as superintendent, Cape Otway Lighthouse. He was then thirty years of age.

Ford could have had no inkling as he rode over the sandhills toward Cape Otway that December day in 1848 that this remote coast, backed by dense forest, would be his home for the next thirty years. For the time being he had left his wife and children in Melbourne.

Upon his arrival, he was concerned — perhaps more for them than for himself — with the dank plaster hanging off the bedroom walls of his residence. His mention of this to his superiors in Melbourne is recorded on the first page of the Cape Otway Lighthouse letter book.

Writing to Henry Ginn:[4]

"I have the honour to inform you that I arrived here on Saturday night last and found everything quite correct ... I find that the bedroom of my Quarters is quite uninhabitable on account of the damp coming through the end wall as the plaster is all hanging with moisture and that I shall endeavour to put a shed or something of the kind to break the weather from off the building but am very much at a loss for some rough carpentry tools."

1. *"West away from Melbourne dust holidays begin, —*
They that mock at Paradise woo at Cora Lynn —
Through the great South Otway gums sings the great South Main —
Take the flower and turn the hour, and kiss your love again!"
— *Kipling.*

The road to the lighthouse near its junction with the Blanket Bay track.

The peeling plaster was a minor problem compared with the task of establishing procedures for the operation of the lighthouse. The Public Works Department kept up a barrage of correspondence in the first six months of 1849, presumably not wanting another Lawrence on their hands. Ford was told; [5]

" ... it is to be expressly understood that although a large quantity [rations] is now at the Cape, the strictest economy must be observed and that for each adult, the following scale only will be allowed [how often is not clear from the directive] 10½ lbs of flour, 10½ lbs of meat, 1¼ lbs of tea, 2 lbs of sugar. You will please to state the number of children you have, [they and his wife had now joined him], and what quantity of rations you intend to draw for them as your own; your wife and children's rations are all chargeable against your pay; and as it is presumed that you have retained the cooking utensils for your own use, they also will be surcharged on your Salary; the Government not providing furniture or utensils."

To this untouched coastline were brought the accepted conventions of the 1840's: [6]

"When giving orders or instructions to the Keepers you will at all times address them by their "sir" [sic] names and maintain the respect due to your situation by causing them to use the word "Sir" when replying or addressing you."

The assistants had no quarters of their own; presumably they lived in the various temporary buildings erected while the lighthouse was being built. Not until the end of 1850 would new but spartan quarters be erected for them; in the meantime Henry Ginn set down guidelines for social intercourse: [7]

"Monaghan will be permitted to erect a chimney in the single mans room after which he is not to intrude in the quarters of the Married Keeper."

As there was neither church nor school at Otway, Ford was instructed to "read the Church of England prayers every Sunday at which all persons in connection with the Lighthouse must attend."

In Melbourne Ginn pleaded pay claims from Ford and his keepers with La Trobe, pointing out that they were receiving less than a labourer's wage while they were

2. Henry Bayles Ford, Superintendent Cape Otway Lighthouse 1848 – 1878.
"I arrived here on Saturday night last and found everything quite correct …"

3. Mary Anne Ford. A former governess to the La Trobe children. This remarkable woman journeyed to Cape Otway in January 1849 and remained thirty years there. She bore seven children at this remote lighthouse, cared for shipwrecked sailors and tended the lighthouse herself when her husband's assistant keepers deserted to the gold fields. A true pioneering woman of Australia.

"necessarily compelled for the greatest portion of the year to live on salt provisions." Monaghan and his wife left before a reply to these claims was received.

La Trobe visited the lighthouse only two months after Ford arrived there. His plan was to proceed there from the abandoned Wesleyan Mission Station near Birregurra on foot over the ranges via Roadknight's track. The horses were to be escorted by way of Colac around to the coast to his former campsite at the mouth of the Gellibrand River. There, after La Trobe's visit to the lighthouse, the parties could reunite and proceed around the coast to Warrnambool and Portland, where La Trobe had business. Setting out from the Mission station La Trobe records that there were stockyards along the track at which those droving cattle could secure the animals and make camp. Although La Trobe's notes for the journey read cryptically, it is evident that he was enjoying himself — it was summer and his lighthouse was established: [8]

"The Fern-tree forest, on by a very fatiguing road to next stockyard. Reach 3rd stockyard about ½ p.3. and here camp as no water was reported ahead. Very fine night. The enormous trees. The beauty of bark."

La Trobe reached Cape Otway via Apollo Bay on the 23 January 1849. Ford had only been there five weeks. La Trobe noted — "Find Ford and all right." Not surprisingly La Trobe took the opportunity to inspect the lighthouse in operation. Doubtless he saw the place where he had driven the spike in to mark the original site. Perhaps he remembered his elated words: "Receding line of coast, on both sides, E. to Cape Patten and W. to Moonlight Hd." Now the lantern turned close behind him. At the crest of the gentle hill that leads away from the tower, the lighted windows to Ford's house could be seen. It must have been with a feeling of satisfaction that he walked back to the quarters.

La Trobe's party remained at the Cape one night. Next day they visited Roadknight's new station and then set off along the coast, later remarking "No one had come from the Westward since our party." Ford accompanied them to the Joanna, parting there and returning to Cape Otway. The journal shows a preoccupation with an injury sustained by Henry Dana, but then notes in interested vein that wax candles were still coming ashore from the *Joanna.* After surmounting Lion Headland and struggling up Nettle Pass behind Milanesia Beach, La Trobe discovered some trees that his party had marked in 1846. Reflecting upon that day he wrote "had a day of the most severe exertion I ever encountered." Here one might well remark on the extraordinary vitality and fitness of the man!

While working along the ridge toward Moonlight Head next day, they were forced to seek shelter from a bushfire. They scrambled down onto the coast and waited. Located two days later by the anxious party that had been waiting for them at the Gellibrand, they rested at the intended rendezvous before pushing on for Warrnambool. Of that night and the next day, La Trobe wrote: [9]

"Sou'wester [native trooper] kills a brush Kangaroo, which we eat without salt."

29th January,

"On to Allan's and I push on to Warrnambool to get a note off to S. [Sarah, his wife]. The deputation sit till 10 p.m. though I never had my clothes off for 8 nights."

Ford, in later disagreements with the Government over his salary, recalled assurances given him by La Trobe on the 1849 visit. After La Trobe had returned to England in 1854, his assurances meant nothing to his successor. Ford was never to receive a salary review.

The lighthouse remained hemmed by the almost totally unexplored forest and the lonely track to civilization was often threatened by fire. With the Otway Forest at his back door it must have comforted Ford to have a sea-link to Melbourne — uncertain though it was. Every twelve months, oil for the lamps, tools, equipment, foodstuffs were landed through the surf at the Parker River Inlet. A tramway, long since gone, was built up the hillside and a windlass used to winch stores up to the main track. A bullock team and wagon then slowly took them on to the lighthouse, three miles away. For all the keepers this was a long hard day's work commencing immediately after the lantern room had been cleaned at daylight. With no shed to store supplies in, goods could not be left at the Parker without risk of damage. By nightfall the light was to be watched again; only on the following day could a few hours sleep be sought before the remainder of the stores had to be fetched.

Occasionally fresh **meat** could be procured from Roadknight's intermittently occupied *Glen Aire* station under an often contested contract the Government had with him. [10] Little business was done with Apollo Bay, though the settlement there was growing as timber mills increased. Trees that were amongst the tallest in Australia were hauled down out of the ranges though much of the forest was destroyed in the January 1851 fires. The fragility of Ford's overland link becomes apparent in this description by an unknown traveller of the track and Apollo Bay three weeks after that fire; [11]

"As we ascended through the thickening timber all view of distant hill or plain was shut out — everything except the immediate forest foreground. It soon began to drizzle, and continued raining during the whole of this dismal lugubrious day of toil and travail. We were, in fact, not under a cloud but *in it.* At first a few reeds and ferns bordered our path; but these soon disappeared, and of all the rich and characteristic vegetation that formed the under-growth of the forest three weeks ago, no trace now remained ... On all sides were gigantic trees, tall and running up a hundred feet without throwing off a single branch. The trunks were completely charred externally, the flames having reached up perhaps a hundred feet, as they fed upon the undergrowth, but he loftiest tops appeared to have escaped. The tops, however, were lost in cloud and mist, so that accurate observation was impossible. Nothing could be more desolate and cheerless ... But the difficulties in our path soon engrossed all attention. The track, formerly well-defined and easy, was now almost effaced; to follow it was out of the question, for it often lay beneath a chaos of huge fallen trunks and branches intertwined. Often it became necessary to make a long detour to avoid these prostrate Goliaths of the Forest, which, two or three hundred feet long, would occasionally arch over a ravine, and leave a passage beneath.

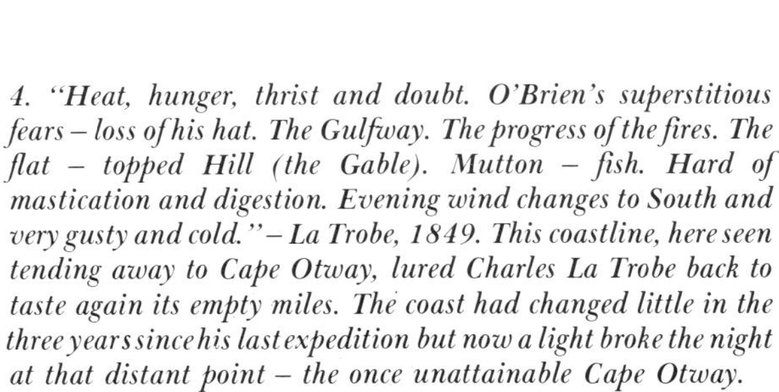

4. "Heat, hunger, thrist and doubt. O'Brien's superstitious fears — loss of his hat. The Gulfway. The progress of the fires. The flat — topped Hill (the Gable). Mutton — fish. Hard of mastication and digestion. Evening wind changes to South and very gusty and cold." — La Trobe, 1849. This coastline, here seen tending away to Cape Otway, lured Charles La Trobe back to taste again its empty miles. The coast had changed little in the three years since his last expedition but now a light broke the night at that distant point — the once unattainable Cape Otway.

5. A survivor of the retreating Otway forest. 1980.

The main point of interest in this wonderful forest is the magnificent growth and almost incredible size of the trees. Some that we roughly measured were fifty and sixty feet in circumference, five feet from the ground. From thirty to forty feet was perhaps the average girth ... The larger trees are generally hollow near the roots: sometimes the interior forms a vast cave ... The colossal limbs and roots, roughened by huge excrescences and fantastically contorted, often assume the most grotesque and *bizarre* forms. All the foliage is at the summit, and thus enjoys the influences of light and sunshine and wind ... There was no voice of bird nor chirp of insect – all animal life appeared to have perished in the universally raging flames.

At nightfall we halted under the lee of a hill. ... The tent, begrimed with charcoal, was spread out on the wet earth, and we lay down before the fire on a slippery steep, wet and miserable.

The little terrier nestled up close to the blazing logs. The horses, fagged and starved, were tied up near us. The night was pitch dark; the rain pattered on the leaves; the wind moaned through the tree tops. It was the very *ideal* of lonely dreariness.

Next day they neared the coast,

"At length we heard the roar of breakers, at first dull and distant; then nearer and louder. Here the forest was merely singed, not burnt up: and presently we passed the limits of devastation and entered a green alley cut through the undergrowth.

After five miles of these green shrubberies, with huge gums and stringybark trees shooting up three hundred feet over our heads, we descended to the beach by the last glimmer of twilight. Old ocean welcomed us with his roar. A little stream was distinguishable wending its way along the beach to the sea. A light on the coast a mile distant showed the spot where the *Margaret* lay stranded ... Camped on a little open platform, by a shrubbery of blue gums.

At daylight, opened our eyes on Apollo Bay ... A party of men were repairing the *Margaret* cutter, lying on the beach. A gang of splitters had also just arrived, with their wives. Our guide had been living here for twelve months when he was burnt out by the fires of Thursday and everything he had destroyed. On the beach was a stack of timber ready for shipment, which had escaped the flames."

At Addis Bay, adjacent to Cape Patton, an attempt had been made that January to burn a fire break in the surrounding hills, however the wind shifted in the afternoon and the fire "came down on the settlers with resistless fury, annihilating everything in their way." The fire must have been as bad as any ever experienced in the Otways because timber millers were driven to shoulder deep water in the sea and "the[12] flames, coming from the forest three quarters of a mile distant, scorched them as they stood in the water ..."

The lighthouse survived the fire unscathed but the author of the earlier account resignedly notes:[13]

'We did not attempt to reach the Cape, the fires having, we were told, rendered the road difficult or impracticable. For the first two miles the track lay through thick shrubberies and underwood. These were succeeded by the limitless burnt-up forest and scrub."

Isolated as they were at the Cape men's tempers could become frayed. Ford charged one Otway man with threatening him with a pair of scissors when at the Parker. Following another similar incident, a rare rebuke to Ford was sent by Ginn after referring it to La Trobe:[14]

"His Honour regrets very much you should have so far lowered yourself by using the disgraceful language attributed to you and which you have admitted to be in part correct."

In such an environment it was often more than tempers that broke. Keeper Thomas Ricketts' tragedy was recorded in Ford's letter book:[15]

"I beg leave to inform you that the Keeper Thomas Ricketts proceeds to Gelong [sic] or Melbourne tomorrow and his wife has become insane and is very dangerous – attempting to destroy herself & infant. I have requested him to remove her to the Asylum and should he not go farther than Gelong he will post this letter, but should he have to come on to Melbourne you would perhaps be so kind as to give him instructions how to proceed in his case, as he must return immediately on account of his helpless children it appears that the woman has been in an Asylum in England some 9 years ago. As to the man I could not wish for a better hand it would be an act of charity to still continue him in the service for the sake of his helpless family Sir, 5 boys at the Cape and one at service."

Ford had been in his position for three years when the Gold Rush brought hundreds of ships past Cape Otway. In 1851, the year gold was discovered, 712 ships arrived in Victoria from overseas. In the following year 1657 ships arrived. Ford had needed an increase in staff, but as it was, Keepers simply disappeared from the lighthouse to the diggings. A report from Ginn, made after a visit by Burns at the beginning of 1852 describes the situation:[16]

"the Assistant Keepers informed him [Burns] that if their pay was reduced they should leave their situations, they having a knowledge of the gold discoveries at Ballarat.

.... I may incidentally remark, that the Foreman of Works [Joseph Burns] did not inform the Keepers of the gold discoveries at Mount Alexander and of which they were not aware when he left."

The majority of ships arriving during the Gold Rush

6. "... at daylight opened our eyes on Apollo Bay ... a bold rocky coast, densely forested hills, reaching down to within a mile of the sea – a heavy surf thundering in upon a broad sandy beach – a glassy stream running parallel to the line of breakers ... wild and desolate, yet not without beauty ... A party of men were repairing the "Margaret", cutter, lying on the beach. A gang of splitters had just arrived with their wives." – an anonymous wanderer, 1851.

This sketch was done five years later by Edward Snell when he visited Apollo Bay to inspect the mill supplying railway sleepers for the Geelong Melbourne Railway line.
Reproduced by courtesy of the La Trobe Library.

78

were captained by men who were strangers to Bass Strait. They were pressed by passengers anxious to reach Melbourne before the diggings closed. In these circumstances it was essential that Cape Otway Lighthouse be maintained as the leading light to Bass Strait. Such replacement Keepers as could be obtained sometimes stayed only a matter of days. La Trobe recognized that men who did stay deserved fair treatment: [17]

"Any of the men employed at the lighthouse who can be certified by the officer in charge to have stuck by him and done their duty during the period in question may receive the full amount of pay claimed. They have deserved it in every way."

In addition to his normal duties Ford was expected to be able to offer succour to shipwreck victims and even to render assistance in possible rescues. In 1854 he reported to the Chief Harbour Master the wreck of a vessel inward-bound from England: [18]

"I beg leave to inform you that the Brig 'Jenny of Hull' from Hull bound to Melbourne was wrecked on the 26th of February last at Brown's Creek near the Johanna River about 12 miles by coast from the Lighthouse to the West. I have been to the wreck with horses and have brought away the clothes of the people that they saved. The vessel is a total wreck, there is nothing of value now on the beach but a large boat which was being brought out as a lighter for the vessel and to get that away is almost impossible as there is always heavy surf running on the beach."

The crew of twelve was saved. Ford accommodated them in the second assistant's quarters and store rooms. A month elapsed before they could depart to follow Roadknight's track over the ranges. They went then without a guide, as no man could be spared from the understaffed station. Nor could Ford reach the wreck itself: [19]

"The River Ayr [sic] having burst at its mouth it is not practicable to get the horse to the wreck for some time to come. I believe that I have managed to fetch from the wreck the principal part of the Crews personal effects."

As the 1850's drew on it was all too apparent that the erection of the Cape Otway Lighthouse had not brought an end to shipwrecks. The last land seen by many of the high masted vessels that now signalled Ford a greeting had been the Cornish coast as it slipped over the horizon. Crowded with new settlers, all borne on a wave of hope, every one was a potential *Cataraqui*. Masters strange to the western entrance failed to appreciate the wisdom of making a landfall west of Cape Otway, then working around to Port Phillip. Worse, too many vessels continued to stumble upon low lying King Island while looking for the high cliffs or light of the Otway.

At least at Otway there was a light that was never allowed to fail. On King Island there was only the darkness. Some men saw that the situation had to be remedied.

QUOTATIONS AND REFERENCES

1. V.D.L. Col. Sec. to N.S.W. Col. Sec. 16/1/1846. Published P.P.G.
2. H.R.A. 1/1/1848. Grey to Fitzroy. P. 134.
3. ibid. P. 412. enclosure.
4. Cape Otway Letter Book. 1849. D/114. Held by Dept. of Transport Commonwealth Govt. first letter, dated 11/12/1848.
5. Col. Arch. Letter Book. No. 180 Page 67. 8/5/1849 P.R.O. VIC.
6. ibid. No. 198. 20/3/1850.
7. ibid. No. 412. 12/10/1849.
8 and 9. La Trobe's Memoranda. H. 93166. La Trobe Library, Journey No. 59. 22/1/1849.
10. Typical conflict described in Col. Sec. Arch. Letter Book. No. 37. Page 14. 5/3/1849. P.R.O. VIC.
11. The Australasian. VOL. 1. 1850-51. P. 461 ff. Mitchell Library REF. No. 352/A.
12. ibid. P. 466.
13. ibid. P. 465.
14. Col. Arch. Letter Book. 1850-1852. Page 85. 20/9/1850.
15. Cape Otway Letter Book. 29/11/1853.
16. Col. Sec. Letters In. BOX 172. 52/27. 3/1/1852. P.R.O. VIC.
17. ibid. 53/4240.
18 and 19. Cape Otway Letter Book. 22/3/1854.

ILLUSTRATION SOURCES

1, 2, 3, 4, 5 D.M.W.
6. M.S. 8970. La Trobe L. The Life and Adventures of E. Snell from 1849 – 1859.
7. Greenwich Maritime Museum Neg. No. P. 7330.

7. *"… the sea has rarely time to gain the enormous height it now had with us – a height frequently of forty feet – regular waves rolling in the direction of the wind and incomparably high peaks and crests produced by crossing waves." A description of a storm in the Southern Ocean while bound for Bass Strait. With such seas and weather accompanying them masters peered hard for the Otway. (See page 80).*

...ON DECK TO SMELL THE LAND...

10

Emigrant ships of *Cataraqui's* era had kept to the Roaring Forties in crossing the Indian Ocean. Slower but easier on passenger and ship, this route often incorporated a stay at the Cape of Good Hope. It had remained largely unchanged for sixty years. But a new route was favoured in the decade of gold and its adoption coincided with a revolution in naval architecture. Suddenly the eyes of the world were on the fledgeling colony of Victoria. The great ships racing out to her.

As word of each new gold discovery reached an incredulous England, people rushed to book passages — some to emigrate, others just to try their luck. The shipping columns of the *London Times* multiplied to accommodate the number of sailing notices advertizing ships bound for Melbourne and Portland.

The lure of gold was so strong that passengers were attracted to the fastest vessels. Their demand led to the development of the "clipper" ship. Most of these great ships were built in North American yards, where softwood was readily available and where streamlined and raked masts were rapidly proving themselves. Sail was piled on sail. Nautical dictionaries soon embraced such terms as *moon sail* and *sky sail*. All the canvas that safety would allow and often more, was set by ships' masters in their efforts to add extra miles to the distance logged each day. One ship the *Schomberg* lost at the entrance to Bass Strait by Captain "Bully" Forbes on her maiden voyage in 1855, could carry *3.3 acres* of sail! Before the disgrace brought upon him by the circumstances of this wreck, Forbes name had been a household word. In 1852 he had brought the famous clipper ship *Marco Polo* to Port Phillip from Liverpool in the unheard time of 68 days. Jammed aboard were over 900 emigrants.

To attain these fast passages a new route to Bass Strait was developed which capitalised on the fact that the earth is a sphere and that the shortest route on it are arcs of "great circles".

Because a true great circle to Bass Strait passes through the Antarctic Continent it was necessary to adopt a compromise route that would take a vessel as close to the great circle as ice and the strength of the ship would allow. This became known as the composite great circle route. Vessels taking it passed 800 miles south of the old Capetown stopping place and 800 miles south of Perth.

Having swung so far south they had to haul up north eastwards to enter Bass Strait. But here the sun was often concealed from them. Lacking determination of latitude and longitude by noon sextant sights, they had

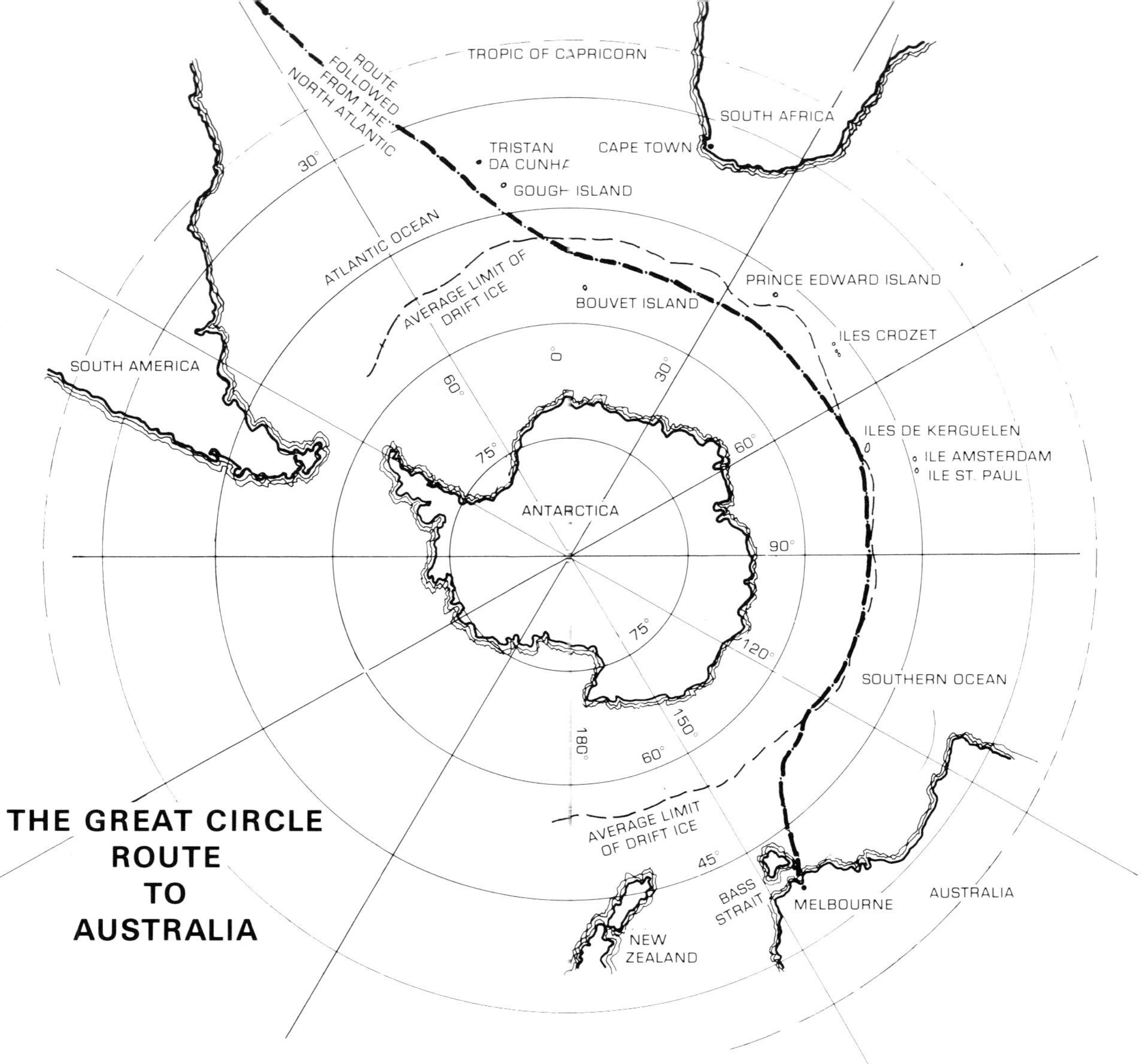

1. *The Composite Great Circle Route. By employing the arcs of great circles, ship's masters were able to satisfy the calls for faster passages as they skirted the Artarctic pack ice before heading north east for the approach to Bass Strait.*

set up its dominion over these lonely waters. An account written by John Dill recalled his passage as a child, far south on the *Monarch of the Seas* in 1857: [3]

" ... we got into what is called a white squall south of the Cape, lost our mainmast and mizzenmast. Sails torn to shreds, and only the vessel was a good one no doubt it would have been all up with us. We were becalmed for three weeks on the line and afterward got too far south and got among the ice. I shall never forget that part of the voyage. The day previous an old sailor said to me, "we are too far south, and the Captain is out of his reckoning; if you stay up tonight you will probably see ice." Like most boys I was fond of the sailors and spent a good deal of my time with them. Consequently after the conversation with my old sailor friend, I decided on staying up and was well repaid for doing so, as at about 12 o'clock at night we got into sheet ice. The grating of the ice on copper of the vessel made a terrific noise, at least so it appeared to me at the time and no doubt was very alarming to the passengers of whom there were about three hundred. The deck soon presented an appearance not easily described and impossible to forget with so many passengers men and women and children all in disable who had rushed on deck thinking we were about to be wrecked. Among the passengers were about eighty Welsh people who could not speak a word of English and the screaming of women and children and din of noises, is still vivid in my memory.

The passengers were all ordered to their cabins and some of them had to be forced down and the hatches closed over them. One very big woman rushed up to the first mate, threw her arms around his neck and asked him to save her. The following morning we found we were pretty well surrounded with sheet ice and that there was a large iceberg about a mile from us. Our course was altered at once and we got clear of the ice in a few hours."

Some vessels did not escape. The *Guiding Star* had been advertized before she departed Liverpool in late 1854 as about to make "the quickest passage on record." Instead she disappeared without trace in the freezing seas of the Southern Ocean. Her secret is still kept there and with her the fate of the 480 emigrants seeking passage by her to Melbourne. When hailed by a Boston whaler in the South Atlantic, the last reported sighting, the clipper's master stated his intention to go as far south as possible.

The knowledge that well built vessels such as the

to fall back on dead reckoning to estimate their whereabouts. Course corrections for Bass Strait's contentious currents were hopefully made according to the master's experience of the western approaches.

Besides the perils of the mountainous waves that girdled southern waters, masters had to contend with pack ice and drifting icebergs. The temptation to go further south than the last passage was to many masters irresistible, but the ice obeyed no man as year by year it

Guiding Star could fail to arrive at their destination served to remind all those crossing these seas, at what risk they journeyed. To the passengers, often battened below decks in the appalling weather, it must have seemed as though the Southern Ocean had everything in its favour as it gambled with the ship's master for their lives. It is a testimony to the quality of the masters and their ships they commanded, that relatively few ships did founder in these seas en route to Bass Strait.

Many ships emerged crippled from their encounter with the Southern Ocean. In a brief statement the *Argus* for September 30, 1859 reported the dismasting in "a hurricane" of the White Star ship, *Ida* off St. Paul's Island:

2. The Torrens, seen here in 1896, survived an encounter with **an iceberg in the Southern Ocean. The Guiding Star, forty years earlier while bound for Melbourne with over 450 emigrants aboard was not so fortunate. She was last seen in the South Atlantic about to make her easting but months later had failed to arrive at her destination. It is presumed that the Guiding Star struck an iceberg but the Southern Ocean has yielded no clue to her exact fate.**

3. A Chronometer and sextant typical of those carried by sailing ships bound for Australia. Weather and sea permitting, a ship's master was able to plot his route and make appropriate adjustments to his course. Very often no land would be sighted between leaving the English Channel and Cape Otway. Finding the entrance to Bass Strait remained the last challenge for the voyage.

amplified trough or peak did not assist passenger comfort. The frequency of poor weather on the approach to Bass Strait and the southerly current setting toward King Island, led to the keeping of an anxious lookout for land. With two or three months of ocean behind, each master who saw the Otway's flash climbing up from the wave broken horizon, thanked God for Ford's light.

In such uncertain landfall waters it is not surprising that ship wrecks continued. At an enquiry in 1853 the new Victorian Legislative Council addressed itself for the first time to the question of making the passage into and through Bass Strait a safer one: [3]

"Your Committee ... were unanimously impressed with the extreme importance to this Colony, the commerce of which has increased since the discovery of Gold to so unparalleled an extent, of taking prompt measures for obviating as far as possible, the loss of life and property by shipwrecks on our coast, and rendering our ports easy of access."

At this enquiry the Port and Harbour Master of Melbourne, Captain Charles Ferguson stated when asked about the sufficiency of the Otway light: [4]

"Cape Otway is a most valuable light; but it being situated at the entrance of the Straits, vessels in trying to make it, run a certain risk with respect to King's Island. A ship has to run down so much longitude without seeing land to know his position; for this purpose a light placed upon Cape Bridgewater, or Nelson, would be of great service."

The Harbour Master at Portland agreed: [5]

"Its erection would entirely obviate the great uncertainty that exists with commanders of ships making the light at Cape Otway, in stormy weather, from its proximity to the western coast of King's Island; and if a light were erected at Cape Nelson, it would be hailed by seafaring men as a great boon conferred on the shipping at large."

When the Committee had heard further opinions they recommended the construction of a stone lighthouse at Cape Bridgewater. Further it was considered a lighthouse at Point Lonsdale was essential to mark the entrance to the Heads, Cape Schanck it was believed could be left unlighted until use of "Western Port

4. An iceberg in the Southern Ocean. Floating silently, their high grey walls would appear out of the night. "... we are too far south, and the Captain is out of his reckoning; if you stay up tonight you will probably see ice." – a crew member's words to a small boy in 1857, bound for Australia.

" ... [the hurricane] which commenced from N.E. and suddenly veered around to N.W. during which the ship plunged into the sea and carried away her bowsprit, all top masts and top gallant masts, with yards. A very heavy sea was running at the time. On the following day during the gale, a seaman named James Drever, native of Scotland, while engaged in clearing the wreck, fell overboard and was drowned."

Reduced to little more than a hulk, the *Ida* reached Melbourne one month later.

Long following seas such as those described cross the continental shelf and drive into Bass Strait. But their regular pattern has always been disturbed by the preceding waves rebounding off King Island's long western coastline. Mariners recognized the confused sea as a warning of land close by while the occasionally

5. *Not only mountainous seas and icebergs were to be faced. In 1874 the Cospatrick caught fire south of Capetown. Of the 500 persons aboard, only two survived.*

Cape Otway Lighthouse – a squall passing

should render it necessary for approaches to the Harbour." Wilson's Promontory was the third recommended site. The question of the unbuilt Gabo Island tower did not have to be raised as the New South Wales Government had recently agreed to erect a prefabricated lighthouse there following the loss of the *Monumental City* on adjacent Tallaburga Island.

1853 gave way to 1854 and in this year still more ships were lost attempting to "thread the eye of the needle". On King Island, the *Brahmin* was wrecked in the May of that year on the west coast. Seventeen lost their lives, including the captain and the first and second mate. The twenty five survivors remained on the island for five months before they were rescued.

It is not surprising that by the beginning of 1855, the Victorian Government considered the continued unlit condition of King Island intolerable. In the September another Board reported to it on the same problem: [6]

"We deemed it our duty, before closing our survey, to ascertain the number, the nature and circumstances attending some of the most remarkable of those shipwrecks that have occurred along the western coast of King's Island during the past two years, which we have gleaned from parties resident on the Island, and sufferers from the earliest of these catastrophes.

Thus we have ascertained that within the past eighteen months the following vessels have been wrecked on the western shores of King's Island, viz:– ship *Brahmin;* schooner, *Waterwitch;* schooner, *Agnes;* ship, *Whistler;* brig, *Maypo;* schooner, *Elizabeth;* and it is not merely a conjecture when we express our opinion that three of these calamities would, in

6. *"Flung wide and far across the world*
Till out of many oceans, many storms,
I came on a golden autumn afternoon
With the long swell to this shore. To north, to south
The fortress walls of the last continent
Slept in the sun unguarded."

— *Nan McDonald, The Lighthouse.*

7. *Point Lonsdale Lighthouse marks the entrance to Port Phillip Bay. The present tower was erected in 1902. However a beacon has operated here since 1854 and served to reinforce Cape Otway's greeting to ships near the end of their long voyages from Europe.*

all human probability, have been avoided had a light been erected prior to that period. These vessels, the *Brahmin, Maypo* and *Whistler,* were driven on shore at night by the force of strong north-westerly gales and a current which we have ascertained to be singularly influenced by these winds.

Their commanders were ignorant of their position; yet within the orbit of that beacon, even in misty weather had it been erected, they drifted on unsuspectingly, and in three instances adduced, not only were the vessels and cargoes lost, but they resulted also in a lamentable loss of human life.

Again we would, before closing our Report, urge the necessity of a light house being erected on King's Island; fragments of wrecks cover its coast, doubtless the remains of vessels missing, whose fates have never been ascertained, and we are convinced it is a measure the importance of which can only be appreciated by actual examination of the localities, and the result of this examination has convinced us that within the compass of our duties lies an earnest recommendation to your Excellency that this great work be speedily accomplished."

The three Board members personally inspected the most suitable sights for the lighthouse. They went to the extraordinary measure of setting up an experimental beacon of burning tar barrels on the New Year Islands. From Cape Wickham they recorded them as being plainly visible. This encouraged them in the belief that the more highly elevated Wickham ridge would afford the maximum range to any light placed there, and be seen by ships approaching from the east and west in good time. Suitable building stone was felt to be easily won but local timber was "wholly useless for building purposes, being crooked and stunted in growth." Water was readily available, "we are glad to report that good spring water is ... abundant and near at hand."

Throughout 1855 Melbourne newspapers continued to emphasize the need for a light on King Island. The *Argus* reported a meeting of the Melbourne Chamber of Commerce at which it was agreed that a [7] "committee be appointed to bring the question under the early notice of his Excellency the Governor of the Colony." The article continued by reporting the impressions of a Chamber member who had recently returned from King Island:

8. King Island. The haze obscured New Year Islands with Victoria Cove in the foreground. Debate continued before and after its erection as to whether Cape Wickham Lighthouse would have been better located on the northernmost of the New Year Islands.

9. One of the vessels lost on King Island before a lighthouse was erected, was the Waterwitch.
"I am perfectly confident that had there been a lighthouse upon the New Year Island ... the Waterwitch, which I had the misfortune to belong to, would not have been wrecked there." – Capt. Burdge. 1855.

" ... the captain of the *Whistler* and mate of the *Maypo* returned with me in the *Corio*. As it is, I shall never be surprised after a gale on the coast to hear of disasters there unless steps are taken to place some guide to the fleets of vessels passing by the island. A glance at the chart of the coast will show how near is the track of most of the vessels bound to Victoria, Van Diemen's Land, and New South wales, from all parts of the world.

The recent wrecks, tis tru, bring the urgency of the matter more closely to our notice; but, instead of expressing surprise that they have occurred, we should rather do so that the numbers lost have not been greater. ... The whole beach on the south side is now strewed with the assorted cargo of the *Brahmin*, and the materials of the *Waterwitch*. The *Agnes* schooner, that came down to assist the *Brahmin*, also left her bones on the New Year's reefs ... and judging from the appearance of the beach on the south shore, with the large quantities of spars, pieces of rigging, sails and figureheads, many vessels that have never been heard of have been wrecked on the treacherous reefs that line the whole length of the coast of King's Island."

Sensitive to growing public uneasiness over maritime safety yet alert to the differences of opinion respecting any lighthouse on King Island, the Victorian Government conducted another enquiry and sought the views of sixteen men familiar with Bass Strait waters. Their answers were presented to the Legislative Council in February 1856 and with them correspondence respecting the proposed cost sharing arrangements between the colonies for any lighthouses erected there. The last opinion quoted was David Howie's — surprisingly he thought such a light house as contemplated at Cape Wickham would be "prejudicial" to the safe landfall sought by vessels. When asked his experience of these waters he said he had: [8]

'.. lived 14 years on the Island; [had] piloted vessels constantly and saved life to a considerable extent."

If such a lighthouse was erected, then Howie felt it should be on the New Year Islands not Cape Wickham, so as to be seen further to the south. He also identified a "strong southerly current on the west side of the Island which ... led to the wrecks of the *Isabella, Brahmin, Waterwitch, Whistler* and *Maypo*."

On Boxing day of 1855, another shipwreck occurred– this time on the Otway coast. Not just any ship, or any master but the beautiful *Schomberg* under the controversial but revered "Bully" Forbes.

The *Schomberg* had been built as Great Britain's challenge to the floating grey hounds such as *Marco Polo, Flying Cloud, Lightning* and *James Baines*, from North American ship yards. Her masts stood over 200' above the deck, higher than a 16 storey building, while her main yard arm later washed up near Blanket Bay was over 100' long. She carried 16,000 square yards of sail. For the furnishings no expense had been spared: [9]

"the lower cabin contains sixty large staterooms, finished with white and gold ... the ladies cabin is inlaid with rosewood, set off into Grecian arched panels, and ornamented with pilasters, paper mache cornices, gilding and flower work, the windows filled with transparencies."

Yet "Bully" Forbes lost this queen of ships, just east of

Peterborough, on the Victorian coast. To the waves her diagonal triple planking was as nothing. Her 400 volume library and velvet pile carpets were spilt into the surf. That no lives were lost may be attributed entirely to good fortune – the *Schomberg* had been stranded off an open beach less than a mile short of the first high cliffs of the Otway coast. Had she struck there almost inevitably all would have perished.

Forbes, with the aid of a clever counsel, evaded official censure at the enquiries but he left Victoria with his reputation in tatters. He never recovered nor commanded so fine a ship again.

Many had hailed the *Schomberg* as representing a new age in ship construction. They were sadly disappointed. One of the principal lobbyists for improved standards in ship construction in Melbourne was James Ballingall. This was an era when all intercolonial movements were by sea. Families and relations could only come to the Australian Colonies by sea. In consequence James Ballingall as founder and secretary of the Port Phillip Immigration and Anti-Shipwreck Society, received considerable publicity from his public meetings and lectures. He laboured the wisdom of using "solid bottoms" on ships, and adopting the same construction standards as common on warships. Ballingall sought to expose the alleged collusion between the various parties more interested in a ship being lost than arriving safely. He saw the ordinary passenger as an incidental victim of this conspiracy. A competent speaker he could quote from wide research: [10]

"If the ship arrives safely into port, the insurers receive their money the merchant profits by his venture, and is able and willing to pay it. If the ship goes down, the insurers pay the money, and the merchant is indemnified to the amount of his insurance. If ships go down, they must be replaced and the ship builders do not care how many go down. If the cargoes are sunk, there is more employment for the manufacturers, as the order must be completed 'de novo', and the manufacturers, do not care how many cargoes go down. If the year has been tempestuous, and the losses at sea very numerous, all the better for the shipbuilder and manufacturer, and none the worse for the merchant, who is insured; and strange to say, all the better for the insurance brokers, who are never sorry to see two pages of casualties on Lloyd's books, for premiums mount up immediately, and the present loss is more than indemnified by future profits."

When speaking on aspects of naval architecture he lost none of his vehemence:

"solid bottoms to vessels of war have, in many instances, preserved them and their crews from being lost by shipwreck ... It is clear that if solid bottoms were adopted in merchant vessels, similar means would produce a similar effect ... It surely is the duty of Government to preserve British subjects from being drowned, whether they be drowned in small numbers or in great, as we have recently had so many lamentable instances of, in weak, fragile, and unsafe merchant vessels. It is in vain to expect those who profit by unsafe vessels will voluntarily possess themselves of safe ones."

With so long a fight behind him Ballingall greeted the construction of the *Schomberg* as the vindication of all his theories. He wrote to the *Argus:*

"I added together the thickness of the planks and found that they formed a solid body of wood fifteen inches thick."

Bass Strait ferried some of this planking as far away as New Zealand — stronger ships still needed good beacons and prudent masters.

Coincident with Forbes arriving back in England without the *Schomberg*, the Victorian, Tasmanian, South Australian and New South Wales Governments were exploring the possibilities of managing Australian Colonial lighthouses jointly. In 1856 a joint Parliamentary Committee was formed to implement the proposal but it was to be another sixty years before the concept came to fruition, for it proved impossible to gain co-operation between the colonies.

Before this conclusion was reached the Commissioners heard from some forty men acquainted with the Australian coastline. For the coastline of each colony, lighthouses were recommended for certain locations. Regarding Victoria, it was Cape Schanck and Wilson's Promontory that were considered to most need lighting.

The report contained the collective opinion of many masters of famous sailing vessels. Captain Anthony Enright, successor to "Bully" Forbes as master of the *Lightning,* remarked of King Island's dangers: [11]

"I have considered them and thought it strange that there was no lighthouse on that island. The first voyage I came from the southward and westward, and the wind happened to be from the eastward, and of course if I had approached King's Island I should have been on a lee shore. I approached King's Island and had a very heavy gale of wind, which tore the best part of my sails away, and I was obliged to keep to windward. I was afraid to approach Cape Otway, so that I was obliged to keep in the mid channel as much as possible, but then I could not keep far enough away from the coast because I was afraid of setting over to King's Island."

Captain Enright's answers to questions throw dramatic light on the difficulties of Bass' Strait:

"Do you think in coming from the westward in your large ships a light about Portland would be of service; say on Cape Bridgewater or Cape Northumberland? – I never tried to make that coast. We generally keep on the parallel of 45°.
And come up in your great circle course? – Yes.
And that frequently necessitates your making King's Island? – Yes, we haul up as much as north-north-east.
That is sailing on the arc of the great circles? Yes.
What is the highest southern latitude that you touch on that arc if you can keep it? – 51°
Then you would approach the land of New Holland from that latitude coming up north-north-east? – We begin to haul up about 25° or 40° east from the cape."

The last two questions Enright answered without elaboration:

"Do you know where the *Schomberg* was lost? Yes, just to the westward of Cape Otway.
Then a light upon Cape Bridgewater or Cape Nelson would not have been of the slightest service to her? No."

The Witness withdrew.

Charles Ferguson, Harbour Master of Melbourne, opted for the northern New Year Island as the site for a lighthouse. He remarked that from his discussions with Guthrie, the surviving officer from the *Cataraqui,* [12] "the cause of the wreck in his opinion was that the ship was considerably south of the position they calculated she was in."

Ferguson further contended that the *Rebecca,* wrecked in September 1843 would have been saved had a light been in operation on the New Year Islands.

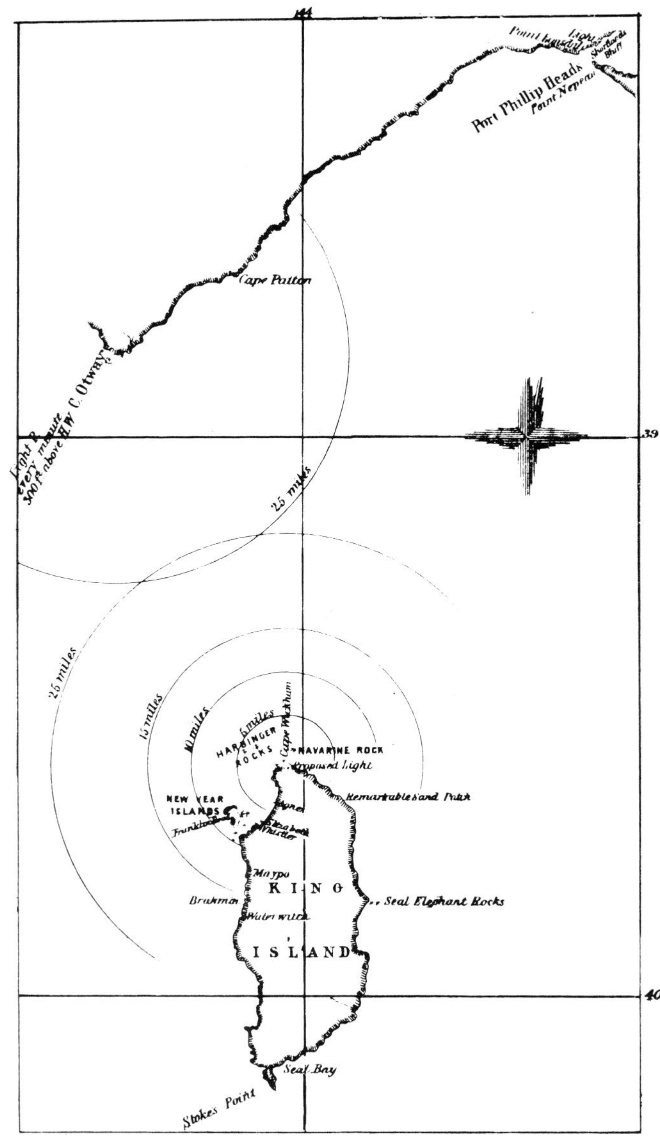

11. Portion of the chart presented with the 1855 enquiry into the necessity for a lighthouse at King Island. Only miles wide "the eye of the needle" was the final great challenge for vessels bound for Bass Strait.

Captain Charles Langley of the *Annie Wilson* out of London volunteered: [13]

"Supposing your chronometers were not quite correct and you were a little further to the eastward than you imagined yourself, you might, in thick weather, make King's Island, and consequently a light upon King's Island differing from that at Cape Otway would of course guide you."

If the Commissioners had had any doubts as to the wisdom of lighting King Island, they were at once dispelled by the Lloyds agent in Melbourne, Barnard R. Matthews. On being asked whether he himself had ever contemplated the necessity for a lighthouse on King Island, Matthews replied with conviction as he recollected how in 1852, in command of the mighty *Great Britain*, he sought the entrance to Bass Strait: [14]

" ... the wind was very scant and I was afraid I should have to shave King's Island very close. I was timid when near the west end of it, in consequence of the rocks which are there. I was getting short of coals. If there had been a light there I should have made the island and saved a little time, but fortunately as I was approaching the land the wind came up and I fetched the Otway."

On Wednesday, 20 August 1856, the last evidence was taken, Captain Joseph Lawson of the clipper ship *Ocean Monarch*, the witness. When so many experienced masters had given evidence before this, it would have been easy to dismiss this captain who had only made two voyages to the colonies. However, the Commissioners soon found themselves listening to a story of near disaster. The incident had occurred in those very circumstances and at the very place on which the Committee was concentrating. An irate Lawson was heard with the minimum of interruptions: [15]

"Yes, I have seen [King Island] on both occasions [voyages] and on this last occasion it made such an impression upon me

12. 1855 Light House Enquiry chart.
"... I think in all my experience I have never seen anything so dangerous as King's Island in its present unlighted condition."
– Capt. Lawson of the Ocean Monarch. His ship had narrowly averted King Island's west coast after he mistook the northernmost New Year Island to be Cape Wickham and sailed inside the Harbinger Reefs as he tacked away from the land.

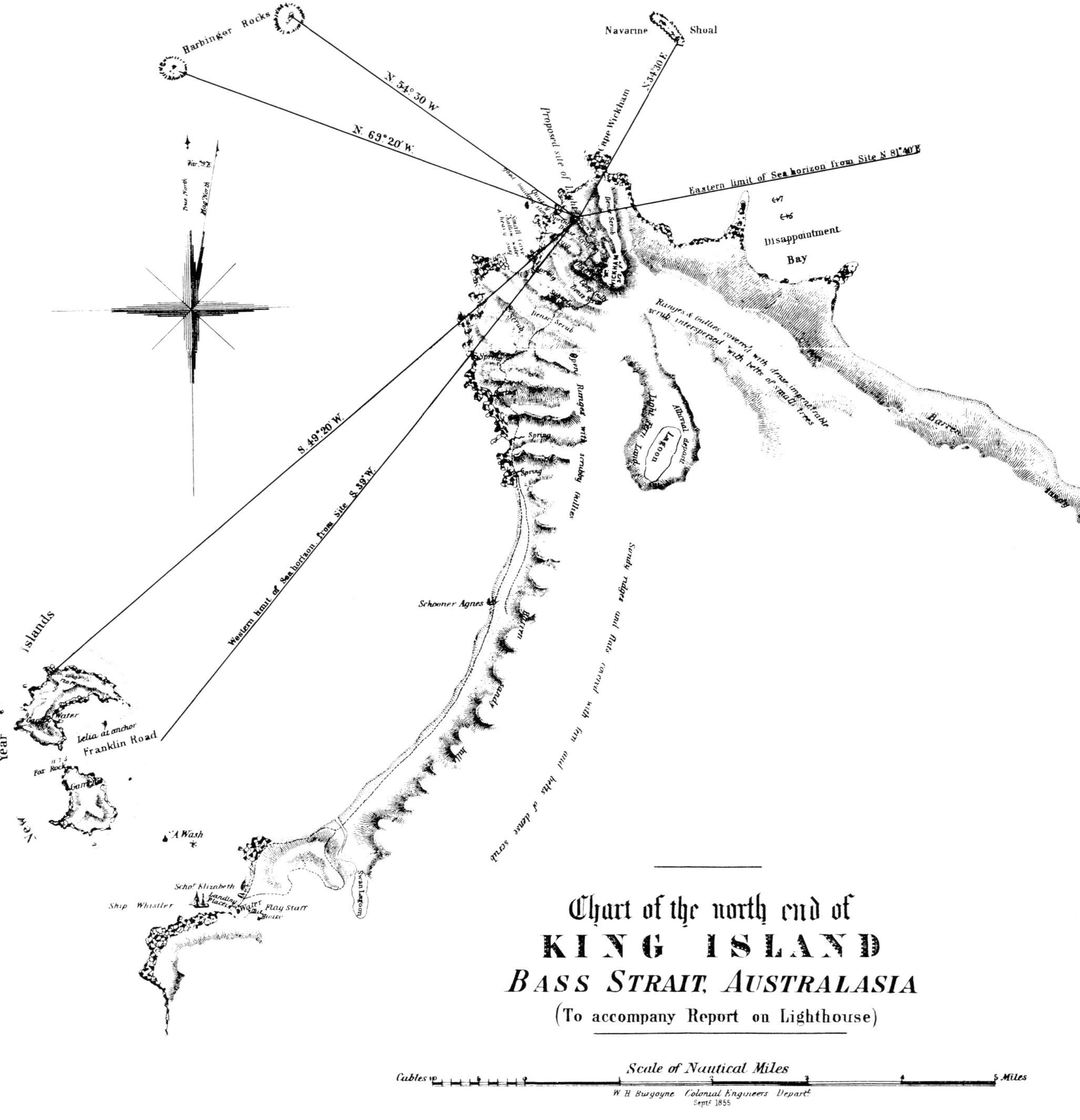

that for other troubles that occurred afterwards, I should have written to the newspaper about it. On Friday, the 30th May, I shaped my course for Cape Otway, bound for Port Phillip, during the middle of the night the vessel broke off from her course and laid down with her head towards King's Island; I found the vessel breaking off during the night, and being satisfied of my position I stood on towards the island I made the land about daybreak, and judging from my experience, I thought I was a good deal farther off than I afterwards found I was, I stood close in and put my helm down with what I considered the New Year Island, bearing north-and-by-east-half-east by compass. At about what distance ? – I should say at the distance of five or six miles, I could not recognise the place by the bearings at all, I could not make out where I was even then, not dreaming I was in the bight at all. I stood close in until I had the New Year Islands bearing north-and-by-east-half-east as I thought, and then I tacked and I suppose after I had stood out at least four or five miles, I was thunderstruck to see the Harbingers on the weather beam, about two or three miles distant, with the sea breaking mast head high over them. Then standing out again, when I began to open the land outside the New Year Islands I at once saw where I was, and I was so astonished that it almost made my blood curdle."

The *Ocean Monarch* had escaped disaster only by yards, In the night Lawson had sailed past the New Year Islands and almost become embayed in Phoques Bay south of Cape Wickham.

Captain Lawson's warning would remain with the Commissioners long after he took the *Ocean Monarch* back to sea: [16]

"It was only as to King's Island that I wished to express a strong opinion, because I have had a great opportunity of judging of it, and I have seen the absolute danger of it; the Harbinger Reefs are fearful reefs. I look upon it as one of the most dangerous places I ever saw unlighted in my life."

The Committee had heard enough. To procrastinate further was courting disaster. A lighthouse was needed quickly!

The Commissioners concluding remarks demonstrated their appreciation of King Island's dangers and they proceeded to carefully document the safest way for vessels to make a landfall – to thread the "eye of the needle:" [17]

"In advising the erection of a Lighthouse on this [King] Island the Commissioners wish to guard themselves from affording the public any reasonable supposition that this Light can be at all considered in the position of a great high way Light for the navigation of the Straits. The South coast of New Holland, and the western entrance to Bass' straits, being free from dangers, affords, in their opinion, the safest shore for the prudent mariner to approach, and they conceive that the Light on King's Island is only to be regarded as a beacon for warning navigators of danger, rather than as a leading Light to a great thoroughfare."

13. The Great Britain steam ship leaving Prince's Pier, Liverpool, for Australia. Her design was far in advance of other ships, but she nearly came to grief on King Island. Her master leant his support to moves to have a lighthouse erected there by giving evidence at the 1855 enquiry.

QUOTATIONS AND REFERENCES

1. Don Charlwood. *Wrecks and Reputations Angus & Robertson.* 1977 Melbourne.
2. Unpublished Journal held by PRO VIC. in Shipping List for **'Monarch of the Seas.'**
3. Vict. Parl. Papers. Select Committee on Lighthouses. 22/12/1853.
4. ibid. P. 4.
5. ibid. P. 6.
6. Vic. Parl. Papers., "Lighthouse on King's Island" Report, 15/9/1855. (general remarks)
7. *Argus.* 23/6/1855.
8. Vict. Parl. Papers. "Lighthouse on King's Island and Light Dues." Report 20/2/1856.
9. **Don Charlwood. P. 43.**
10. Victorian Pamphlet Series. Anti Shipwreck Society. 10/5/1854 and "A Retrospect of Shipwrecks", 13/7/1858 by the same **author. La Trobe Library.**
11. Vic. Parl. Papers. Joint Parliamentary Enquiry. "Australian Lighthouses" 1856 P. 75.
12. – 16. The various witnesses heard are given at the beginning of the enquiry.
17. ibid. P. XI. Summary.

ILLUSTRATION SOURCES

1. D.M.W.
2. Edwardes Collection. State Lib. of S. Australia.
3. Science Museum of Victoria.
4. Dept. of Science, Antarctic Division.
5. Edwardes Collection. State Lib. of S. Australia. Vol. 19, No. 50.
6. D.M.W.
7. Capt. C. Jackman.
8. D.M.W.
9. **Maritime Museum Liverpool, Photographic Collection No. 32292.**
10. ibid. Vol. 19, No. 38.
11. Victorian State Parliamentary Papers. 1855 Enquiry into King Island Lighthouse.
12. ibid.
13. La Trobe Library. Picture Collection. H. 31728.
14. D.M.W.

14. "The fortress walls of the last continent
Slept in the sun unguarded."
The higher and more prominent Victorian coastline was the safest landfall coast to seek. This practice led to the completion of a further lighthouse at Cape Nelson. King Island was to be avoided.

... THE SHELL BURRED CABLES CREEP ...

11

1. *"... a still more exciting indication of our approach to land was the light on Cape Otway, the cape before we turned toward Port Phillip Bay. There was a stunning shout, the Captain said, "Thank God! We have made no mistake'!"*

While enquiry after enquiry continued to investigate King Island, it was agreed that the Cape Otway lighthouse served its purpose well. As the Ford family drew to the end of their eighth year there they were still occupying the original three roomed cottage built for the superintendent in 1847. In 1850 the assistant keepers' quarters with its party wall and two single rooms had been commenced and, tower aside, is today the oldest surviving building at Cape Otway.

Although Ford had complained of the state of his house in his first report to Williamstown, it was not replaced by new quarters until 1857. In the following year Messrs. King and Brown contracted to build a new assistant keepers' quarters at a cost of £3214. The extraordinarily high cost can be explained by Cape Otway's remoteness and the fact that the Parker River quarries had to be re-opened. The builders built well and both quarters are still in use today. Ford's old quarters were demolished but the assistants earlier rooms became emergency accommodation for victims of shipwreck and were then absorbed into a larger storeroom which was added onto the east end. The original shingle hip roof of the assistant keepers' quarters may still be seen within the "new" (1860) roof structure of the adjoining storeroom. Drawings of Ford's and his assistants' quarters show that the roofs of the main residences were in Welsh slates. Corrugated asbestos cement now serve in their place. It seems likely that improvements to quarters at the lighthouse contributed largely to a decrease in the turnover of assistant keepers – Otway was no place to live with inadequate shelter.

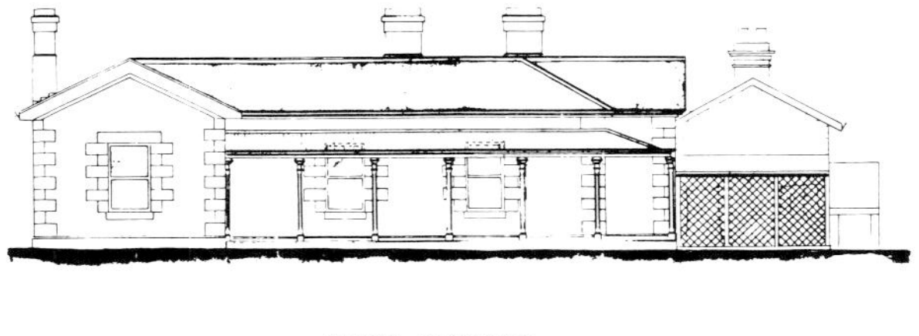

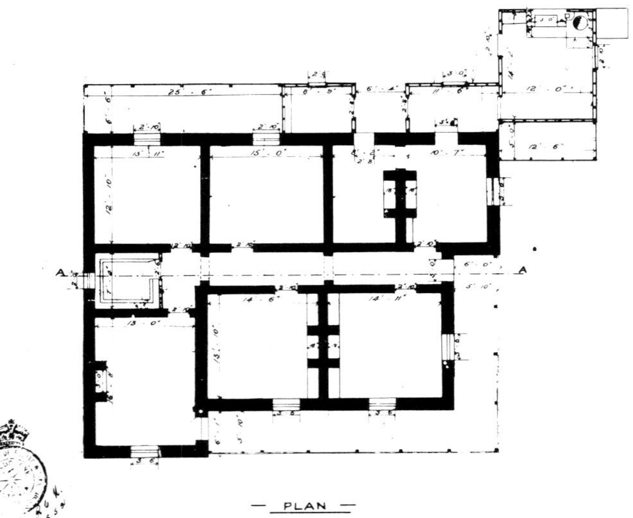

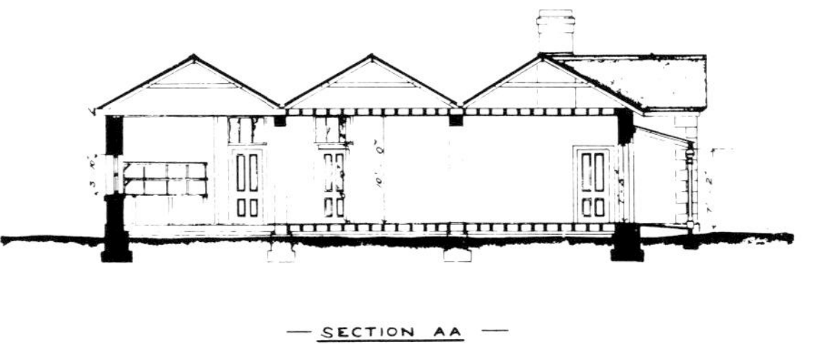

2. Cape Otway Lighthouse, Principal's Quarters. This residence was built in 1856 and although much modified speaks well of the durability of Parker River sandstone and the men who built it. Unfortunately the sandstone was painted some years ago and now presents a continous maintenance problem. The noble slate roofing has gone; replaced with graceless corrugated asbestos cement.

3. Window Detail of Head Keeper's Quarters.

— ASSISTANT LIGHTHOUSE KEEPERS QUARTERS —
— CAPE OTWAY. —

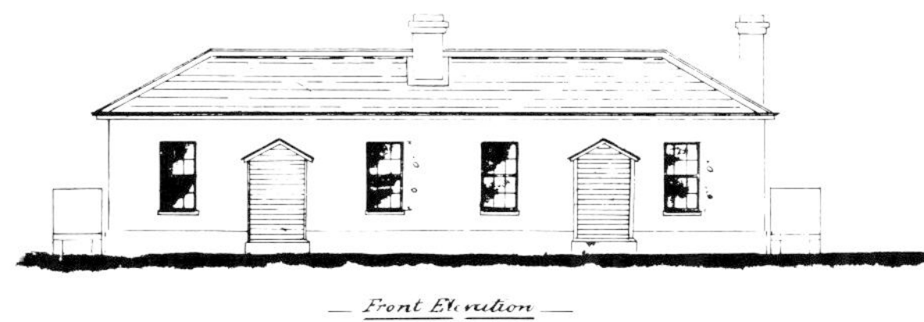

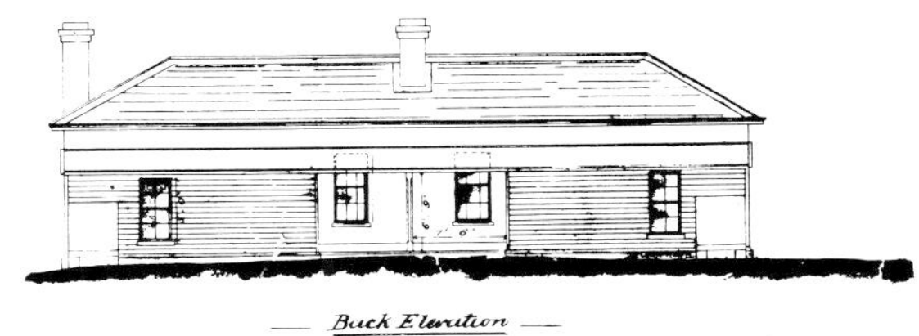

4. Assistant Keeper's Quarters, Cape Otway. Built one year after the Principal's quarters this building housed two families in separate residences. Terminating above the bed of Superintendent and keeper alike, a signal tube led to the tower, 200 yards away. When a keeper was to be woken for his watch, the duty keeper would blow down the tube and the awakened keeper was required to give an answering blow to signal that he was out of bed and on his way.

5. Much altered, today this houses only one keeper and his family.

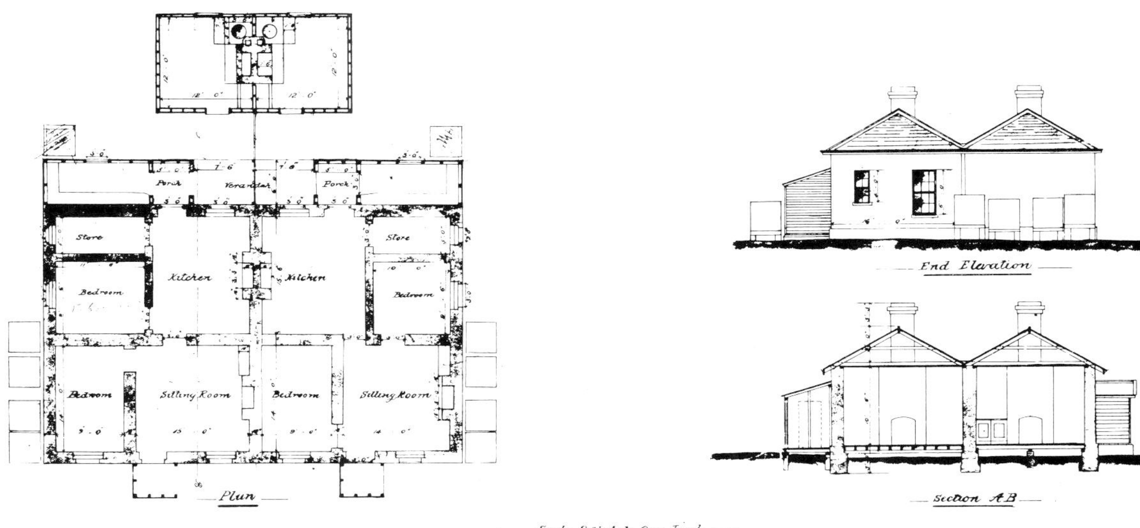

As the number of vessels making a landfall at Cape Otway increased, so did the pressure to improve communication with the outside world. The advantages of being able to communicate with any lighthouse erected on King Island were obvious. The months it had taken for word of the *Brahmin's* fate on King Island to reach Melbourne was evidence enough of that. By 1854 the infant Post and Telegraph Department had completed a telegraph line between Melbourne and Geelong but no further.

Agreement was reached with the Tasmanian Government on the advantages of laying a submarine cable for communication between the two colonies. A Launceston based syndicate formed a company to fund the undertaking. The Commercial advantages of taking such a inter-colonial link through Cape Otway and Cape Wickham were apparent to all. As ships passed Cape Otway they could identify themselves. Melbourne's waiting business community could then be informed by telegraph of their likely arrival time. Not only matters of commerce, but of the colonies defences also promoted the installation of the telegraph line and cable. In the shadow of the Crimean War there was widespread concern in Victoria that a Russian Naval Squadron could blockade or bombard sea ports and attack British shipping. Telegraph stations at the entrance to Bass Strait were thus seen as performing important surveillance work and hence any private company willing to undertake such a project was encouraged to do so.

From Geelong the telegraph line reached the coast in the region of present day Anglesea. From here it was taken around the coast to Apollo Bay and on to Cape Otway. The Cape Otway signal station with its splendid tower and wide verandahs was built by Gibson and Swan of Geelong for £2459. It was mentioned in 1865 in the Illustrated Melbourne Post: [2]

"Next in importance to the lighthouse stands the electric telegraph and maritime signal station, built upon a grassy knoll some 400 yards to the eastward of the lighthouse."

Thousands of arriving emigrants were greeted by its signal flags. One was Mary Anne Bedford, arriving on the *Champion of the Seas* in 1864: [3]

"A most beautiful morning. We were awakened about 4 o'clock by the shouting of land. It was Cape Otway about 100 miles from Melbourne and there is a lighthouse on it. We had a head wind or we should have been there in a few hours. As it is we have been rocking about all day and they have turned the vessel around eight or nine times today to keep us off the land. They have gone very close to it and we could see the lighthouse. Our captain put up many flags. They put up theirs and they let us know that the *Anglesea* had landed on Sunday the 13th. You will see that we passed it on our way. It is a great disappointment to our Captain that we did not get there the first. They also told us that the *Marco Polo* was a hundred and twenty days going and that it had just landed. They telegraphed from here to Melbourne to let them know of our arrival. They would hear of us in four minutes from the time they telegraphed Melbourne. We have seen small brigs today."

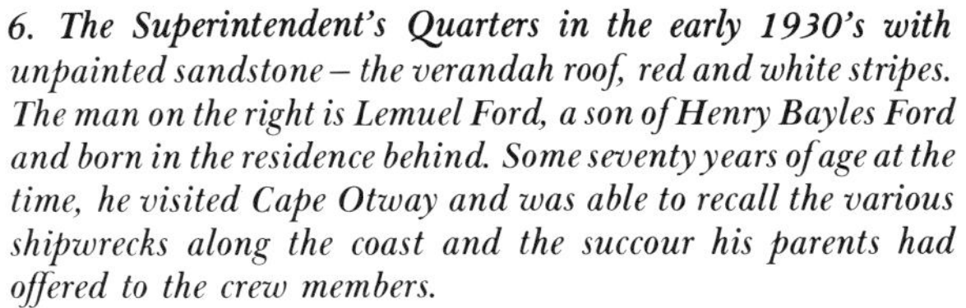

6. The Superintendent's Quarters in the early 1930's with unpainted sandstone – the verandah roof, red and white stripes. The man on the right is Lemuel Ford, a son of Henry Bayles Ford and born in the residence behind. Some seventy years of age at the time, he visited Cape Otway and was able to recall the various shipwrecks along the coast and the succour his parents had offered to the crew members.

7. The Cape Otway Signal Station with lighthouse beyond. Although greeted with enthusiasm by the lighthouse keepers for the break in isolation it offered, the telegraph proved a burden as well as a blessing. Light house staff members were reduced on the pretext that Telegraph Station staff could be employed to keep watch in the lighthouse. By 1894 the telegraph station had ceased operation and minus its tower and verandahs, today awaits a new calling. (See opposite page)

No traces remain today of this or of the other six test houses along the telegraph line's route to Geelong.

The main cable laying operation was completed on the 12 August 1859 by the principal contractors Mac-Naughton & Co. of Launceston, aboard the cable laying ship *Omeo*. The first tests showed the cable to be damaged but after repairs to the section between King Island and the Otway coast had been completed, the contractor's Melbourne agents released the following telegram transmitted from — [5]

"Parker River Inlet 21 September 5.30 p.m. Finished shore end Victoria Cove and came here yesterday morning and finished tonight. Signals from Cape Wickham perfect. We have been detained by bad weather. May return to King Island tonight to inspect there and Three Hummock Island. All's well. Will soon be back. All on board "Storm Bird" [presumably the *Omeo*] satisfactory. Unfavourable weather has detained us longer than we expected."

The first message between Melbourne and Hobart was transmitted on 29 September 1859. The facility was hailed in the newspapers as ushering in a new age for Bass Strait communication and on the 3rd October 1859, Launceston and Hobart had a public holiday to celebrate its completion. Hobart's Mulgrave battery fired a 21 gun salute in honour of the new link.

Though launched with confidence, the line to King Island failed within weeks and the venture was soon to end in costly anti-climax. Various sections of the cable were replaced or relocated and the line re-opened on 22 December 1859. Intermittent breakdowns continued until on the 28 April 1860 the section between King Island and Circular Head failed completely. After more fruitless attempts to repair it, it was abandoned in the following year. The cable laying had cost £53,000 and would not be attempted again for another ten years.

Although its link with King Island had failed, the telegraph station at Cape Otway was retained as a Lloyds Signal Station able to report rapidly to Melbourne. Today this building – a valuable link with the past – is derelict. The look-out tower was removed in 1910 but the windows of the unmaintained station still gaze seaward.

The cost of the line where it pushed through the Otway ranges was £50 per mile. On King Island, through a now vanished forest, an overland section of the link was laid. It crossed the island to Sea Elephant Bay on the east coast and from there another submarine cable ran southward to Three Hummock Island from whence it was continued on to Launceston via Stanley.

At the Cape Otway end the cable terminated at the Parker River Inlet where a test house was provided, a building measuring 6 feet square: [4]

"the floor to be 8" above the ground. A panelled door, hinged fitted and properly furnished ... The whole to be fitted and fastened together with screws and to receive 3 good coats of the best white paint – externally and internally."

—TELEGRAPH STATION—
— CAPE OTWAY —

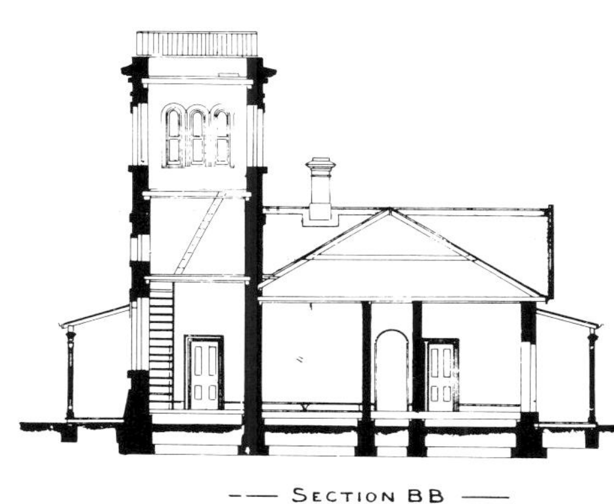

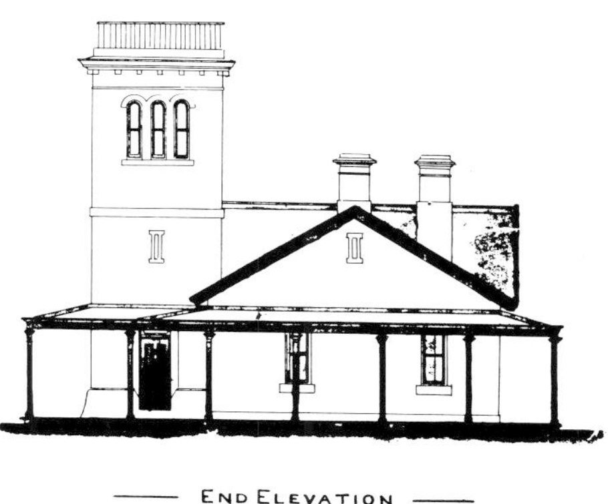

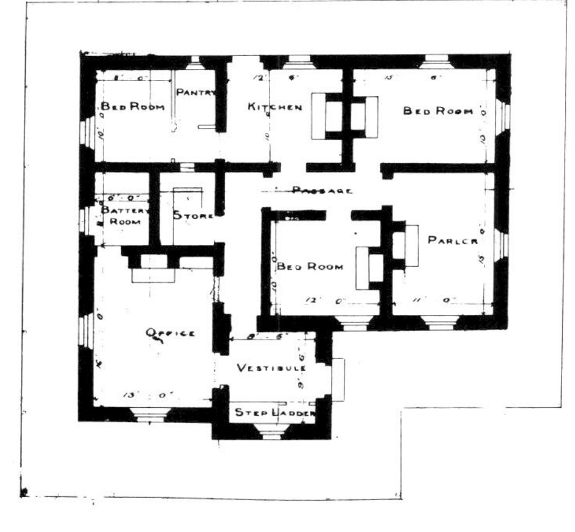

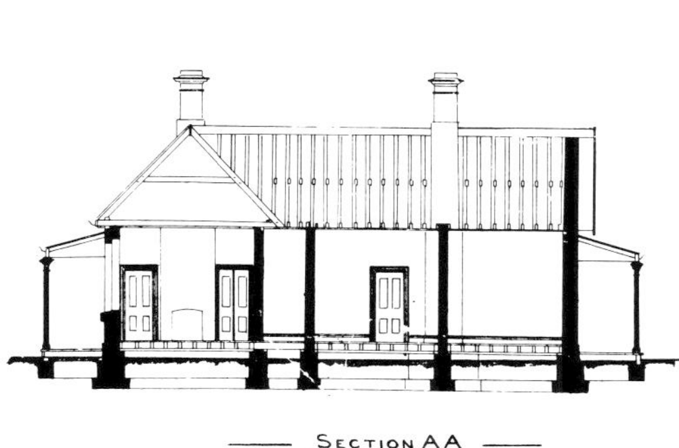

10. With a tower that once competed with the lighthouse as a landmark, this building was recognized by mariner and traveller alike for the link it offered with Melbourne.
Architect's drawings of the long since abandoned Telegraph Station.

10. *Tower and verandahs long ago removed, ugly additions now scar this once fine building.*

The first Telegraph Operator at Cape Otway was Joseph William Payter. Appointed in August 1859 on a salary of £250 per year, he and his family shared the Ford family's isolation. No records have survived of the operation of the station and the lighthouse records make only passing reference to it, but supplies were presumably landed for it by the lighthouse supply ship. Ford was instructed not to use the telegraph unless some urgent matter vital to the continued operation of the lighthouse arose.

In his report for 1864 S.M. McGowan, Director of Post and Telegraphs for Victoria, described the difficulties in maintaining this fragile link between Melbourne and its gate keeper: [6]

"The only line showing an excess of interruptions beyond the usual average is that between Geelong and Cape Otway on which section the interruptions during 1863, amounted to 13 days, the damage was occasioned in each instance by falling trees, blown over by the hurricanes which visited the district in the months of January and December of last year. On the last mentioned occasion upwards of 3 miles of the line were destroyed, when it was estimated that nearly 200 trees were prostrated by the violence of the gale, a fair idea may be formed as to the difficulty attending the maintenance of this line if it be remembered that its course lies through some of the most rugged and densely timbered portions of Victoria; that it crosses eleven precipitous ranges, varying from 1000 to 1500 feet in height; that the route is in several places during the winter season, quite impassable even for packhorses; and that along fully sixty miles of the route, the wire and other materials used in constructing the line, had to be transported on the backs of the workmen, as the only practicable means of performing the service required."

While Signal Station records have not survived, Fords lighthouse letter book for these years deals largely with mundane matters that concerned both establishments. It lists supplies required; information on the lighthouse cattle and the erosion they had caused; the condition of the tramway from the Parker River. The letter dated 16 June, 1857 is typical, as is Ford's lack of punctuation therein: [7]

11. *"That this house was never intended for two occupants is evident from the fact that it only contains one room capable of being used for culinary purposes . . . only one set of apartments between us renders domestic affairs very uncomfortable for both myself and assistant and should the latter marry this discomfort would be greatly augmented." – Kelsall, 1871.*

"Sir,

I beg leave to acknowledge the receipt of your instructions to report of my Department, per mechanic Samuel Hale on the 13th instant who arrived that day travelling by the coast from Apollo Bay, he had no little difficulty in so doing he states that he lost some of his tools and gear by the way.

2. The Buildings, Lighthouse and Quarters. There is no alteration taken place since my last report.

3. The Lantern is very much troubled with smoke and heat for the want of proper means of ventilation, I would suggest that 4 sheets of copper be sent next opportunity there will be of a mechanic coming here direct. These sheets to act as a double roof under the holes that have been cut formerly for ventilation, the same holes now being stopped up on account of drops of water being driven through by the wind and dropping on the glasses and destroying them.

4. The Lamps are very much worn that is those now in use and all of the spare lamps have become unfit for service.

5. The reflectors are very much discoloured by smoke and heat and I find it very difficult to keep them bright, and they do not show any appearance of the silver wearing off and showing the copper under it. I was in hopes that the mechanic would be able to get the flues of the pipes brazed but for the want of a forge it could not be done. Mr. Maplestowe I believe has taken the measurement of the iron platform and steps for the interior of the lantern, it will also require a set of steps for the balcony for the purpose of cleaning the plate glass outside, as doing it by the ladder that I have made it is dangerous.

6. The Machine shortly after your leaving it went very indifferent in short it would not go when wound up unless it was started by hand first. I increased the weights about 28 lbs. and that made very little improvement. April 2 I removed the cup of the small spindle and eased up the rollers of the large spindle and then put them together again the machine has gone well ever since and by twisting a needle full of thread over the worn and screwing up the nut (that was loose) over it, it has remained firm ever since.

7. Tram Way for getting the supplies up from the Parker River was erected in Jan. 1851 and now the posts are nearly all rotten it will require to be remade and also there is a great need for means to fetch the truck up the hill. I would suggest something of a capstan to be worked by the horses on the top of the tramway."

I have the honour to be
Sir,
Your most obedient Servant
H.B. Ford
Overseer of Lighthouse

In the letterbook Ford, or occasionally another member of his family, has copied requests for information on subjects as diverse as earthtremors; their nature and timing; the gathering of seaweed samples for Ferdinand von Mueller; the rise and fall of tides and the influence of the wind.

All this Ford did while directing the lighthouse establishment and acting as a link with the few settlers inland of Cape Otway. The nearest station was situated three quarters of a mile to the west near Point Flinders and belonged to Lawry and Chapple — one of the Lawry children is buried in the Cape Otway cemetery.

Often Ford was instructed to watch for the victims of the Strait his lighthouse presided over. A letter from Melbourne's Chief Harbour Master dated 19 January 1859 read: [8]

"*H.M. Brig Sappho* having been seen about the 18th February last off Cape Otway bound to Sydney and no further account having been heard of her, it is supposed she was wrecked either on the coast from Cape Otway to Cape Howe or on some of the islands or rocks in the straits.

With a view of trying to throw some light upon this unfortunate circumstance, will you endeavour to search along the beach in your locality as far each way as practicable and should you find any pieces of wreck likely to have been belonging to a man of war write me full particulars at your earliest convenience, be good enough to instruct any persons near the coast to search should they be near the beach."

Grates that might have come from the *Sappho* were later picked up, but Bass Strait has never yielded the rest of her secret. Presumably she foundered with all on board.

The request to Ford to search the beaches was made with the knowledge that parts of wrecked ships were often washed ashore along the Otway coast. In 1863 Ford recorded picking up on the beach: [9]

"part of a ships name from off a head board. There was no paint on it. I made out its name to be *Paxton*."

Ford could not have known but this nameplate had floated over 10,000 miles from the east coast of Canada where a ship of that name had been wrecked eighteen months before.

In 1860, Ford wrote to the Harbour Master at Williamstown giving a breakdown of duties for himself and his keepers: [10]

"The time employed is as follows: The assistants in charge of the lights from 10 P.M. until sunrise in two watches and immediately after extinguishing the lights, the lamps are all trimmed ready for lighting which according to the time of year will be done between 8 P.M. and 9 A.M.
Wednesday and Saturday all the gear of the lantern is cleaned and overhauled. That will be done about 1 P.M. or 2 P.M.
The other free parts of the day during the week are employed cleaning and boiling glasses, getting fire wood, carting home the stores (when landed) painting, keeping things in order in short anything I should deem necessary to be done to keep the place and buildings in repair or order.
Myself in charge of the light from lighting up to 10 P.M. and throughout the day overlooking and directing the works on hand and a general supervision of the issue of stores and throughout the whole of the Department. During the afternoons I endeavour to have nothing to be done unless in case of necessity or emergency."

By now just fifty miles to the south, the building of the Cape Wickham lighthouse was commencing. The primary need there and at Cape Otway had been spelt out by the Harbour Master at Melbourne, Capt. Payne four years earlier:

"... the first and most prominent object [is] a clear and powerful light at all times from sunset to sunrise."

13. *Cape Otway Lighthouse looking seaward; Bass Strait to the left and the Southern Ocean to the right.*
"... many Masters of Vessels who have visited the Port for the first time ... have informed me that they were not aware of the existence of a Lighthouse on Cape Otway and I have not seen published in the English papers, Gazettes or periodicals ... the directions which were originally drawn up relative to this Lighthouse ..." – Ginn. 1853.

QUOTATIONS AND REFERENCES

1. This information is drawn from the Colonial Architects Letter Book PRO, VIC. and the C. Otway Letter Book Dept. of Trans.
2. *Illustrated Melbourne Post.* 25/11/1865. P. 175.
3. Diary of Anne Bedford held by Mr. W.F. Renshaw, Melbourne.
4. – 6. This information is drawn from the Victorian Post & Telegraph Dep't. annual report to Parl't. contained in Parl. Papers for 1859 – 1864. Col. Arch. letter book 1859 – 1861. PRO. VIC.
7. C. Otway Letter Book. Dep't of Trans.
8. ibid. 59/4 Harbour Master to Cape Otway.
9. C. Otway Letter Book.
10. ibid. 2/5/1860.
11. ibid. 19/9/1857.

ILLUSTRATION SOURCES

1, 3, 4, 6, 8, 9, 10, 11, 12 and 13 D.M.W.`
2, 5 Dept. of Transport.
7. Illustrated Melbourne Post 25/11/1865. P. 175.

...THAT GRAVEYARD OF SHIPS...

12

As soon as the Victorian and Tasmanian Governments had accepted the recommendations of the 1856 Joint Parliamentary Lighthouse Enquiry, the preliminaries to building a lighthouse on Cape Wickham were begun. Before drawings and cost estimates of the work could be prepared, a detailed inspection of the site was essential. The enquiries had been dominated by naval men; now engineers from the respective Public Works Departments would carry out the work.

At the request of the Hobart Marine Board, inspections were made late in January 1857 by the foreman of the Public Works Department of Tasmania, Robert Henry. He was accompanied by Capt. Chas. Nicholson of the H.M. Schooner. *Beacon.* Henry restricted himself to commenting on practical questions likely to be of concern to tenderers and to the successful contractor;

Capt. Nicholson on the other hand disagreed with the proposed site altogether. He believed that a lighthouse on the northernmost of the New Year Islands would not only afford earlier warning to vessels closing on King Island's west coast, but would more easily be kept supplied by ship. Nicholson's objections concluded: [1]

"I would beg to give an opinion that if Cape Wickham *should* be decided upon as the Site, that the only way of conveying the material for building; oil, rations etc. to the place would be by pack Bullocks or Horses, as I do not think any cart could travel through the heavy sand on the beach, and I consider that there should then be a Depot on New Years Island for landing the stores etc., and the person in charge should be supplied with a good Boat, that he might be able to go across according to the weather, and supply himself, as a vessel carrying the stores might be detained weeks before she could effect a landing on King's Island independent of the risk.

On leaving King's Island on the 31st January during a fog, I could see the New Years Islands distant 3½ miles and I could not see King's Islands but only the surf breaking on the beach dist[ant] 1 mile."

Portion of Henry's detailed report reads as follows: [2]

"On the whole I foresee very considerable difficulties in the way of carrying out the undertaking, first from the uncertainty of landing especially landing materials — secondly the distance to be traversed, and the heavy soft nature of the soil, in fact for a loaded cart to reach the site, it would be necessary in many places to form a sort of corduroy road for which plenty of timber which would answer the purpose can be found about the lagoons — there would be plenty of feed for the cattle, and this would be no doubt much increased by burning off the scrub."

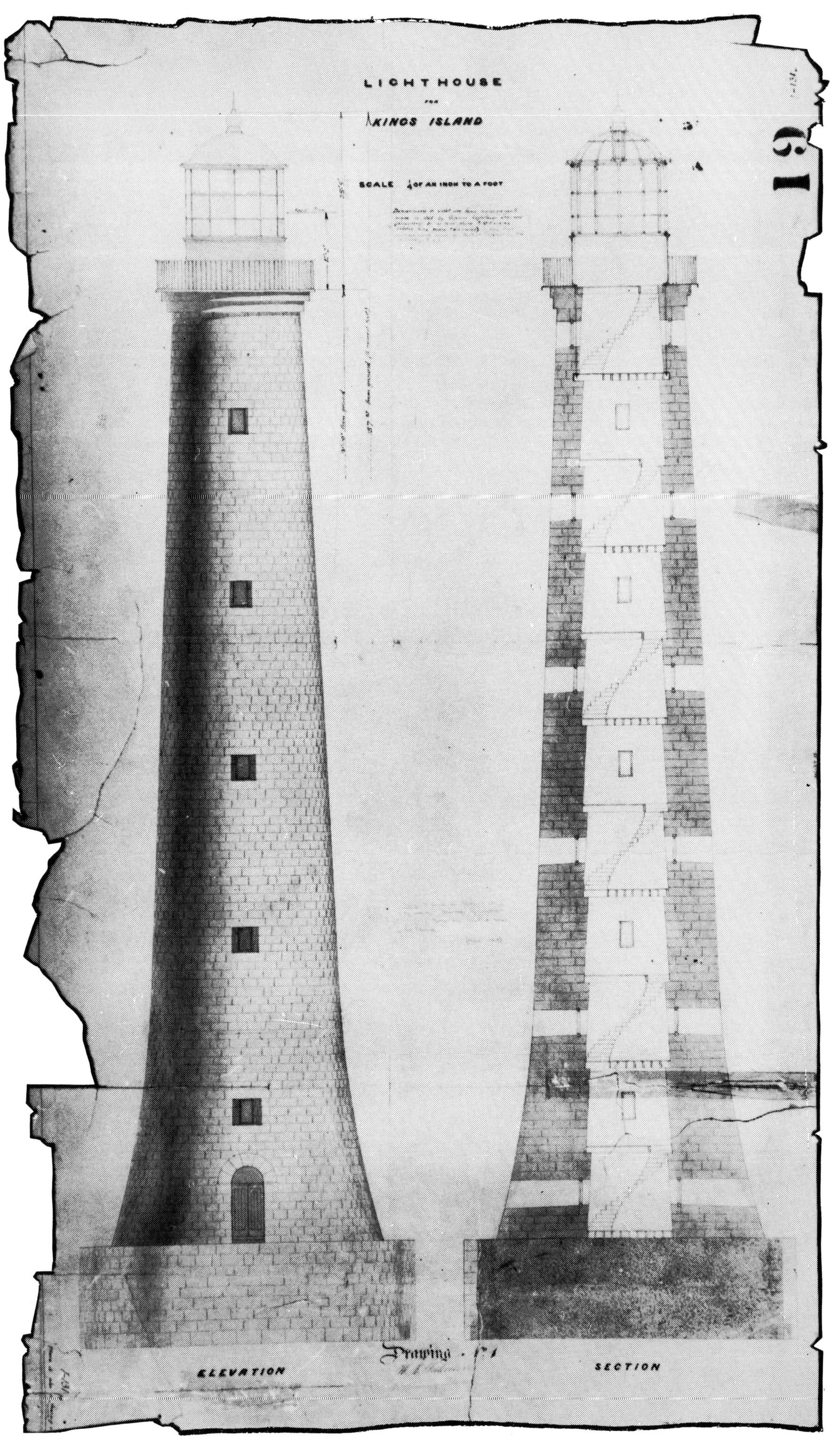
61
LIGHTHOUSE
FOR
KINGS ISLAND
SCALE OF AN INCH TO A FOOT
ELEVATION
SECTION
Drawing No 1

1. *The original working drawings of the Cape Wickham Lighthouse, King Island.*
"... the north end of King's Island is unquestionably the best site for a lighthouse ... the light when erected, will embrace within its circle a still greater range of the compass, while at the same time it will be distinctly seen over the New Year Island." – 1855 Enquiry finding.

2. *Phoque Bay with the New Year Islands in the distance. "A beacon of tarbarrels was burnt on the New Year's Island, distant seven miles in a direct line from the site of the proposed lighthouse, and was found of sufficient power to have been visible at a considerably greater distance while at a lesser altitude, than the site chosen for the light on King's Island." – 1855 Enquiry finding.*

These discouraging reports were noted by the Marine Board but the decision to build at Cape Wickham as the original enquiry had recommended, stood. The drawings were begun by the Public Works Department of Tasmania but when the question of a prefabricated cast iron tower was raised as a possible solution to the site difficulties, it was decided to appoint a consultant to the work. A Launceston Engineer, W.B. Falconer, was then requested to take over the documentation of the plans, prepare fresh estimates of alternative design solutions and report to the Hobart Marine Board when he had visited the island.

Falconer seized upon the project enthusiastically but was not treated kindly by King Island during his visit. His report is a catalogue of the west coast's blows at an invader come to see how it might be tamed: [3]

" ... 20th September. New Years Islands, and landed on King's Island near wreck of "Whistler" and camped half way to Cape Wickham ... [Falconer spent the 21st and 22nd inspecting the proposed site] ... 24th went on board "Victoria", 25th landed Mr McGowan, Victoria Cove, heavy surf and obliged to return soon. [McGowan as Director of the Victorian Posts and Telegraph department was inspecting proposed routes for the submarine cable on King Island and Three Hummock Island.] 26th New Years Islands, blowing hard. 27th, Ditto, 28th Ditto, 29th better, 30th Sept. New Year Islands, but surf too heavy at Victoria Cove to land, went on to Disappointment Bay, sea calm and no appearance of surf, tried to land with eleven others in boat, upset in in heavy surf, one man drowned, others nearly so, self saved by getting hold of oar, men attempted to get off, upset again, taken off by barge under point to south of Disappointment Bay, self went on with [an] Island Hunter to camp at Cape Wickham. 1st October ... I got on board "Victoria" in evening 2nd October. Steamer off Victoria Cove ... landed ... surf rather heavy boat upset ..."

Falconer had seen at first hand the difficulties any contractor would have in maintaining a regular supply to workmen at such a place as Cape Wickham. The lot of future keepers could only be imagined. He estimated a building cost of £19,507. A prefabricated cast iron tower of similar height, shipped from England and erected, was estimated to increase the project cost to £23,743. These figures reflected all he had seen and experienced of King Island's nature. This extraordinarily high figure was to prove accurate.

Before the drawings that bear his signature were completed, Falconer informed the Hobart Marine Board of the importance of attracting the right men to the project, once construction had commenced: [4]

"I conceive that if a *good* Contractor can be obtained in Tasmania, he will tender for the work at much less than one from Victoria, as he will base his tender upon Tasmanian prices, and even if he has to obtain Masons from Melbourne, will have his Labourers, Quarrymen, and Sawyers, at much less rates, and many of the Tasmanian Quarrymen are better than Masons at dressing ironstone; besides I do not think any but fourth or fifth rate Contractors from Melbourne, would be inclined to leave Melbourne for King's Island unless with certainty of making a very handsome profit; one of the fourth or fifth class built the additions at Cape Otway Lighthouse and I thought his price enormous, and work very inferior.

In my estimate I allowed for a Resident Superintendent, being constantly on the spot, and while the Tower was building he would require never to be absent, as without a doubt the centre of the walls would be built up with sand in place of lime; such a Resident Superintendent will require to be a perfectly trustworthy man and one who can be implicitly

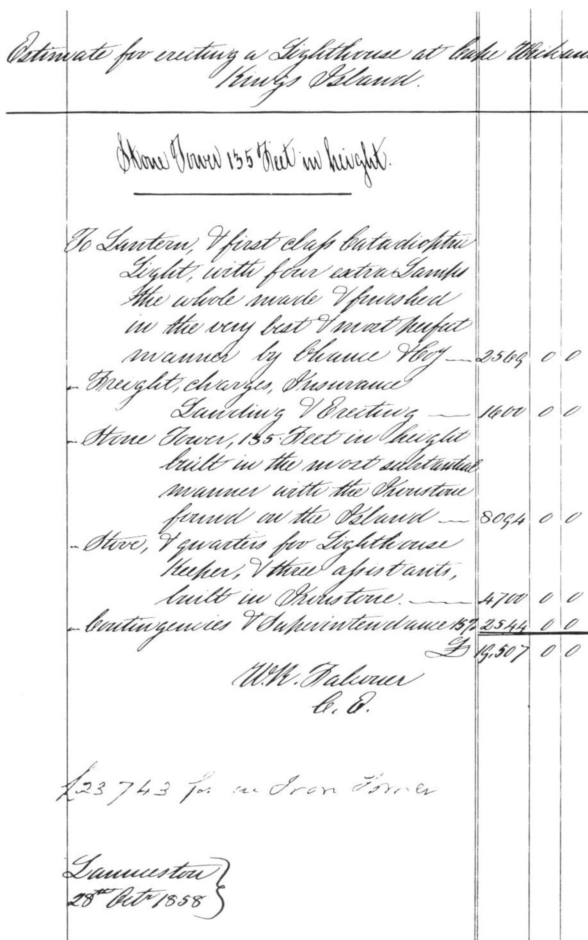

depended upon, and I have no fears about finding such; – the principal matter is where to find a *good trustworthy* Contractor."

Falconer, it is evident, was aware of the setbacks suffered at Cape Otway. But Kirkland and Co. of Melbourne were the successful tenderers. What Falconer thought of this is not known. That the immense lighthouse still stands today in so inhospitable a location is sufficient indication that they built well. Granite for walls eleven feet thick at the base was quarried one mile inland from the lighthouse and brought by tramway to the site. The changing dunes have rolled over much of the route, but in places traces of the cuttings are betrayed by their makers love of straight lines. As predicted, all other building materials had to be brought through the surf. The total project cost of £18,533.1.8. showed that Falconer had done his work well. Victoria, as the State with most commerce in the Strait, paid all but a small portion of this. The Hobart Marine Board assumed responsibility for manning as well as supplying the lighthouse, adding it to the earlier Bass Strait towers it already supplied.

The day after Cape Wickham Lighthouse commenced operation news that Burke and Wills with companion Gray had perished in Northern Australia reached Melbourne. Naturally the newspapers were preoccupied with the explorers' tragedy and it was some weeks before a report appeared that King Island had finally been lighted.

Five years after the last evidence had been given to support its establishment, the Cape Wickham log book was opened: [5]

"Friday November 1st 1861 a.m. to noon, moderate fine weather. Noon to Sunset, Fine. At sunset light exhibited for the first time from this Station. Bright fixed light. Elevation of tower 145 feet and elevated above the sea 280 feet. Wicks require trimming every five hours obscuring the light six and seven minutes. Watch relieved at 10 p.m. Midnight all well."

The mechanism was a catadioptric one. This meant that only one, instead of Ford's twenty-one lamps, had to be tended. It was a fixed light to enable mariners to be able to differentiate positively between it and Cape Otway.

In the middle of the next month severe gales tested the tower. The journal records: [6]

"Midnight. Heavy Gale. S.S.W. 10 p.m. called relief. 10.12 relieved. Midnight. Heavy gale, framework of lantern vibrating allowing the rain to ooze thro' sash work. Otherwise all well in light room. Heavy surf on. Neal laid up .. a barque off the Harbingers, frequently altering her course."

These short daily entries were to continue for the next sixty years until the light was converted to automatic operation in 1921 and the residences were demolished.

For some twenty of the manned years – from 1862 – the resolute E.C. Spong served as lighthouse superintendent. Like Ford, he was a former sea captain. On clear nights Ford at Cape Otway was able to see the light across the fifty miles of Bass Strait's western entrance. It is unlikely that he and Spong ever met, but there was between them the strong bond of their duties. The link that they might have had – the abandoned submarine cable – lay silent on the sea floor. It had offered much but now its building at nearby Victoria Cove only mocked Spong and the other keepers. From the test house there Spong's predecessor, Captain Drugan had tried repeatedly to contact Joseph Payter, then the officer in charge of Cape Otway Signal Station. On Tuesday Nov. 19. 1861 Drugan wrote: [7]

"Made many attempts to get the current in the cable without success, from experiment with coils, find the damage is about three miles from this terminus. Strong earth currents ... Sunset, lighted up, dusted lens and set the watch ... Midnight all well."

In the winter of 1863 – Spong's second year the construction of the tower was fully tested: [8]

"Dark gloomy weather ... Noon. Blowing a tremendous gale, rooting up much vegetation and damaging roofs of cottages.

The widely held opinion that the light on Cape
Wickham could be confused with Cape Otway was well-
founded. When high waves broke the horizon, a fixed
light could well be mistaken for a flashing light. Added
to this, the dangerous New Year Islands lay between the
Wickham light and ships approaching from the west. In
1865 the three masted schooner *Arrow* mistook Wickham
for Otway and was lost on the west coast of King Island.

The *Arrow* was wrecked not far from the lighthouse.
Spong records a number of incidents concerning goods
salvaged illegally from the vessel: [9]

5. *Cape Wickham Lighthouse and quarters (circa 1915). The
Superintendent's residence can be seen on the left of the picture, the
chapel stands alone, the three assistant keepers' residences are to
the right.*

"Saw the *Ben Bolt* Cutter 5 miles down the East coast, standing for the lighthouse, hoisted landing in Cove [signal flag indicating which beach to land on] 8. [o'clock] launched whale boat, 9. Boarded Cutter in the offing, Vessel working up for the anchorage. 10. Cutter anchored. Capt. Leggett, Mr. Lambert C.D.C. George Town and two Constables came on shore and proceeded to search the cottage of William Weight the Head Assistant where they found quantities of stolen property from the wreck of the *Arrow* ... loaded up the property identified by Mr. Leggett as taken from the *Arrow*. 2 p.m. carted the above down to Cove, and took them off together with Constables, William Weight a prisoner in their charge."

The episode did not conclude there. One month later Mrs. Weight was preparing to leave the station: [10]

"10 [o'clock] Employed carting down the baggage and sundries of Mrs. Weight, 4. two horse dray loads down and one more to come. I objected to the employ of the assistants, horses and dray, in carting, or boat in taking off. Two packages of old copper sheathing weighing about [blank] cwt. unless the women signed a declaration, that it was no part of the wreck of the *Arrow*, this she refused to do – Richard Leggett Assistant identified a table on the dray as belonging to the *Arrow* which he took charge of. From the large amount of baggage and sundries this woman has (treble the quantity brought down in Sept. 2. 64.) I have no doubt there is much stolen property among it. The woman has been most insolent since her husbands arrest, trying to annoy me in every possible way."

Times do not change. In recent years much of King Island's maritime heritage has been smuggled off the island to be melted down for scrap or to grace private collections. Few wreck sites remain unplundered.

Although the lighthouses at Cape Wickham and Cape Otway guarded the western entrance to Bass Strait, the entire west coast of King Island was unlighted. This coast fronted the gales of the Roaring Forties and was directly in the path of any ship from Europe that wandered south of track while running its easting down. Such a ship was the 944 ton *Netherby* lost on 14 July 1866, with 452 emigrants and a crew of fifty, this ship saw no light at all and struck the western shore of the island twenty-three miles south of Cape Wickham at 7.15 p.m. She was one and a quarter miles south of present day Currie harbour. By a combination of good

6. *"Notice is hereby given that a Circular Stone Tower, one hundred and forty-five feet high, and painted white, has been erected for a Lighthouse on the hill near Cape Wickham, at the north end of King's Island, in Bass's Straits and from which a fixed white light will be exhibited on and after the 1st day of November next." – Notice to Mariners, 31st August, 1861.*

fortune and skilled use of the ship's boat, every person was brought ashore. It was clearly evident that a lighthouse on King Island's western shore would in all probability, have saved her. Spong learnt of the wreck when a party of nine survivors led by Second Officer Parry reached the lighthouse. Parry and three men then prepared to cross Bass Strait in the lighthouse whale boat. Spong quickly victualled them: [11]

"fifty pounds of biscuit, six cooked wallaby, cakes, jam, bread, pies, apples, tobacco, matches, water etc. enough stores to last them a week. Tea and sugar they refused to take, and openly stated that they had all they wanted."

In the meantime Assistant Keeper William Hickmott was sent south to inform the other survivors of what steps were being taken to obtain help. After covering the distance in only sixteen hours, Hickmott led 117 male survivors north to the lighthouse next day. By telescope Spong saw the bedraggled expedition making its way around the coast when still ten miles away. He rode out and greeted the party with a large sack of cabin biscuits. The men were billeted in and around the four houses.

Spong kept a scrapbook for the twenty odd years he served at Cape Wickham. In it, he and his family pasted cuttings of newspaper articles dealing with King Island. One account recorded the part they had played in the *Netherby* story and continued with a description of the life at the lighthouse: [12]

"At the lighthouse station every care and attention was paid to the comfort of the shipwrecked people, not only Mr. Spong himself, but also by his three assistants. A number of the most respectable of the lot was quartered in the superintendent's own house, while others were similarly treated by the three assistants, who not only gave up their own rooms, but put themselves to much trouble and great inconvenience, which in every instance, was not repaid by the recipients of so much real kindness and true hospitality. A small chapel and the telegraph station were filled with men, so that one and all had quarters alike, comfortable and commodious. The superintendent is Mr. Edward Nash Spong who has three assistants under him. The position of a lighthouse-keeper residing on some out-of-the-way land has often been a subject of commiseration, but the little community on King's Island are perfectly happy and contented with their lot in life. The superintendent resides in a good well built eight roomed stone house, and has all his family around him. The assistants have also stone cottages of their own, neatly and comfortably furnished. There are a few cows, pigs, fowls, etc., which belong to the superintendent, and at a short distance from the habitations there are several gardens, in which a few flowers and vegetables of all kinds are grown. The Island is full of kangaroo and wallaby, which the assistants hunt three times a week, and any number of black swans and wild duck can be obtained for the trouble of shooting them, so that perhaps under all these circumstances Mr. Spong, the superintendent, might quote from "Gil Blas," and say, "I am quite my own master, agreeably lodged, perfectly easy in my circumstances. I am contented with my situation, and happy because I think myself so." A small church, built in the orthodox ecclesiastical style, and with a steeple too has been constructed, and in this edifice the islanders assemble for prayers every Sunday morning. The country is very undulating and in parts thickly wooded with a sort of white maple and blackwood. The scrub, which consists of brushwood and ti-tree, about 9 feet high, is very thick and difficult of penetration. Some very picturesque spots were seen in the journey from the rock to the lighthouse, not unlike a gentlemans park in the old country, with the undulations of thick belts of timber."

The passengers of the *Netherby* were feted upon their arrival in Melbourne. Their original destination having been Brisbane, they were given the opportunity of continuing on there, or remaining in Melbourne.

Even before the loss of the *Netherby*, the need for a light on King Island's west coast had been voiced, by 1874, nothing had been done. That year great loss of life again highlighted the need. The ship, the *British*

7. Cape Wickham quarters and reserve. "... all the station kept open house to the shipwrecked passengers, and gave them ... their private stores as well as those of the Tasmanian Government ... by doing so they deprived themselves for months to come of many comforts that they had procured from Hobart Town, the store-vessel being sent only twice a year." – a newspaper account of the treatment received by the survivors of the Netherby in 1866. This photograph was taken in approximately 1904, the signal mast may be seen to the right.

Admiral, nearly twice the size of the *Netherby,* was on her maiden voyage; she carried 88 passengers and crew. At 2 a.m. on 23rd. May this iron clipper struck a reef two miles off King Island's western shore. The *Australasian Sketcher* described what followed: [13]

"the ship struck heavily, and for a few minutes it was expected that the masts would go by the board in consequence of the manner in which they swayed to and fro. Up to this time the passengers had been totally unacquainted with any possibility of danger, but the severe shock of the ship striking brought them rushing on deck, and a most heartrendering scene

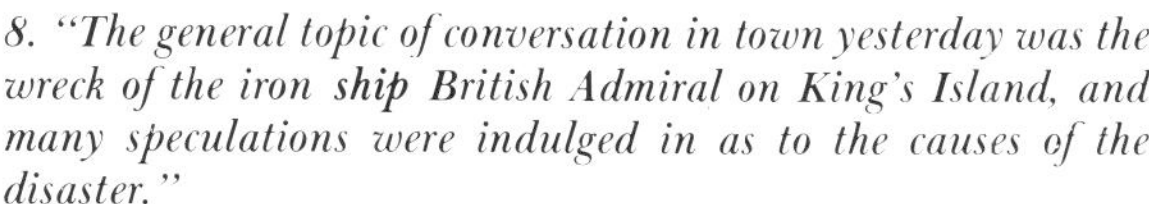

occurred. There were several women on board – one of whom was far advanced in pregnancy – together with many young girls and the screams and prayers for rescue from these were appalling. The women and children had congregated on the poop, and were clinging to the mizen rigging within a few minutes of the ship striking, having been awakened from their sleep by the shock."

The *British Admiral* was unfortunate to be lost. The captain, fearing his chronometers to be out, had ordered a close look out for land. When it was sighted the helm was put down and the vessel began to claw her way seaward. But no person aboard knew that an offshore reef lay between the ship and the open sea. The *British Admiral* struck the reef full on. Holed below the water line, she sank into deep water.

Slowly bodies and wreckage began to reach shore and by late afternoon goods were piled there in confusion. Local wallaby hunters reached the scene and buried as many of the bodies as they could. Later it was to be alleged that they stripped many of the bodies of valuables. The underfed hunting dogs, beyond restraining, made the task of burial doubly gruesome.

Newspapers wrung all they could from the story of one passenger – a girl named Tilly Dale: [14]

"Upon one of the pieces of timber which formed the structure [hunters shelter] was hanging the hand muff of Miss Tilly Dale, a young lady eighteen years of age, whose body was found on the shore, partly mangled by dogs, a few days afterwards, and was buried by the survivors and hunters on the bluff overhanging the beach. As her fair form, with hair still flowing down her back – the last vestiges of fleeting beauty – was buried, naked, beneath the cold sod of that scene of desolation, all around the grave sighed and wept at her melancholy fate. McEwan cut an inscription on a piece of wood, which was placed over her grave as a headboard."

This mawkish account concluded with the story of how, some days later, a sea chest belonging to Tilly Dale was washed ashore. It bore the label, "Not Wanted on Voyage." A cabin passenger who lost his life was William Dalzeil Nicholson, third son of a former Victorian Premier. The Nicholson family erected a monument that still overlooks the long beach that had been covered with the remains of the ship, her passengers and crew. It reads: [15]

"To the memory of William Dalzeil Nicholson, third son of the Hon. Wm. Nicholson, who with 78 others, perished in the wreck of the *British Admiral*, 23rd May, 1874. Age 25 years. To live in the heart of those we leave behind is not to die."

The Nicholson family lent their weight to the call for a second lighthouse on King Island. Spong pasted in his scrapbook one article which suggested again that had a lighthouse been on the New Year Islands in lieu of Cape Wickham, the *British Admiral* might have been warned in time of her close proximity to land: [16]

"It is admitted by all seafaring men that the erection of a lighthouse on Cape Wickham has been a mistake. North New Year's Island would have been the most advantageous position, and would not only have guarded the entrance to Bass's Straits, but also have warned mariners off the iron-bound western coast of the island. It is, of course, a matter of impossibility to move the light now existing from Cape Wickham to New Year's Island, but in view of the casualties that have occurred on King's Island during the past few years, it becomes a question with the Imperial and Colonial Governments whether another lighthouse should not be erected on that coast. The most suitable position for this would be the projecting point on which the ill-fated ship *Netherby* was lost about six years ago."

On the 22 February 1875 a document entitled *Report of the Board appointed to enquire into the necessity for the erection of a second lighthouse on King Island, and*

10. British Admiral Beach, King Island and the memorial erected to William D. Nicholson. Following this shipwreck new doubts arose as to the wisdom of having one lighthouse so far north at Cape Wickham. "It is admitted by all seafaring men that the erection of a lighthouse on Cape Wickham has been a mistake. North New Year's Island would have been the most advantageous position ... [to] ... have warned mariners off the iron-bound western coast of the island." – The Argus.

as to the best means of avoiding shipwreck thereon was presented to the Commissioner of Trade and Customs of Victoria.

Annexed to the report were the opinions of thirty shipmasters and others connected with the Bass Strait trade. Advice from masters of vessels seeking a landfall at the entrance to Bass Strait after the long voyage from Europe were decidedly in favour of the second lighthouse. As if to reinforce their opinions the 889 ton barque *Blencathra* was wrecked outside Currie harbour even while the Committee sat. Fortunately there was no loss of life.

Of the many masters giving evidence Captain Alexander McPetrie of the *Ben Voirlich* expressed views that were typical, he had seen the *Blencathra* ashore: [17]

"Do you think that, had a light been upon Netherby Point, that vessel might have been saved by it? If a distinctive light had been there she would have been saved."

Questioning of McPetrie then turned to one possible cause of faulty navigation.

"You have been a long time in iron ships?" "Yes, I have."
"You Know thoroughly the effect of hauling to the north ward after running down your easting; the compasses become polarized?" "Yes, they do that every voyage."
"Therefore there is a tendency directly you haul to the northward to make more easting?"
"Coming along this voyage I tried to make a forty miles northing course, which I thought I did, having good observations; and at noon the next day I found I had made forty miles the other way, making eighty miles out. That was in about 115°E. longitude."
"You tried to make your land-fall forty miles to the north?" "I intended to make a course forty miles of northing, and instead of that I made forty miles southing. I have found that to occur several times."
"This error applies the more as you get more to the eastward?" — "Yes."
"Assuming that to be the case, this is not generally known, except by men of great experience coming out here?" — "Strangers, of course, coming here do not know it."

Captain James Elmslie, of the 2131 ton *Sobraon*, gave his reasons for making an early landfall on the Australian main land, then remarked: [18]

"At present there are very few who make Cape Wickham in making the land. I have only seen King Island once, it was last year coming in. I had a strong north wind, which kept me from getting more to the north-east. I came up here late in the evening, and passed within ten miles of Cape Wickham. I ought to have been, according to my noon and afternoon sights, ten miles further north; it was very hazy, and I could not see any stars."

Captain George Burrell felt that a lighthouse on the west coast of the Island, "might possibly lead men who are not very careful to come and see the light dragging them to the southward." Somewhat distracted from King Island he remarked, "I call that Cape Otway light a magnificent light." With evident frustration the quest-

ioner attempted to steer the discussion back to King Island: [19]

"The question we have to get your opinion upon is that, with the number of vessels that have been wrecked staring us in the face – 805 lives having been lost – upon this very coast, can you suggest some means by which, in the future, if a ship came into that position, to save life and the ship?

11. *The sailing ship Ben Voirlich. Her master in 1875 was Capt. Alexander Mc Petrie and he gave evidence at the enquiry into the necessity for a second King Island lighthouse. McPetrie stressed the difficulty masters of iron ships had in compensating for the influence of magnetism in their ship's hull upon the compass, while making their easting to Australia.*

Captain Burrell's reply cannot be said to have made sense:

"If the weather were thick he would be close in before he could possibly see the light, therefore it would be useful. In thick weather perhaps is the only time that it is required. If that is the object, why you may place lights all over the coast!"

Captain Charles Grey of the *Loch Maree* felt that the mainland coast rather than King Island should receive a second lighthouse; somewhere in the region of Cape Nelson. He did not believe that a lighthouse on King Island's west coast in gale conditions, could afford enough warning to allow a vessel to take avoiding action. But his questioner persisted, not believing that Grey meant what he had said. He was asked: [20]

"Would that light have helped to save you?" –
"No, not in the least. With a gale of wind how could she [Loch Maree] have got off? Even if you are very smart, it takes at the very least an hour to reduce sail to close-reefed topsails. Now my ship would run twelve miles in that time, and by that time I should be in such dangerous proximity that nothing could save my ship, for I could not heave up upon either tack to clear the island. Suppose the light were upon Point Netherby, I could not clear it upon either tack, and could not clear the other points either, and before the ship would be under proper canvas I should not be able to get clear of it. I really do not see how it would be any good, it simply might induce captains of ships to run into danger, and when they saw the light it would be far too late to save any ship. Of course, that is only my opinion."

The Committee knew that the *British Admiral* had been able to go about in sufficient time. The weather conditions had been admittedly milder than those envisaged by Capt. Grey, but the vessel was only lost

12. "... in making my bed discovered that the bottom of my berth was full of water, the salt water from the beams dripping into every part of it and my bedclothes litteraly [sic], wet through . . . Ye Gentlemen of England who live at home at ease how would you like sleeping in a wet bed with an oilskin for a sheet." – The diary of an emigrant to Australia in the 1850's.
This photograph records Cape Horn weather as experienced by the Imperator Alexander. The Southern Ocean was no less kind to a ship and her crew enroute to Bass Strait.

13. Cape Nelson Lighthouse erected in 1884. This tower satisfied those who considered the need for it to be greater than that for a lighthouse at Currie Harbour, King Island.

because, in moving away from the shore, she had struck the Waterwitch Reefs. This may explain the careful questioning of Grey.

Master after master laboured the wisdom of making an early mainland landfall; some the advantages of erecting a lighthouse at Cape Nelson to aid early landfall. Captain Colin Brown, a veteran of the 1855 enquiry, avoided the choice: [21]

"I think there ought to be both. I do not think a light upon Cape Nelson would be sufficient in the face of the losses; one big ship tumbling in after another; it is fearful, and something ought to be done."

In its findings the Board strongly recommended that a lighthouse be erected at Netherby Point on King Island and considered that, "a light on Cape Nelson, or some prominent cape on the Australian coast to the westward of Cape Otway is of the utmost importance." Next a recommendation was made to revise the sailing directions for entering Bass Strait, masters would be warned to avoid a King Island landfall "in all weathers." The unreliability of compasses in iron ships was recognized and the necessity for masters to take corrective action stressed.

Edward K. Barnard, Master Warden of the Hobart Marine Board and Chairman of this Enquiry had written to the Colonial secretary of Tasmania before any evidence had been heard. The degree of his concern is shown by his closing remarks: [22]

"Whatever may be the action in this matter after the evidence that is about to be taken by the Commission, of which I have been named the chairman, I record my own opinion, feeling that in the future that if any such terrible sacrifice of life and loss of ships again take place, I have, without reference to any other theory or expressed opinion of those with whom I co-operate, given what I trust will not only be considered the correct one, and induce the Governments of the several colonies interested to establish *a warning light on Netherby Point King Island.*"

The lighthouse comprised an 80 foot prefabricated steel tower with a spiral stairway of ninety steps. A Victorian contractor Johnstone & Co. completed the structure in 1879 and it was located so as to remain visible northwards until the Wickham light could be picked up.

On 1st April, 1880 the Netherby Point Lighthouse commenced operation and joined Otway and Wickham to face the Southern Ocean. As the light swung around the horizon it touched Cataraqui Beach away to the south — that place of tragedy thirty-five years before.

14. Currie Harbour Lighthouse — to the south of here is Cataraqui Beach.
"... re the graves of the passengers and crew lost in the Cataraqui in 1845 ... the place was afterwards visited for the Port Phillip Government, but all traces of fencing have long since disappeared, from lapse of time and bushfires. The tablet is in a very corroded state from the action of sea water and the lack of paint for so many years." — a description by E.N. Spong in 1881 of the Cataraqui graves.

QUOTATIONS AND REFERENCES

1. Marine Board Records. 1857 – 1882 (MB. 2/5/5) Arch. O. of **Tas**. Report on King's Island addressed to Capt. George King R.N. 13/2/1857.
2. ibid. Report on King's Island by R. Henry 1/3/1857.
3. ibid. 14/10/58. Falconer to Maxwell.
4. ibid. 15/11/1858.
5. Cape Wickham Log Book D/077. Dep't of Transport. Navigational Aids.
6. ibid. 15/12/1861.
7. ibid.
8. ibid. 4/7/1863.
9. ibid. 16/4/1866.
10. ibid. 18/5/1866.
11. Spong's Scrapbook. Page 3. Illustrated Melbourne Post Article.
12. ibid.
13. *Australasian Sketcher*. 13/6/1874.
14. ibid. and in Spong's Scrapbook.
15. Monument. British Admiral Beach. King Island.
16. ? Argus article. Spong's scrapbook. P. 3.
17. Enquiry as named. Question No. 128 ff.
18. ibid. Question 285.
19. ibid. Question 312.
20. ibid. Question 400.
21. ibid. Question 490.
22. ibid. P. 10.

ILLUSTRATION SOURCES

1. Dept. of Transport
2. Mr. Col. Cotter.
3. Archives Office of Tasmania. 1857-1882. (MB 2/5/5)
4. Dept. of Transport.
5. Mr. R. Russel. King Island.
6. **Mr. Alan Simm Apollo Bay**.
7. Archives Office of Tasmania.
8. La Trobe L. Australasian Sketcher. 13/6/1874. .
9. Edwardes Collection. Library of South Australia. Vol. 79, No. 76.
10. D.M.W.
11. **Edwardes Collection. Vol. 15. Sect. 1.**
12. Edwardes Collection. Library of South Australia.
13. Capt. C. Jackman.
14. & 15. D.M.W.
16. Chance Bros. Birmingham.

15. Currie Harbour Lghthouse commenced operation on 1st April, 1880. The King Island Historical Society have, with the assistance of the Tasmanian National Parks Association, converted the surviving 1880 keeper's residence into a historical museum. In the foreground a plaque commemorates the keepers who served at Cape Wickham prior to automation, and the burden they shared with their mainland brothers at Cape Otway.

16. The lighthouse for Currie Harbour, King Island sitting in the builders yard in England, before being shipped out to King Island.

...ALL IN GOOD ORDER...

13

While the long struggles for the Wickham light and then the Currie light were proceeding on King Island, Ford continued at Cape Otway. What is known of daily life there in the 1860's and 1870's is derived from Ford's faithfully kept letter books and the few notes of infrequent visitors to his outpost. The trivial and the important receive mention in the letter books: shipwrecks and survivors, disputes between keepers, the demands incidental to living in an isolated place — all are preserved over his 30 years at the Otway. The pages blur the years but the approach of the 1860's saw one battle won over the Otway Ranges: the bringing of the Telegraph to the Cape in 1859. This had represented an important turning point for all stationed there. The isolation was no longer total. Coincident with the telegraph line, a more direct track was cut to Apollo Bay and the occasional visitors found their way to the Cape to avail themselves of the Ford's hospitality.

The tracks had been improved in 1864 when a Geological Survey Party led by Charles S. Wilkinson set out to "correct information regarding the topographical outlines, characteristic features and geological structure of a portion of Victoria hitherto but very imperfectly known." The party spent some six months in the district cutting a new track as far west as Moonlight Head and completing the first accurate survey of Roadknight's "tolerable road" — as La Trobe had called it. Like Henry Allan before them they had to contend with the Otways in winter. Wilkinson, writing from Apollo Bay, remarked: [1]

"The season is very much against our examining the district with such expedition as I should like to do. At present the creeks are very high and the sides of the ranges densely scrubby, making it very slow work getting along them; otherwise, in the summer time one could easily get along the beds of the creeks.

All our party are in good health. I could not have done well without Murray's assistance, and he is a thorough bushman. The men are both willing and do their work well. I would not wish for better men."

The Murray, Wilkinson referred to, was R.A.F. Murray, then only eighteen. He was destined to become Government Geologist for Victoria.

The maps prepared from this survey work indicate the magnitude of distances the men travelled. In the September the party made the first recorded crossing south to north of the western end of the Main Dividing

1. Charles S. Wilkinson.
This dedicated surveyor and geologist wrestled with the Otway
Ranges to produce the first accurate maps of the areas he could
penetrate.

Range – referred to by Wilkinson as Mount Chapple, no doubt named after Ford's nearest neighbours. [2] "From here the ranges begin to fall towards the north of the Gellibrand River." Three nights later they reached the Colac-Warrnambool Road at a point "ten miles from Colac, which township we arrived at late in the evening, in by no means an enviable state as regards the condition of vestments." Lawry·and Chapple from the Cape Otway Station had accompanied them, doubtless pleased to find a shorter route that they could use to reach markets in Colac.

Wilkinson succeeded in cutting a bridle track to Moonlight Head from the Johanna River over the intervening La Trobe Range – a name that unfortunately has not survived. La Trobe's own track, cut nearly twenty years previously, had all but disappeared. Regular communication westward to the mouth of the Gellibrand River and on to Warrnambool was now possible.

The party must have spent some time at Cape Otway itself. Writing of the sandstone thereabouts, Wilkinson remarks: [3]

2. Reginald A. F. Murray – an assistant to Wilkinson. Murray
married Jane Louisa Otway Ford, daughter of Henry and Mary
Ford in 1869. They had met five years prior to this when
Wilkinson's party was staying at Cape Otway.

"Some of it ... is very durable as shown by that used for the Cape Otway Lighthouse, built in 1848, and in which the chisel marks even on the steps are only slightly effaced."

Wilkinson's preliminary report conveyed his thanks to:

"Messrs Lawry and Chapple, and Mr. Ford of Cape Otway, for the kind assistance they have always rendered us since we have been in this district."

Unmentioned in the report is the meeting of the then 18 year old Reginald Murray and Ford's daughter Jane Louisa Otway Ford. They were married five years later in January 1869.

A glimpse of the lighthouse settlement at this time is afforded by another visitor, Mrs. Thomas Roadknight. It had been her father-in-law and husband who had pushed the track through to Cape Otway in 1846. Visiting there in 1863 she recorded her impressions of the Ford family. The description of Ford himself throws light on a man otherwise only known from his letter books: [4]

"Leaving the telegraph office we returned to the Fords (we had called there on our way). They are kind hospitable people – Mr. Ford rather rough with the slightly bumptuous dogmatical manner of a sea captain which I believe he has been – then I suppose he considers himself the Head of the Cape community. Mrs. Ford is a truly kind sensible woman, not educated but with so much common sense and innate kindness of heart that you feel you could at once make a friend of her – she has only nine children (the two eldest are grown up and visiting in town just now) and they seem well behaved and nicely brought up – scarcely ever having seen any other children."

"Only nine children", in that remote place! As for her education, the La Trobes had thought her a suitable governess for their children.

The letter book describes several clashes with staff in which Ford's somewhat uncompromising manner may be sensed. In 1872 there was a particularly drawn out disagreement concerning the role the Telegraph station staff were to play in the running of the lighthouse. Memoranda passed back and forth between Ford and Kelsall, the Telegraph Officer, arguing the relative importance of the telegraph and the lighthouse. Apparently an agreement existed between the two responsible departments for the assistant telegraph officer to take one of the lighthouse watches. This worked until Ford realized that on occasions this man had to leave the lighthouse during his watch, and walk the 500 hundred yards to the Telegraph Office to contact Melbourne, "which", as Ford pointed out, "entirely destroys that order that no keeper is to leave the Lights during his watch."

Ford only had one assistant keeper for much of the time and had no option but to rely on Telegraph Station staff for assistance. He felt doubly let down because one

3. Portion of Wilkinson's map of 1863-4. The main track from
Apollo Bay to Birregurra still followed Roadknight's route cut
fifteen years before.

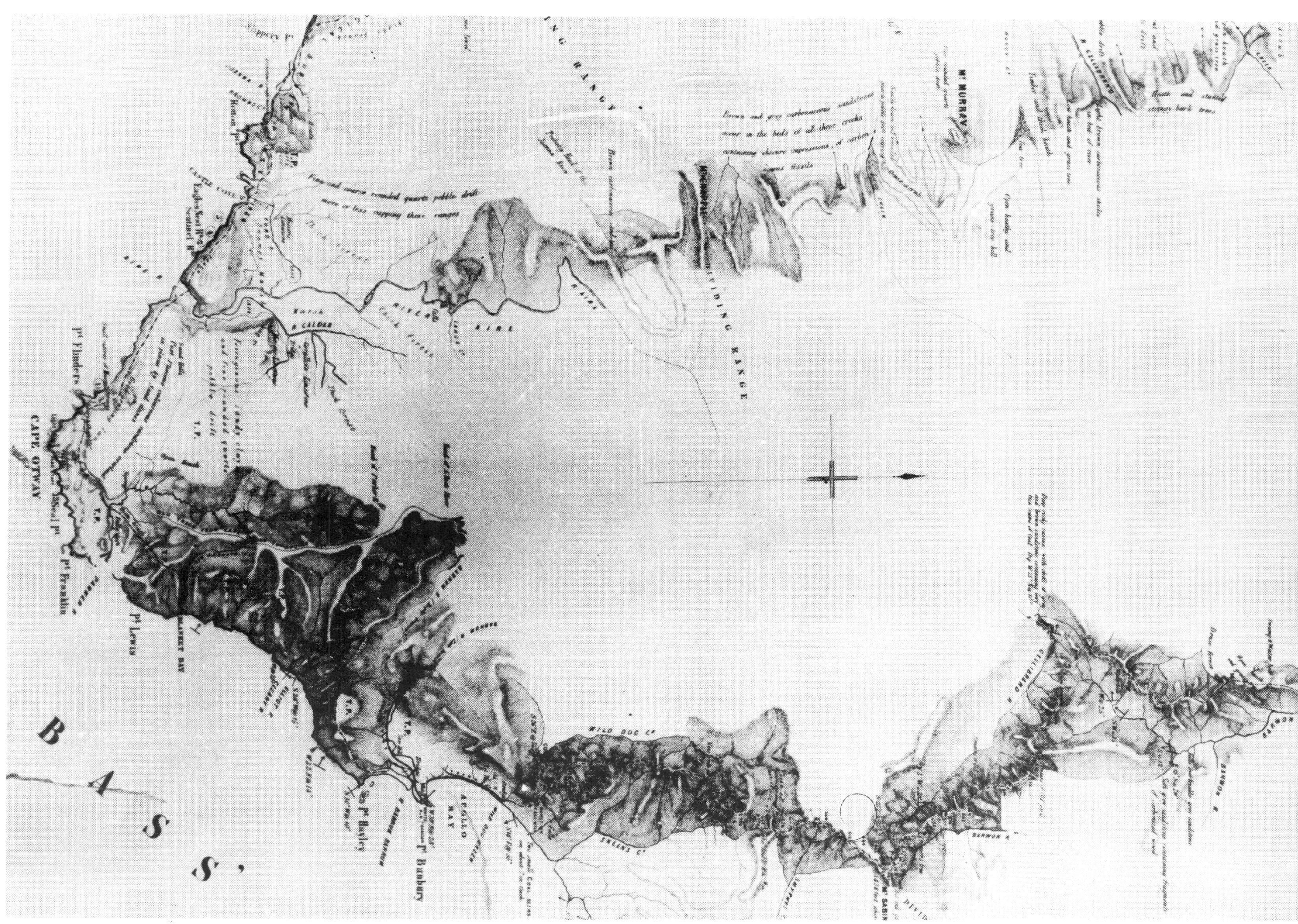

Slippery Pt
DIVIDING RANGE
Mt MURRAY
Brown and grey carbonaceous sandstone
occur in the beds of all these creeks
containing obscure impressions of carbon
plant fossils
DIVIDING RANGE
Fine grained coarse rounded quartz pebble drift
more or less capping these ranges
R. CALDER
AIRE
MILL
Pt Flinders
CAPE OTWAY
Pt Franklin
Pt Lewis
MARKET BAY
Irregular sandy clay
and fine rounded quartz
pebble drift
B   A   S   S'
WILD DOG Ck
APOLLO BAY
Pt Bunbury
SKENES Ck
Mt SABINE
DIVIDING
BARWON R.

On the night of the 13th ultimo or morning of the 14th I saw the assistant returning from the telegraph at 12.40 a.m.

Kelsall replied in reasonable terms to the charges made by Ford: [6]

"I do not defend the practice, on the contrary I admit it to be defective as the mail watch alone if properly kept is quite sufficient to engage the attention of one person but I maintain that it is the most workable arrangement that presents itself under present circumstances."

Eventually Kelsall was instructed by the General Post Office to comply with Superintendent Ford's wishes: [7]

"There should be no difficulty and as the Telegraph officers get overtime they must do the work or pay the other officers for doing it."

Ford also reported word for word a disagreement with one of his assistants over the erection of an "unauthorized structure." Keeper Morwich wanted to build a fowlhouse with old timber and iron from a recently demolished structure: [8]

"I have to complain of his disobedience of my orders at several times and setting me at defiance by purposely doing what I have requested not to be done ... I then told him that none of the Government property could be appropriated to a private purpose, he said, he would have some of the iron. I informed him I had orders to have it stacked – he replied that I had too many orders and fifty contractors should not take the iron and with a little of the bully about him."

The trouble had started a week before when Morwich wrote direct to Capt. Payne, the Chief Harbourmaster complaining of injustices at the establishment. The letter was returned unopened, accompanied with a warning that a repetition of such communications "will be dealt with as a breach of the regulations." The unopened letter concerned repairs being made at that time to the quarters: [9]

"I beg to submit that the plans ... proposed for the repairs to the quarters of Assistants at the lighthouse have been materially altered very much to the prejudice of convenience of the assistants and I believe through the instigation of Mr.

4. Separated by only a short distance at so remote a location as Cape Otway, the Lighthouse staff and Telegraph Station staff answered to different masters. They doubtless drew comfort from each others presence but on numerous occasions memorandums passed back and forwards across this gap instancing one department's grievance against the other.

of his own daughters had learned telegraphy and served as assistant at the station when another operator could not be procured. Finally on the 11th April 1872, he wrote to the Chief Harbour Master: [5]

"Now as this affair of leaving the lantern when on watch and going up to the telegraph to attend at the same time to the mail watch has become so notorious that I have ceased to take any record of it. I had hoped that after what had occurred at the General Post Office when I was in town it would have ceased or if not then certainly it would when the new assistant began his duties but after his arrival it went on just the same. Mr. Senior [chief lighthouse mechanic] must have been aware of it as he was here at the time.

Ford for his own advantage. Instead of the addition of kitchen and other conveniences promised, one room is to be left without plaster and the front fence the posts of which is [sic] so decayed that they cannot be straightened for fear of their falling to pieces, is simply to have a few of the old pickets renailed. The locks to all the doors are thoroughly worn out but only about half of them are to be renewed. The only gate which was to be supplied I requested the Inspector to place in front of the door but he states that it cannot be done. While Mr. Ford is getting a quantity of new fencing with no less than seven gates where neither gates nor fencing are much required. You would be the better able to see the injustice of these alterations were you on the spot yourself.
The old iron which is removed from the roof of the assistants quarters Mr. Ford has ordered to be carried to his yard. I have retained a portion of it and do not intend to give it up unless requested by you.
I make this statement not altogether for the benefit I should myself receive but because I consider it my duty."

Ford then records the circumstances under which he returned the letter to Morwich. [10]

"June 13. This afternoon I went to Morwich and said that you have sent a letter to the Chief Harbour Master and he desires me to ask you for an explanation, why you sent it in an irregular manner and not through me – he replied, show me the letter – I said, that was not an answer to my question I had asked – he then said, I told you I had written – yes I said, that was when it was being sent back – then he said that he should write how and when he liked to who he liked – I then drew the letter from my pocket and handed it to him saying there is your letter returned."

Next day superintendent and keeper were working in the lantern room together when Morwich asked Ford if he would now be prepared to forward the letter through to Williamstown. Ford's account resumes: [11]

"I replied, he must write to me to do so – I saw two papers lying on the window sill and thought they were as I expected – he left the Lighthouse and did not hand them to me at all. After he was gone I looked at them and found that they were two letters for Capt. Payne. On first thought I did not think I would take them but secondly I thought it would be better to forward them on."

Poor Morwich! His previously returned letter was accompanied by the following brief note: [12]

"Sir, Will you please to inform me whether it is right to report a superior officer concerning his conduct on any point and that report to go through himself. As regards any letter, has it to be handed to my superior sealed or open?
I will strictly follow your orders when received."

By telegram read by Ford, Morwich was instructed to comply with Ford's wishes. This he did replying, "he had shifted the fowlhouse and would erect no more." Morwich, with his family, left the next summer.

But Morwich was not the last assistant keeper to find himself apologising to Ford. After being charged with being "drunk and disorderly at the Parker" the long serving keeper William Evans wrote to the Harbour Master: [13]

"Sir, In reply to a communication received from Mr. Ford charging me with being drunk and incompetent at the Parker landing place on the 21st instant I yesterday pleaded guilty. I have nothing to say in defence or justification of my conduct upon that unfortunate occasion except that previous long abstinence and the heat of the weather aided very considerably in bringing me to the state I was in.
I most earnestly and sincerely express my sorrow for what has passed and steadfastly promise that I will never be guilty of such conduct in future – as a proof of my firm determination to adhere to this promise I respectfully inform you Sir that I have enrolled myself as a member of a temperance society and have taken the usual solemn pledge to abstain totally from intoxicating liquors of all kinds.
To show that I am able to keep this most Solemn engagement I may mention that from February 1873 until a few weeks ago I voluntarily and without any pledge or promise whatever totally abstained although at the landing of Stores in 1874 and on various other occasions liquors were in my way and offered to me had I chosen to indulge.
Any punishment however light inflicted on myself would be severely felt by my innocent family – we have had a very hard struggle Sir to recover from losses incurred during my temporary removal from the Govt. Service and we are only now just emerging from pecuniary difficulties.
I therefore entreat you Sir for the sake of my young ones who have not offended, in consideration of my long service, 15 or so years and previous good conduct and the assurance of my temperance pledge as a guarantee against a repetition of the

5. *"The only gate which was to be supplied I requested the inspector to place in front of the door but he states that it cannot be done. While Mr. Ford is getting a quantity of new fencing with no less than seven gates where neither gates nor fencing are much required."* – Keeper Morwich. 1870.

6. Assistant Keeper William Evans and his wife Katherine. The Evans family served at Cape Otway for over twenty years but two of their children are buried there. The headstone over the grave indicates that the children died within twelve months of each other.

7. "My object in obtaining leave is to be able to spend my time on the Aire River or wherever else I may be disposed to seek recreation ..." – William Evans.
This photograph was taken of the Aire River in 1891.

8. The grave of the Evans children in the Cape Otway cemetery.

recent Sincerely regretted exposure, to pass over the present offence and allow me an opportunity to redeem the past."

William Evans served longer (1858 – 1868 and 1872 – 1884), than any other assistant keeper at Cape Otway and his descendants settled in Apollo Bay. His letter to Ford has a desperate sound to it. Already Cape Otway had taken two of his children. their grave stone may still be seen in the small station cemetery. Ford simply noted one of the deaths with the words "Keeper Evans child died today."

The routine of lighting the lamps, trimming the wicks, polishing the brass reflectors, cleaning the chimneys, timing the revolutions, never varied from night to night. Ford lit the lamps and took the first watch which lasted to 10 p.m. A third keeper, or the telegraph assistant, took the next watch which lasted until 2 a.m. Ford's assistant keeper took charge at 2 a.m.,

"and the duties [of this watch] are not done in the Lantern and Lighthouse before 12 o'clock in the forenoon and sometimes later and a great part of the cleaning is done in his watch."

There were compensations in living in such an isolated location as Cape Otway but many men could not tolerate the ceaseless routine of the establishment. William Evans obviously appreciated the beauty of the country from which the other assistants and Ford himself, invariably attempted to escape during leave of absence. In 1877, when questioned as to his intended leave arrangements, Evans wrote: [14]

"As there appears to be a misunderstanding with reference to my previous application, I beg respectfully to state that it is not my intention to remain at the Lighthouse station though I do not propose going to Melbourne. My object in obtaining leave is to be able to spend my time on the Aire River or wherever else I may be disposed to seek recreation and during my holiday I wish to be able to camp out or otherwise live away from the quarters – probably during that time I may return to the quarters occasionally but only to obtain supply of provisions.
As it is now more than four years since I returned to Cape Otway during which time I have had no leave whatever, I sincerely trust that this application will meet with your approval."

So that year Evans and his family declined the passage back to Melbourne aboard the supply ship.

It was the practice for the *Pharos* and later the *Lady Loch* to signal with their ships horn when ready to begin unloading stores off Blanket Bay or the Parker River. The Inlet ceased to be used for landing supplies after 1877 when a new store shed was completed at Blanket Bay. Although no lives had been lost at the Parker since 1847, its narrow entrance gave limited room for a boat's crew to time their run in, consequently the broader, but more open Blanket Bay was used.

The arrival of the department's mechanic on the supply ship provided a welcome opportunity for the keepers and their families to learn the latest postings, and promotions, or changes in a Melbourne they only visited once a year. Unexpected visitors always appear to have been most welcome.

In 1869 the lighthouse's hospitality was tested to the limit when the crew of the French barque *Marie Gabrielle* reached Cape Otway after a fearful scramble from Moonlight Head. The master, having run the risk of

9. The opening of the new lighthouse supply shed at Blanket Bay in 1877. It is likely that Henry Ford and William Evans are among the uniformed men at the rear of the group. Bullock teams were used to haul the supplies from Blanket Bay to Cape Otway.

altering course while close to land to rescue two Aboriginals in a bark canoe, was caught in a south-westerly and driven irrevocably toward shore. He chose to beach his ship, thus saving his crew of eleven men. They headed toward the lighthouse, but most of them were exhausted by the time they reached a hut on the Aire River. There, all but the four fittest waited. These four struggled on until, at Cowrie Beach, two miles short of the lighthouse, they came upon Lemuel and George Ford gathering shells. To the children their tattered clothing and their strange and agitated speech was alarming. They fled to their father: [15]

"Late in the afternoon my young son came running home stating that he had seen four men coming from the direction of Moonlight Head. The other son came home later and informed

me that there was a wreck and that these four men had left seven others behind and that they had not had any food for four days. Mr. Lawry had started to meet them with provisions after lighting up. Morwich went over and brought two men to his house and got blankets from me.

Monday at 7 a.m., I went over to Mr. Lawry's and saw the Captain of the Marie Gabrielle [Auguste Evaine] and obtained the particulars, these I forwarded by telegraph. The other seven men and one boy came to the squatters.[most likely the owner of Glen Aire Station.] I had mentioned to the squatter I would endeavour to see him remunerated – in the afternoon I went over to Mr. Lawry's and then it was arranged to divide the rest between us – Telegraph taken 4 men, Morwich has 2 men, Lawry had the Captain, 1 man and 1 boy. Myself has 1 man and 2 boys. I have informed them that they should have blankets but at present Morwich is the only one that has any."

10. The Cape Otway store-shed and workshop; in the distance the abandoned Signaller's residence. The two rooms in the near end of the store-shed were built in 1850 as the quarters for the assistant keepers. A portion of the original shingle gable roof may be seen when standing inside the extension. After 1857, when the present assistant keeper's quarters were constructed, these rooms served as accommodation for victims of shipwreck.

11. In this 1890 photograph the Cape Otway signaller's residence and flagstaff can be seen.
"… my son picked up on the shore under the Lighthouse a board about 10ft. long with a ships name cut into it, apparently off the quarter …" – Ford 1876.

The spare quarters kept for shipwrecked crew were prepared and there the crew was accommodated for four weeks before they left for Apollo Bay to return to Melbourne aboard the *'Pharos'*. Lemuel Ford was to later recall with pleasure the French cooking they were treated to during that time. The men fished and made new clothes for themselves out of blankets, but were quite unable to accustom themselves to the numbers of snakes that Cape Otway has always been known for. Captain Auguste Evaine could speak and write English; he corresponded for many years afterwards with the Fords. The letters ceased after the Franco – Prussian War.

Walking and playing on the beaches the Ford children sometimes found more than shells. In September, 1876 Ford informed Williamstown: [16]

"On the 6th instant my Son picked up on the shore under the Lighthouse a board about 10 ft long with a ships name cut into it, apparently off the quarter – name as per margin."

In the margin opposite, Ford wrote in deliberate upper case lettering. W. GORDON. He could scarcely **have guessed that the brigantine,** *W. Gordon* **had left** Ardrossan on the Firth of Clyde in ballast, bound for South Australia via Capetown. She had departed Capetown in mid June 1875, but nothing further was heard of her or her crew of ten.

Among the visitors to the Cape Otway region was an 1873 survey party. Their task was to report to the Minister of Mines on the extent of coal deposits on the Otway coast. The report was a discouraging one: [17]

" ... we saw nothing which would justify the Government in expending moneys in sinking or boring."

They did, however give an interesting description of the Apollo Bay country at the time: [17]

"Some years ago the fine forest of trees extending back from Apollo Bay attracted the attention of parties engaged in timber trade, and led to the construction of a temporary wooden jetty inside Point Bunbury, and of a wooden tramway, some two or three miles in length, leading from this jetty up the small valley of the Barrum-barrum River to the base of a mountain spur. A good deal of timber of a size suitable for

conversion was cut down and sent from this place to Melbourne, but so much trouble and loss of time were incurred by the difficulty of loading in the open roadstead, and the unsafe nature of the anchorage in easterly winds, that the trade was eventually found to be unremunerative and was abandoned.

In such portions of this district as are found to possess the necessary conditions of good soil and shelter from the force of the westerly and south-westerly gales, the timber, mostly bluegum, attains a large size, and many trees are to be found of 5 and 8 feet diameter and 200 feet in height. We measured several trees of these dimensions in the sheltered gullies near Apollo Bay, and also about four miles from the bay on the track to Cape Otway, and on the more elevated sites upon this track much fine timber was found from 3 to 5 feet in diameter, and about 130 feet in height, and numbering from twenty to twenty-five trees to the acre."

12. The Elliot River in 1890. The caption on the photograph stated: "This picture was taken as we journey on horse back from Apollo Bay to Cape Otway. The Elliot River is four miles from Apollo Bay and here is situated the Ballarat Timber Co. mills. The tramway crosses the gully on high tressels. The trucks with logs are drawn up the hill by means of steam winding gear at the top. Tramway, hut, ferns and trees form a charming picture."

The jetty had broken up by 1873 and the idea of a breakwater was advanced as being the only way to encourage small vessels to engage in the timber trade by an assurance of safety. The timber resources of the district were still largely untouched: [18]

"The four sawmills (those of Messrs, Fulton, Silk, Pyle and Hall and Co.) erected in this forest, work almost exclusively messmate timber ... In the proximity of the coast the great timber wealth has had some attraction, but after the removal of the sawmills at Apollo Bay, the more valuable kinds of wood – bluegum and blackwood have not been gotten in any quantity, while owing, to the utter inaccessability of most of the inland valleys, the axe has been idle since a venturous party of splitters terminated a short lived subsistence on shingle-splitting some two or three years ago."

Two years later Ford's son-in-law, R.A.F. Murray led a further survey party that added to Wilkinson's work in the Otways, "suggesting the best means of facilitating the development of the resources of the district, as for instance by the cutting of tracks." Within another five years the first land was offered for selection.

Among the last visitors to enjoy the Ford's hospitality were two university students. They were attempting to walk around the coast from Warrnambool to Cape Otway. Having misunderstood the distance from the Aire River to Cape Otway, one later wrote under the pseudonym, "a Wandering Maniac": [19]

"By the time we had negotiated the sand, darkness had fallen, and no lighthouse could yet be seen. Our spirits fell below zero, the piercingly cold sea breeze and want of food, aiding them to a certain extent. After losing the way several times, and going many ways in our endeavours to find it, just as we were resolving upon a cold night's lodging on the bleak cliffs, we, as a forlorn hope, ascended a neighboring eminence and much to our delight caught sight of a distant ray on the horizon, and after crossing a boggy place, arrived at the lighthouse gate at about 9 p.m., tired and hungry. We were received in a manner I shall never forget. everything that could be done for us Capt. and Mrs. Ford did. We went up into the lantern that night to watch the machinery in operation. There are twenty one lamps, and the light they emit is exceedingly brilliant. I was ashamed of my appetite the next morning, but couldn't help it, having been on short allowance so long, and worked hard on it. After a tour through the station and inspection of the wonderful furniture Capt. Ford has made entirely from forest wood, and which surpassed in beauty almost everything of the kind one sees about Melbourne, we started on our return journey loaded with every provision that kindness could suggest."

While Henry and Mary Ford served their last year at Cape Otway their son George Ford became involved in probably the most well known wreck along the Otway coast – the ship *Loch Ard*. Cast very much in the mould of his father he was working for Hugh Gibson, the owner of the *Glen Ample* Station near Princetown. On the morning of June 1, 1878 this 1693 ton square rigged ship was near the end of her long voyage from London. Aboard were eighteen passengers and a crew of thirty

six. On this hitherto uneventful voyage the *Loch Ard* was commanded by a Captain George Gibb. A thick sea mist the day before had made an accurate sextant sight difficult to obtain and he thought himself further south in his approach to Bass Strait than he was. Unsure of his position he was now groping along an invisible coast, seeking the Otway Light and entry into Bass Strait.

At 4 a.m., instead of a light tended by one of Ford's keepers, Gibbs sighted the uncompromising cliffs that now bare the name of his ship four miles east of Port Campbell. Unable to put about in time, the *Loch Ard's* stern struck an off-lying reef and almost immediately began to sink. The yardarms dislodged huge pieces of rock from the cliff face which rained down in the dark on passengers and crew alike. One passenger, Eva **Carmichael and one crew member, Tom Pearce, survived.** Eva, only eighteen years of age, lost her parents, her three sisters as well as two younger brothers. They with the other passengers were the last Melbourne bound sailing ship emigrants to perish by shipwreck.

George Ford located the two survivors and spent the rest of the day at the gorge. Under instructions from Gibson he left there at midnight, on a horse he had ridden all day, to take word to Camperdown of the wreck. By next morning he returned with a mounted trooper and the telegram Gibson entrusted to him advising the authorities of the wreck, was already in Melbourne. It read: [20]

"The ship *Loch Ard* was wrecked off this coast last night. All hands and passengers are supposed to be lost except Miss Evalin Carmichael and Tom Pearce (midshipman) who swam ashore. The place of the wreck is about one mile east from the Sherbrooke. I hope protection will be given from wreckers."

The attention of the people of Victoria followed Ford back to the coast as once more, Bass Strait's western approaches had shown how uncompromising a landfall was provided for vessels unsure of their position. Tom Pearce and Eva Carmichael were hounded by the press but when all the medals had been awarded and citations read, George Ford like his father, was overlooked and slipped back into obscurity.

On the 12 October 1878, Superintendent Henry B. Ford wrote to Williamstown: [21]

"I herewith beg leave to inform you that I am now sixty years of age and that my health is fast failing, I have been in charge of the Lighthouse nearly thirty years ... therefore I would most respectfully solicit that I may be allowed to retire on superannuation."

Ford catalogued the times he had been deserted by his assistants; the promises made by La Trobe for salary adjustments then forgotten by his successor; the unauthorized but essential repairs he had made to the lighthouse machinery in July 1854. He concludes: [22]

"there is no record of any failings of the Light since it has been in my charge. I may also remark that I have always tried and done all that was in my power to keep the Government buildings in good order... the evidence is to be seen in the works."

Ford must have had some indication that his request to be superannuated would be granted, for the following month he reminded Capt. Payne that he would need advance warning of the *Pharos's* departure for Cape Otway, as it would be necessary to transport all his belongings and 'household goods down to Blanket Bay.' He concluded: [23]

"I would most respectfully solicit that you would be so kind as to inform me as early as possible the decision of the Government as regards my petition which I pray may be granted as both myself and Mrs. Ford's health is fast breaking up."

Who could guess their thoughts as the wagon trundled away from the lighthouse down to Blanket Bay, the *Pharos* and eventually retirement. If Ford showed no emotion, one can imagine that Mary Ford at least would have seen the faces of those she had fed and sheltered there. She had borne seven children at the place now slipping into the distance, hidden by La Trobe's 'cups and saucers' undulations. La Trobe. They had named their youngest son after him. He was seventeen now – born not long after the signaller's residence had been built. The signaller's residence was the last building they could see as they drew away.

Henry Bayles Ford died at his home in Cunningham Street, Northcote in 1893 aged 75. Mary Anne Ford died at the same address in 1915 aged 93. Both were buried in the Melbourne General Cemetery with their daughter, J.L.O. Murray. No headstone marks their grave. Only the weeds keep watch.

QUOTATIONS AND REFERENCES

1. Geological Survey Report 1865. Vict. Parl. Papers. VOL. 4. No. 44. 25/7/1864. Wilkinson to Director.
2. ibid. letter dated 26/9/1864.
3. ibid. 13/3/1865.
4. Journal of a Visit to Cape Otway. H 5491 La Trobe Library.
5. Cape Otway Letter Book.
6. ibid. 24/4/1872.
7. ibid. 2/5/1872.
8. ibid. 16/6/1870.
9. ibid. 23/5/1870.
10. & 11. ibid. 16/6/1870.
12. ibid. 15/6/1870.
13. ibid. 28/1/1875.
14. ibid. 13/11/1877.
15. ibid. 28/11/1869.
16. ibid. 12/9/1876.
17. Geological Survey Report. 1874. No. 1. Page 115. F.M. Krause.
18. ibid. P. 106. Appendix A.
19. *The Gippsland Independent* 25/4/1879. Article entitled "On the Wallaby".
20. Don Charlwood. The Wreck of the Loch Ard. P. 65.
21. – 23. Cape Otway Letter Book.

ILLUSTRATION SOURCES

1 and 2 Victorian Geological Survey Bulletin No. 23, 1910.
3. Parlt. Papers, Geol. Survey of Vict. 1864-65. No. 44.
4, 5, 8, 10 and 17 D.M.W.
6. Mr. W. Evans, Apollo Bay.
7. Brooke's Photographic Union.
9. Mr. John Tulley.
11. D.M.W. Brooke's Photographic Union.
12. D.M.W. Brooke's Photographic Union.
13. D.M.W. Brooke's Photographic Union.
14. La Trobe Library Picture Collection.
15. Illustrated Australian News. 8/11/1884.
16. D.M.W. Brooke's Photographic Union.
18. E.C. Booth. Australia, Vol. 1 p. 76. Illustrated by Nicholas Chevalier, 1876.

18. Cape Otway.

...PULL BOYS! PULL!...

14

1. *The sadly neglected Cape Otway Signal Station, now awaits a new calling.*

In 1878, the Chief Harbour Master, C.B. Payne, informed his staff at the various lighthouses that long periods of service at one lighthouse were in future to be discouraged. Never again would men and their families be asked to endure as much as the Fords had endured.

Before leaving Cape Otway Ford had recommended his lightkeeper David Simpson for the position of Superintendent Cape Otway. Payne declined Ford's suggestion and appointed a more senior Keeper, William Martin to the post.

During Ford's last years at the Cape, uncontrolled cattle grazing in and about the quarters had caused extensive soil erosion near the footings of the buildings. Martin appealed successfully for new fencing. The already eroded areas were secured with twenty five bullock dray loads of cut ti-tree. Seeds of various plant species including marram grass, sent by Baron Von Mueller, were sown and Martin monitored their progress. The results were encouraging and eventually the erosion was arrested.

For thirty years the Fords had put up with the discomfort of the trip by bullock dray from Parker River and Blanket Bay to the quarters. Perhaps Ford himself was of that passing generation who "knew their place" and spared little thought for their own discomfort. Not so Martin. In 1880 he wrote to his superiors: [1]

"I also desire to point out the Great need here of some description of light Vehicle such as those in use at Cape Schanck and Gabo Island. Female passengers arriving by the *Pharos* are compelled to remain ten to twelve hours on the Beach at Blanket Bay and then ride up on a bullock dray which does not reach the station until long after dark. With such a vehicle and a supply of fodder any person requiring to visit the station could be conveyed to and fro in ample time for the sailing of the Vessel."

Possibly by now senior government officers were beginning to realize that the new country had developed new attitudes. At all events, Martin was granted both horse and buggy.

With Ford's departure the somewhat overshadowed William Kelsall, who had been in charge of the Telegraph Station for over ten years assumed a greater prominence at Cape Otway. In January 1880 G.E. Morrison visited the Cape on his walk from Queenscliffe to Adelaide as a seventeen year old Geelong College school boy. Possibly Martin was away from the station at the time. Morrison records: [2]

" ... On rounding a hill I saw what looked like a church on the top of a hill. I made my way to this and was welcomed in most hospitably by Kelsall, the telegraph operator. He was most cordial, gave me a good tea and a shakedown on the sofa.

Next day, Monday, in the morning I was shown round ... The man in charge showed us the revolving apparatus ... On taking leave of Kelsall I, of course, asked him what the bill was. He seemed quite annoyed at my doing so and asked me what I should think of a man who expected to be paid for a night's board and lodging by the only stranger he had seen for six months. His last few words raised my respect for him."

But the isolation of lighthouse life continued to have serious disadvantages – some of greater significance than others. The lack of schools for the children was an obvious concern. For any education the Ford children might have received at the Cape, they could thank their mother and her former vocation. In 1880, two years after the Fords had left Cape Otway, a petition bearing the signatures of lighthouse keepers and settlers on neighbouring stations was sent to the Education Department. The petition pointed out that the Wilson's Promontory lighthouse had a school and teacher, yet Cape Otway, with sixteen eligible students, had none.

The families at Cape Otway in need of a school were listed as – Cordell (six children), Stevens (two children), Evans (two children) and Kelsall (six children). Cordell

2. *Cape Otway school children, the year was 1908. Seated with his dog is the amazing Theodore Prolius.*

3. *The Glen Aire Station homestead with its wide verandahs and shingle roof. The woman riding side saddle is Miss Ethel Chapman who was a teacher at both Johanna and Cape Otway school at that time. The gentleman in the centre is Mr. B.J. Denny owner of this large property which enjoyed grazing rights as far east as Blanket Bay. This was the holding claimed by Thomas Roadknight after his successful expedition across the Otway Ranges.*

was now the Telegraph Operator. He offered the use of the "12 feet by 10 feet, light and airy front room" at the Signal Station. The petition concluded: [3]

"With reference to the other gentlemen signing the petition, I may state that they are connected with the Cape Otway Cattle Station which is distant from the Government Quarters about ¾ of a mile. There are at present no children at the cattle station.

The same gentleman [Cordell] offers to find accommodation for the teacher and his family and I venture to suggest that as all the male children are young a female teacher would meet our requirements."

Miss Mary Dwyer arrived at the beginning of 1881, the first teacher at State school No 2352, Cape Otway. Three years later a Richard Heath, who signed himself "a rate payer of the district" wrote to the Education Department concerning the supposed "light and airy" conditions: [4]

" ... the childrens health is visibly affected by being confined in such a small room for so many hours daily."

He offered to build a small classroom, "similar to the one at Apollo Bay." For reasons not recorded the offer was declined. By 1885 the numbers attending had fallen to ten children: Musgraves, Whitelaws, Stevens and one child of William Evans. Next year the school closed. The decision to close was due in part to the difficulty the Education Department had in finding teachers prepared to work in so isolated a place. One Janet Swayne wrote when she learnt of her posting to Cape Otway, in 1884: [5]

"It is quite impossible for me to go overland. I cannot endure a sixty mile ride through the Cape Otway Forest. Besides I have neither a horse nor an escort and I could not travel alone for such a distance and over such a bad road."

As soon as the school was closed fresh petitions called for its reinstatement. Force was lent to them by R. (Ren) N. Robinson who was part owner of the *Glen Aire* station and a well known and colourful character – a crackshot, a superb horseman who on at least one occasion rode up the steps and into the bar of the Apollo Bay Hotel. Robinson wrote: [6]

"Dear Sir,
The inhabitants of this locality including four families in the Government Service in connection with the Telegraph and Lighthouse Dept. are very badly in need of a school. It is a great pity that the children of persons who have spent of their lives in serving the government isolated from their fellow men should be allowed to grow up in complete ignorance. The Education Department may argue that there are not a sufficient number of children to keep a school open. The number is ten but yet are placed at a great disadvantage when compared with other children in the colony who are not connected with government in any way If you will do what you can for me in this matter you will greatly oblige me and many others of your supporters. A school there could be made to keep in employment those teachers who require sickleave. The Department could save the expense of paying salaries to teachers for doing nothing.
R. N. Robinson"

Whether this novel idea was responsible for the school re-opening in the following year is not clear from the correspondence files. The numbers continued to fluctuate with closure from 1893 to 1897 and by 1898 only children of the Lawson and Rayler families were enrolled. Members of the Frayne, Franklin, Whitlaw, Skilton, Keyes, Musgrave, Stevens, Prolius, Dunk and Olsen families all attended the Cape Otway school before the end of the century.

In contrast to the only slowly receding isolation of Cape Otway, Melbourne in the 1880's could legitimately claim to be the most exciting capital city of the Australian colony. There was about it a spirit of confidence and adventure. This extended to the countryside and the Minister for Lands was under continual pressure to make more land available for selection. The Otway Ranges were not immune from this demand and in 1879, 160,000 acres were thrown open for selection. 'Wandering Maniac' after seeing the country in his visit to Cape Otway remarked: [7]

"I have lately seen that a large portion of the Otway forest is to be thrown open for selection, and as I have tramped through a good deal of it to the west of the lighthouse, venture to give my humble opinion that the selector who buries himself in that portion of the ranges, will be before long, a ruined man ... Has the Minister of Lands ever seen the way these ranges are timbered? My candid belief is, that in most places I have seen there, if land were given to the selectors free, they would find themselves utterly unable to earn a common livelihood."

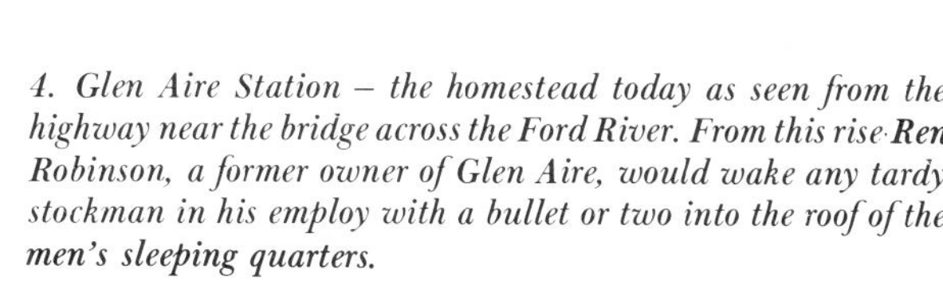

4. Glen Aire Station – the homestead today as seen from the highway near the bridge across the Ford River. From this rise Ren Robinson, a former owner of Glen Aire, would wake any tardy stockman in his employ with a bullet or two into the roof of the men's sleeping quarters.

Many did fail and within a few years walked off their selection defeated by the continual rain, the encroaching forest and the quagmire tracks. Others, the persistent or lucky, stayed on and learnt to adapt to the whims of the Otway climate.

The mood of confidence in 'Marvellous Melbourne' in the 1880's led also to a desire to secure overseas recognition of the state's achievements. In 1880 Victoria hosted its first International Exhibition. Drawn from all over the world, products of the industrial revolution were housed in the newly built Exhibition Buildings.

On the night of 3 September 1880, eighty-four days out from New York, the square rigged ship *Eric the Red* was seeking the Otway Light from the west. Stowed in the holds were the many trade exhibits of those North American manuracturers who had chartered her. Instead of clearing the Cape easily, as the master expected, she struck the Otway reef two miles off the land in a typically heavy swell and was mortally wounded. Merchandise and exhibits were spilt into the sea.

By morning it was realized that four men had lost their lives. There were seventeen survivors. As far as the people of the Otway coast were concerned, the *Eric the Red* was generous. Items of all description floated ashore for easy collecting.

To avoid another such loss, an auxiliary red warning light was fitted near the base of the tower and first operated on the night of 18 July 1881 – a light only seen if a vessel strayed within 3 miles of the Cape. Thus ships were given warning of their close proximity to the Otway Reef. This measure proved effective and no further vessels were lost through "the extremity of danger not being lit."

By now sail was being pushed out of the passenger trade to and from the Australian colonies by a new generation of vessels that were not dependent solely on the wind for propulsion. For auxiliary steamships regular passages of sixty days to Melbourne were commonplace – less after the Suez Canal was opened in 1869. Auxiliary ships wherever possible employed their sails and reserved their engines for use in the English Channel after departure, the doldrums – where potential record passages by clipper ships were so often undone, and for negotiating the entrance to Bass Strait. The risk of being caught on a lee shore when making a landfall on the Otway coast had been reduced. It would not be altogether removed until steam turbines and twin screws came early in the new century.

The Orient Line was a leader in the rise of steam. In 1879 the 5400 ton auxiliary ship *Orient* entered the Australian run and as she and her sister ships became identified with the fastest of passages, Melbourne grew to depend on them for the latest mails from the "mother country." For the previous twenty years news of all sizeable vessels entering Bass strait in daylight had been telegraphed from Cape Otway to Melbourne. Passing vessels remained unidentified at night but public interest in the arrival of Orient Line ships was so high that in 1884 keepers on watch at Cape Otway were instructed to co-operate in reporting their passing: [8]

5. Early morning in a valley just south of present day Gellibrand. In 1846 when Henry Allan struggled past here in an attempt to reach the coast from Colac, these spurs were covered in thick forest. He was to be turned back by rivers swollen from winter rains, within sound of the sea, tantalizingly close to the much sought Cape Otway.

6. An old shed at Glenample station which was formerly a deck cabin on the Eric the Red. This American square rigged ship was lost on the Otway Reef in 1880.

7. Cape Otway, Victoria as the age of sail was passing. Keepers were instructed in 1884 – "The Orient Steamers will use detonating rockets to call attention to their arrival and will then show red and blue lights alternately. The answering signal from the lighthouse is to be a blue light flashed horizontally while burning." (See opposite page).

"The "Orient" Steamers will use detonating rockets to call attention to their arrival and will then show red and blue lights alternately.

The answering signal from the Lighthouse is to be a blue light flashed horizontally while burning.

It is assumed that the detonating rockets will make sufficient noise to be heard from the interior of the Lighthouse, it will therefore be necesssary for the person on watch in the Lighthouse to be on the alert to catch any unusual sound, to look out for the specified signals; when seen to give the answering signal and then call the Signal Station by telephone.

You will exercise your own descretion as to the most suitable situation from which to show the answering signal. I think however it would be best seen from shipboard if shown from the base of the Lighthouse."

By 1888 the original Wilkins Bros. lantern at Cape Otway was over forty years old and had, like the thousands of sailing ships it had greeted, been overtaken by technology.

It had endured the extremities of climate that were the lot of Cape Otway, the tampering of Lawrence and Moneghan. It had known the ministering care of Ford, Evans and many other keepers, overhauls by Burns and later by Senior. In 1891 it was decided to replace the 21 Argand Lamps by a single light source with prismatic lenses revolving around it. In the forty years that had elapsed between the installation of the original and the 1891 mechanism, one thing had not changed, namely the hazard faced in landing delicate equipment from a ship off shore, through the surf. The new kerosene powered mechanism then had to make the same journey from the landing place to the lighthouse. Not only delicate equipment, but foodstuffs, tins of kerosene, tools, building timber, nails, fine white calico polishing cloths, boiled oil – and hundreds of other items – all came ashore in the supply vessel's boats.

Because it was essential that the lighthouse be kept in operation throughout the changeover, a stout frame was built on the ocean side of the stone shaft. The old lantern was then detached and hauled onto this temporary tower. This transfer was, presumably, completed in one day. The new lanthorn was then installed on top of the 1848 stone shaft for commissioning. The old lanthorn and scaffolded tower were dismantled but what then happened to the old mechanism from Cape Otway remains unclear.

The consequent Notice to Mariners stated: [9]

8. *A photograph of the 1848 mechanism at Cape Otway being replaced in 1891.*

9. *The lighthouse supply ship Lady Loch. Supplies were brought ashore in her boats at Blanket Bay, and then conveyed to the lighthouse five miles away by bullock wagon.*

"Mariners are hereby notified that it is intended on and after the 1st April 1891 to exhibit from the old lighthouse tower at Cape Otway, a first order dioptric light, showing white flashes in groups of three every minute, and to discontinue the exhibition of the present catoptric light."

In 1896 a tragedy occurred at Blanket Bay that eventually led to abandonment of the sea supply route in favour of rail and road. This was to become known as the Blanket Bay Disaster. It involved the drowning of three crew members of the supply vessel *Lady Loch*.

One load had been landed safely in the ship's boats, when Franklin, the lighthouse Superintendent, went out in the boat to visit the *Lady Loch*. Her master, Captain Livingstone, was an old friend of Franklins and while still talking they were told that the next load was ready.

As it was customary for the Superintendent to supervise the unloading of all stores, Franklin begged to be excused for the return ashore. Livingstone urged him to wait for the next boat load — the sea was not rough, no trouble was expected and so Franklin stayed on board for a brandy Livingstone was now offering.

The boat cast off without Franklin and headed for the gap in the reef that gave access to the jetty. In charge was the Chief Mate Albert Griffiths, aged 32 of Williamstown, married with two children. While passing through the reef a sudden swell swamped the boat, followed by another which threw men and supplies into the sea. Unaware of how bad the accident was Captain Livingstone took the severely undermanned *Lady Loch* to Apollo Bay. From there he telegraphed Cape Otway and

learnt of what had happened. Alexander Mathieson, Thomas Monks and Albert Griffiths had drowned. Griffiths had been caught in kelp and for half an hour was crying for a rope. Beyond reach of anyone on shore, he was overcome by the rising tide. One of the survivors Jack Dunk, saved a fellow crew member. Later he was to be presented with a pipe. It was inscribed – "The loving hand that saved, Blanket Bay, 21/3/1896". The survivors remained at Blanket Bay for the rest of the tragic day, succoured by 'Old Joe King' a hermit living there. Monks and Mathieson were buried at Cape Otway two or three days later. Griffiths' body was not found until the *Lady Loch* had departed. Later his remains were buried at Williamstown and a memorial to the three men lost was erected in the Cape Otway cemetery.

Long ago though the Blanket Bay Disaster now is, a woman still living in 1980 is able to recall it clearly. Her ex-policeman father had emigrated from Wales and joined the lighthouse service in the early 1890's. Stationed first at Queenscliff, then Gabo Island, they were transferred to Cape Otway in 1894.

Laura McColl or Laura Skilton as she then was – expected to go back to school at Williamstown with the *Lady Loch* the very day the tragedy occurred. She had expected that by late afternoon she would be getting settled in the small cabin reserved for keepers and their families. Instead, as she recalled in 1973: [9]

"Late in the morning, the carpenter that had come down to do odd jobs around the quarters came galloping up the seven

10. Capt. Livingstone master of the Lady Loch at the time of the Blanket Bay Disaster, here seen with his two sons.

11. Blanket Bay with the hills behind, which prompted James Grant to write: "The Land here is truly picturesque and beautiful resembling very much that about Mount Edgecumbe near Plymouth, which faces the Sound. It is moderately high but not mountainous."
However it was here in 1896, that three men drowned while ferrying supplies ashore from the Lady Loch.

12. Mr. Franklin – Superintendent at Cape Otway in 1896.

13. John (Jack) Dunk at the wheel of the Lady Loch. The three Dunk brothers, Andrew, Herman and Jack survived the accident and were sheltered at Cape Otway till fit enough to walk to Apollo Bay where they rejoined the Lady Loch.

14. *A newspaper illustration showing the Lady Loch's boat swamped in the surf at Blanket Bay. Other accidents had occurred in the past but none so serious.*

15. *The men who drowned (left to right), Thomas Monks, Albert Griffiths and Alexander Mathieson.*

16. *The crew of the Lady Loch (circa 1900).*

17. *The pipe presented to Jack Dunk by the crew members of the Lady Loch in appreciation for the help he gave to his shipmates at the time of the capsizing.*

miles from Blanket Bay to the houses, and asked mother if she had any whisky in the house — "the keeper only had a wee drop." Mother said, "There's a full bottle of Mitchells in the cupboard. Whatever's happened?" She knew there must be something if they wanted whisky. So mother gave him the quart bottle of Mitchells whisky and away he galloped back again to give those that had washed ashore and were still alive. One had every stitch of clothing ripped off him when he was dashed amongst the rocks and that was *Jack Dunk*. There were three brothers in that smash and this one was pretty badly hurt and the other one had a steer oar stuck in his stomach and they said he had a bruise as large as a soup plate across his stomach where the oar hit him.

Well the poor fellers were at Blanket Bay for the remainder of that day until the bullock team left in the early evening to travel, you know with a bullock team it wasn't very fast, from Blanket Bay to the Otway Quarters. Some of them came toward our house and said to my brother Will, "Which house does your mother live in," he said "This one," so what number there was came in. Mother was busy baking, I was to get ready to go to town; there were the three brothers [Dunk brothers] and a Mr. Jones all came in and spoke to mother. Well, mother gave them something to eat and made them as comfortable as possible, as early as possible. So all the bedding was stripped off our beds; we youngsters had our kapok mattresses taken and all we were left with was the string mattress. Beds were put all along the dining room floor; a big fire was lit and the poor fellows lay there on the kapok beds on the floor for the night. Mother had a long cretonne curtain dividing the room. They took that down and put that between blankets to help the warmth. So that was how they put them up for the night."

18. Cape Otway cemetery – the monument to those who drowned in the Blanket Bay Disaster. Monks and Mathieson were buried at Cape Otway, but Griffiths' funeral was held in Williamstown.

19. The Signal Station at Cape Otway – unoccupied when this photograph was taken in 1895. Fourth from the left is young Laura Skilton on her horse "Doughboy".

Laura McColl continues by describing the stay of the men at the Cape and their long walk back to Apollo Bay to meet the *Lady Loch* – many of them in borrowed clothing. The remainder of the supplies were landed after the *Lady Loch* was brought back to Blanket Bay from whence she sailed.

Some days later when Laura arrived at the Williamstown jetty aboard the *Lady Loch*, she purchased there a small poem for one penny. It had been printed to raise funds for the families of the drowned men. Remembering Mr. Griffiths for "the nice man he was," Laura mailed the poem to her mother at Cape Otway.

The perils of Blanket Bay and Parker River could be avoided after a narrow gauge railway line was completed from Colac to Beech Forest. From there supplies could be transferred to bullock wagons for the haul down to Cape Otway across slowly improving forest tracks. In 1911 the railway was extended to Lavers Hill and provided an alternative route to the lighthouse.

Laura McColl also recalled names of other Otway characters: Mr. Franklin, the Head Keeper, whose daughter Edith later married Walter Gosney the mailman who rode regularly from Apollo Bay; the Mauritius-born Theodore Prolius, who had been a steward aboard the *Lady Loch* and later a light keeper – he was especially fond of the hotels in Apollo Bay and sometimes became lost. One "morning after" he turned up at the lighthouse riding a blinkered draft horse borrowed from a timber mill at the Elliot River. Prolius had no fear of heights and was known to do hand-stands on the lighthouse balcony for the amusement of onlookers. One can only imagine the outcome had Ford been his Superintendent.

Mrs. McColl's memories reach back to hours spent riding her horse "Doughboy" over the Cape Otway country – there was a muddy slide for him at the Elliot River; other hours learning morse code at the telegraph station, the multi coloured signal flags being run up the lighthouse station mast and she herself signalling to passing steamers with a white table cloth; picnics with Mrs Rainer and the younger children at the Parker River;

20. A poem recounting the events at Blanket Bay. Laura Skilton bought a copy at the Williamstown jetty after disembarking from the Lady Loch. Much creased, that child's purchase survives today.

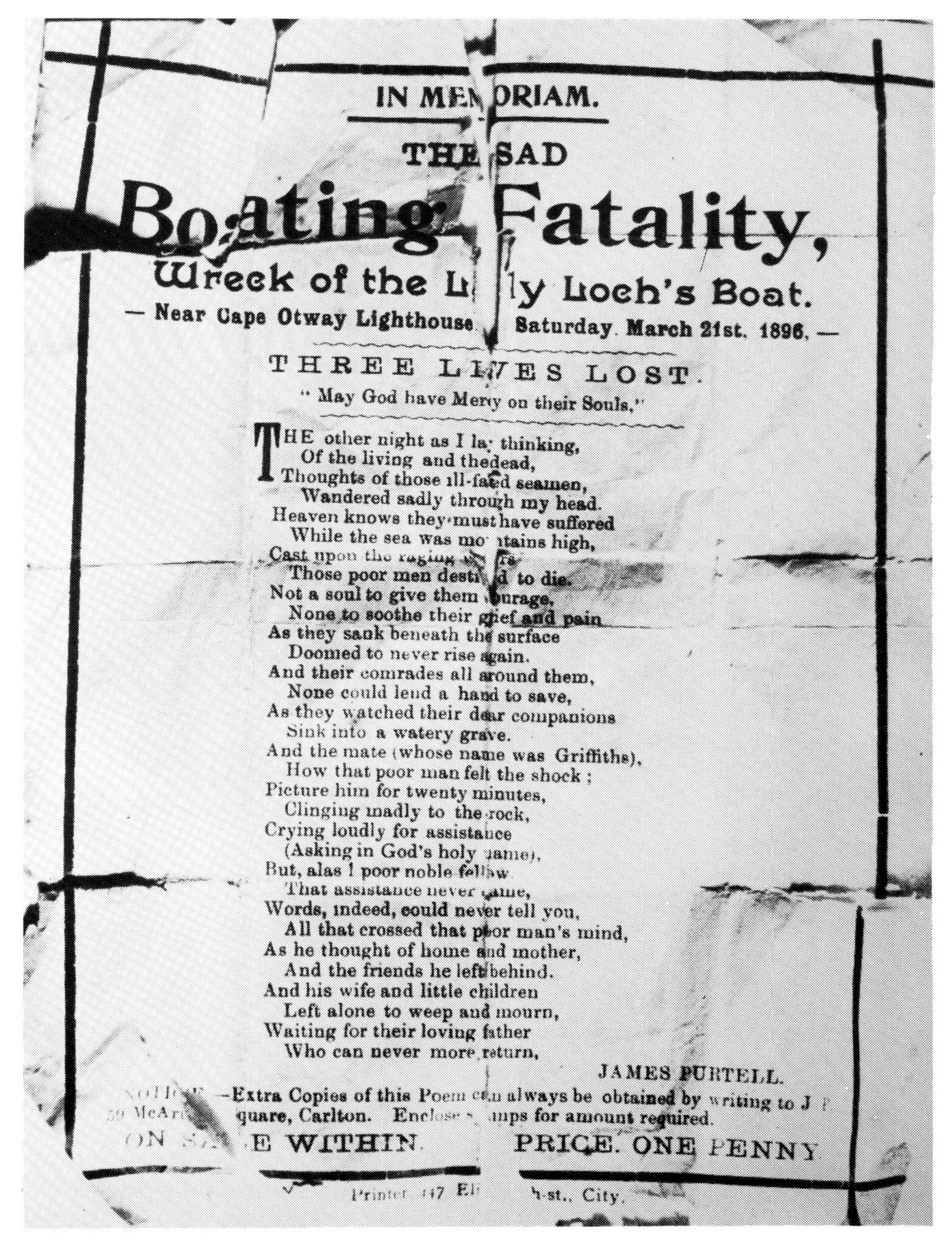

IN MEMORIAM.

THE SAD

Boating Fatality,

Wreck of the Lady Loch's Boat.

— Near Cape Otway Lighthouse, Saturday, March 21st, 1896, —

THREE LIVES LOST.

" May God have Mercy on their Souls."

THE other night as I lay thinking,
  Of the living and the dead,
Thoughts of those ill-fated seamen,
  Wandered sadly through my head.
Heaven knows they must have suffered
  While the sea was mountains high,
Cast upon the raging surf
  Those poor men destined to die.
Not a soul to give them courage,
  None to soothe their grief and pain
As they sank beneath the surface
  Doomed to never rise again.
And their comrades all around them,
  None could lend a hand to save,
As they watched their dear companions
  Sink into a watery grave.
And the mate (whose name was Griffiths),
  How that poor man felt the shock ;
Picture him for twenty minutes,
  Clinging madly to the rock,
Crying loudly for assistance
  (Asking in God's holy name),
But, alas ! poor noble fellow
  That assistance never came,
Words, indeed, could never tell you,
  All that crossed that poor man's mind,
As he thought of home and mother,
  And the friends he left behind.
And his wife and little children
  Left alone to weep and mourn,
Waiting for their loving father
  Who can never more return,

JAMES PURTELL.

NOTICE.—Extra Copies of this Poem can always be obtained by writing to J
59 McArthur Square, Carlton. Enclose stamps for amount required.

ON SALE WITHIN.   PRICE. ONE PENNY.

Printer 147 Elizabeth-st., City.

the nearest doctor — miles away at Beech Forest, Robinson from Glen Aire Station, as a good a horseman drunk as sober; old Mrs (William) Evans who was employed there — still with her Irish accent and her sons Tom and Martin, the latter a stockhand for Robinson; making bread "under mother's watchful eye", the butter preserved in earthenware vessels with brine on top; the one-armed hermit Joe King at Blanket Bay; the travelling Indian hawker; the numerous snakes; mail day (Saturday) when settlers at Johanna would ride to the Cape for their mail; the Signaller's residence empty, except on Sunday when Mr. Franklin's daughters led Sunday School classes there; Mr. Pallamountain the Methodist Minister at Apollo Bay, who would ride out once a month to Cape Otway to lead a church service; the fearful roll of the "greyhound" *Lady Loch*

Three days after the drowning at Blanket Bay, Laura McColl left Cape Otway in one of the *Lady Loch's* boats. Capt. Livingstone stood in the stern, steer oar firmly in hand and pointed the boat out to the ship waiting beyond the reef. A thunder storm was approaching from the ranges to the north: [10]

"When we pulled off in the boat from the shore, the Captain was shouting to the crew, "Pull Boys! Pull!"— because he could see the storm just about breaking. They just got the boat up into the davitts and it broke! It just roared through the timber. I couldn't forget it and you could see the lightning flashing down through all the trees as I stood on the deck of the steamer looking towards the land."

Grant had first seen this land at the beginning of the century now closing, and later many hopeful emigrants had welcomed the sight of that shore, its lighthouse and the brooding ranges behind. Writing as the Otways slipped by, one of the thousands who passed in safety recorded: [11]

"For the present the most conspicuous feature of civilization is the lighthouse on the Cape . . . it is a revolving light, and now, just as the night sets it is right abreast of us."

QUOTATIONS & REFERENCES

1. Cape Otway Letter Book 23/5/1879
2. Rosamund Duruz, *The Long Walk* by G.E. Morrison. PAP. Books, Warrnambool, 1979. P.7 & 8.
3. Education Dep't Files, held by P.R.O.VIC. School No.2352, petition. 26/11/1880
4. & 5. ibid.
6. ibid. 3/1/1886
7. *Gippsland Independent* 25/4/1879.
8. Cape Otway Letter Book.
9. & 10. Tape recording of discussions with Mrs. Laura McColl made by DMW. The remainder of the chapter is drawn from notes of interviews with children of former Keepers at Cape Otway in the 1890's. In particular Mrs. Edith Gosney (nee Franklin) and the late Mr. L. Keyes who escorted Theodore Prolius back from the Apollo Bay Hotel to Cape Otway (circa) 1900.

ILLUSTRATION SOURCES

1. DMW.
2. Mr. & Mrs. C. Speight.
3. Mrs. S. Anderson.
4 & 5. DMW.
6. Judy Spafford , Lower Gellibrand.
Note to accompany this photograph for Edition 3. Sadly this 3m x 2m unpretentious link with the days of sail was destroyed during clearing works undertaken preparatory to restoration work commencing on the main Glenample homestead in the mid 1980's.
7. Australia Illustrated Vol. 1.
8. Miss. Mason. DMW.
9. La Trobe Library. Allan C.Green Collection.
10. Mrs. R. H. Livingstone, Williamstown.
11. DMW.
12. Mrs. Edith Gosney.
13. Mrs. I. Russel.
14. & 15. The Leader, 28/3/1896.
16. Mrs. E. McColl.
17. Mrs. I. Russel.
18. DMW.
19. Mrs. Lawson, Princetown.
20. DMW.
21. Mr. V. Quinn, Burwood.
22. Mrs. Laura McColl.
23. RHSV.

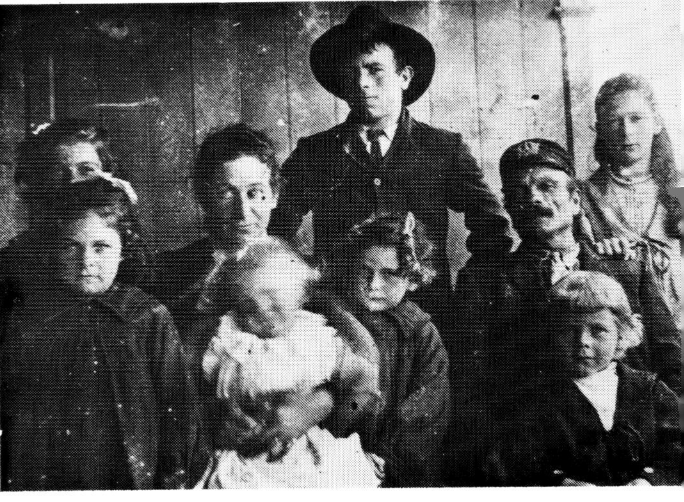

21. The Quinn family at Cape Otway in about 1906.

22. Cape Otway Lighthouse in 1895. The rocket shed housed mainly fog rockets, which were fired from a small platform on the eastern side of the lighthouse. (See opposite page).

23. The age of sail was rapidly passing when this photograph was taken of a large four-masted sailing ship at Geelong wharf, her sails drying. One reason why the great majority of ships such as this and her predecessors reached their destination was because, lighthouses had been erected at the western entrance to Bass Strait. (See opposite page).

Cape Wickham Lighthouse, King Island.

BIBLIOGRAPHY

CORRECTIONS & UPDATING

Dire Strait. C Bateson, A.H. Reed, Sydney 1973.

Settlers under Sail. Don Charlwood Premiers Department, Melbourne , Victoria, 1978. Republished 1997. Burgewood Books. Templestowe

King Island. C. Sullivan, Australian Schools Commission, 1979. Currie.

The King Island Story. R.H.Hooper, Peko- Wallsend Ltd. 1973. Sydney.

Wrecks and Reputations. Don Charlwood. Burgewood Books , 1997.

The Otways Region Symposium Vol 89 Parts 1 & 2. Royal Society of Victoria , " The Aborigines of the Otway Region" by N.H. Scarlett 1977.

The History of Colac and District. I. Hebb, Hawthorne Press, Melbourne.

The Life and Adventures of William Buckley, 2nd ed. Morgan, Heinemann, Melbourne.

The Long Walk. G.E. Morrison, edited by Rosamund Duruz, P.A.P. Books, Warrrnambool, 1979.

The Lighthouse. Dudley Witney, 1975, New York Graphic Society.

A History of the Post Office in Tasmania. Australia Post Office, 1979.

A History of the Colony of Victoria Vol. 1 H.G. Turner, 1973, Heritage.

The World of John Boultbee. A.C. Begg and N.C. Begg, Whitcoulls. Christchurch, N.Z.

Immigration into Eastern Australia. R. B. Madgwick, Sydney University Press.

French Explorers in the Pacific. J. Dunmore .Vol 1 & 2. Oxford 1965.

The Long Farewell. Don Charlwood. Burgewood Books. 1998.

Cape Otway: Coast of Secrets, B.Pascoe, Pascoe Publishing

Chapter 7

Page 63. The correct name for Roadknight's Station was "Gerangamete". It has long since been ploughed under the land it once claimed.

Page 55. Foster Fyans from 1841 on was Commissioner for Crown Lands and Acting Coroner for Portland Bay District. It was his responsibility to investigate incidents of a serious nature between settlers and aborigines. Fyans had instructions from Latrobe to equip Smythe with whatever he needed to pursue Conroy's murderer(s). At the time Native Police were unavailable and so Fyans authorised the arming of the Barrabool men. Latrobe was actually in Sydney for much of this time receiving instructions from Governor Gipps on general matters to do with the administration of the Port Phillip District. Fyans records in his Annual Report for 1846 that he has forwarded a full report on the "affray at the River" to the NSW Crown Prosecutor. This document has not been located.

I am grateful to Mr. Jim Campbell of Box Hill, Victoria who has clarified issues regarding Fyans' and Smythe's roles based on the official correspondence. Bruce Pascoe of Cape Otway has also carried out further investigation work in the course of writing his book Cape Otway: Coast of Secrets and further material continues to emerge on the precise sequence of events at the Aire River. The injustice of the incident is doubled when we remember that less than three years earlier the Katabanut clan had rendered assistance to the stranded survivors of the ship *Joanna* lost at present day Johanna, just west of the Aire River.

Page 55. The settler in the photograph on this page is actually Thomas Roadknight, son of William Roadknight. Father and son took up the Cape Otway Run from the Crown. This lease stretched for over 15 kilometers along the coast, encircling the Cape Otway Lighthouse Reserve.

Chapter 9

Page 77. The incident concerning the keeper's wife who "has become insane" is referring to the Riches family.(note correct spelling). His wife may have been suffering from some form of Post Natal Depression. We cannot know. Descendants advise she died in Sunbury Asylum in 1908.

Chapter 11

Page 93, 94 and 95. In the early 1990's a diary secreted in the Melbourne City Council Archives for over 50 years was discovered to have relevance to the question of precisely who designed many of the lighthouses and associated quarters in this State. The diary was that of Charles Maplestowe, Deputy Architect under William Wardell, Chief Architect of the Victorian Public Works Department.

Reading its pages it quickly becomes clear that Maplestowe was responsible for the design and erection of the new residences at Cape Otway Lighthouses, together with Cape Schanck and Gabo Island Lighthouses.

Chapter 13

Page 118. Quotation 4. The quoted journal was actually kept by Eleanor Parkinson, governess to the Roadknight children at the River Station near Winchelsea. She accompanied the Roadknights on the summer excursion that year to Cape Otway, recording adventures below the lighthouse near the mouth of the caves, camping in the sand dunes. She was blessed with a keen eye and a good turn of phrase.

Page 120. The keeper referred to was <u>Morwick</u> not Morwich.

Assistant Keeper Thomas Morwick with his wife Fanny were stationed at Cape Otway in the early 1870's. He was one of the many keepers who were to clash with Superintendent Ford during the the 30 years his superior was in charge there.

INDEX

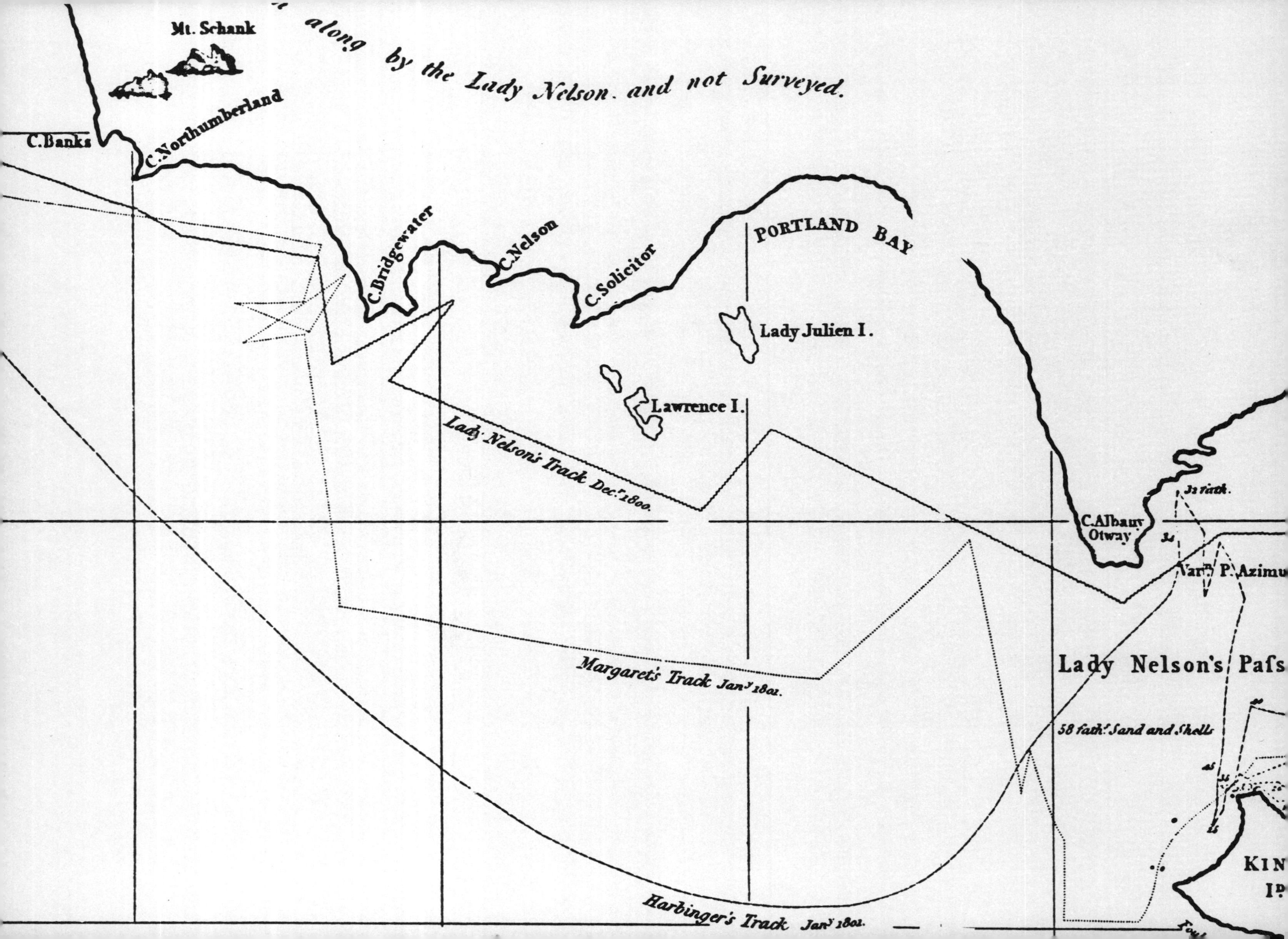

Mt. Schank
C.Banks
C.Northumberland
along by the Lady Nelson. and not Surveyed.
C.Bridgewater
C.Nelson
C.Solicitor
PORTLAND BAY
Lady Julien I.
Lawrence I.
Lady Nelson's Track Dec.r 1800.
Margaret's Track Jan.y 1801.
C.Albany Otway
31 fath.
3¼
Varn.n P. Azimu
Lady Nelson's Pass
58 fath.t Sand and Shells
Harbinger's Track Jan.y 1801.
KIN
I.